Gospel, Church, and Ministry

Gospel, Church, and Ministry

THOMAS F. TORRANCE COLLECTED STUDIES 1

Thomas F. Torrance

EDITED BY
Jock Stein

☙PICKWICK Publications • Eugene, Oregon

GOSPEL, CHURCH, AND MINISTRY
Thomas F. Torrance Collected Studies 1

Copyright © 2012 Thomas F. Torrance and Jock Stein. All rights reserved. Except for brief quotations in critical publications or reviews, no part of this book may be reproduced in any manner without prior written permission from the publisher. Write: Permissions, Wipf and Stock Publishers, 199 W. 8th Ave., Suite 3, Eugene, OR 97401.

Pickwick Publications
An Imprint of Wipf and Stock Publishers
199 W. 8th Ave., Suite 3
Eugene, OR 97401

www.wipfandstock.com

ISBN 13: 978-1-60899-939-2

Cataloging-in-Publication data:

Torrance, Thomas F. (Thomas Forsyth), 1913–2007

    Gospel, church, and ministry : Thomas F. Torrance collected studies 1 / Thomas F. Torrance, edited by Jock Stein.

    viii + 284 p. ; 23 cm. Includes bibliographical references and index.

    ISBN 13: 978-1-60899-939-2

    1. Church. 2. Church work. 3. Pastoral theology. 4. Preaching. 5. Clergy—Office. I. Stein, Jock. II. Title.

BV660.3 T67 2012

Manufactured in the U.S.A.

Contents

Acknowledgements vii

Editor's Introduction 1

1. My Parish Ministry: Alyth, 1940-43 · 25
2. The Church in the World · 74
3. The Humanity of Christ in the Sacramental Life of the Church · 85
4. The Meaning of Order · 93
5. Consecration and Ordination · 111
6. Service in Jesus Christ · 140
7. The Church in the Last Quarter of the Twentieth Century · 162
8. God, Destiny, and Suffering · 173
9. Eldership in the Reformed Church · 182
10. The Ministry of Women · 201
11. Preaching Christ Today · 220
12. Legal and Evangelical Priests · 257

General Index · 271

Scripture Index · 280

Acknowledgements

I WOULD LIKE TO thank T. F Torrance's brother, David Torrance, for a few minor factual corrections to the memoir, for his own writing about his brother's life, and for his encouragement in this and many other projects. Also his nephew Robert Walker, who edited the two volumes of New College lectures (published in 2008 and 2009 as *Incarnation* and *Atonement*), for practical help with sourcing articles, for advice on the project, and for helpful comments on the Introduction. Naturally responsibility for content remains with me.

Helen McLeod, John Russell, and Irene Robertson worked hard to track down the material in chapter 2, and Dr. Timothy Lim gave helpful advice on the state of academic discussion on whether Jesus would have taught using Hebrew or Aramaic. Jason Radcliff interpreted one or two of Torrance's less obvious patristic abbreviations.

The contribution of Wipf and Stock editorial staff is acknowledged in the Introduction.

Most of all I am grateful that Professor Torrance himself was willing to give time, friendship, and encouragement to intending ministers like myself and my wife Margaret, who chose to study theology because of a talk he gave to students at the Edinburgh College of Art.

Editor's Introduction

Conventions and House Style

MOST ACADEMIC BOOKS REFER to a writer like Professor T. F. Torrance as 'Torrance,' which is certainly not wrong. However, the difficulty with it is twofold—it is formal and somewhat impersonal, and one of the emphases of this volume is how in his theology (and his life, for that matter) Professor Torrance regarded God's dealings with us as intimate and personal. The other point is that the Torrance theological dynasty is not small, and there are other members of the family who are also well known.

On the other hand, while, like some of his older students, I was on first name terms with him, 'Tom' is not how I would wish to refer to someone of his stature in a serious book. So I have used the name by which students and staff knew him, and the name by which he is widely known even today, his initials run together as 'TF.'

The original articles have more capitalization than is customary today, but this has been left largely unchanged, except that pronouns for God are now in lower case. TF, like nearly all his generation, used 'man' as a generic term; sometimes it has been simple to change his terminology into inclusive language without loss of meaning, but otherwise it is left as he wrote it.

Often a bit of negotiation is involved when non-Americans use American punctuation, especially when the non-American is used to publishing books for European audiences. The Wipf and Stock editors have graciously allowed a degree of hybridization, for example, in that double quote marks are used where there is a real quotation, but single quotes for emphasis or when the phrase in question is 'so-called'; and they have also allowed the use of British spelling.

Selection of Writings

With someone whose writings are prolific and whose thought makes connections at so many levels it is not easy to make a small selection of writings by TF. In choosing items under the overall title of 'Gospel, Church, and Ministry' the following factors have been kept in mind:

1. This is the first of three planned volumes, and contains writings which are, on the whole, more accessible to the non-specialist reader than the writings on philosophy and theology which will feature in volume 2. However, I would not wish to describe these as 'popular' and 'academic,' since the best popular writing is well researched, and the best academic writing should be clear and not opaque; the divorce between popular and academic is not one that TF himself would have embraced.

2. TF never saw himself primarily as 'an academic.' In his student days he was preparing to serve as a missionary, and his work as parish minister and later in academic positions was undertaken within that frame of reference. One of his favourite teachers, H. R. Mackintosh, had stressed the link between theology and mission.[1] Certainly, his vision of 'being a missionary' changed, once he realized his calling was, in part, to help evangelize the foundations of modern scientific culture,[2] well illustrated by his approach to preaching in chapter 11. This was just one reason why for him theology could never be a detached commentary on Christian doctrine: rather, theology was an engagement of

---

1. Alister McGrath, *T. F. Torrance: An Intellectual Biography* (London: T. & T. Clark, 2006), 31.

2. In his unpublished 2011 University of St Andrews PhD thesis on *The Dogmatics Lectures of T. F. Torrance*, 29ff., Robert Walker spells out this aim in four parts: fashioning a modern Christian dogmatics, reconstructing the concept of reason (not as an autonomous power, but as controlled by its object), the overcoming of dualism, and the reshaping of fundamental presuppositions.

mind and heart and strength with a living God who had already lovingly engaged all humanity in incarnation and atonement.

3. The chapters contain writings that are out of print, though mostly accessible in libraries. The first two chapters are an exception to this, chapter 1 having not been previously published, and chapter 2 requiring considerable detective work to find. These two chapters illustrate TF's passionate concern that theology should service the ministry and mission of the Christian church.

4. These collective writings by TF span fifty-five years, from chapter 2 (1942) to chapter 12 (1997). Chapter 1 is placed first because it describes an earlier period (though written much later), but otherwise the chapters are in chronological order of writing, except that chapter 5 is placed after 4 because it is better understood in the light of chapter 4.

There is a gap of ten to fifteen years, therefore, between chapters 1 and 2, and chapters 3, 4, and 5; and a similar long gap between chapter 5 and chapters 6 to 8. Chapters 9 to 12 cover the following twenty years. The contents in all span well over fifty years.

For readers wondering how TF's thought developed over the years, there may be some advantage in this chronological order, but it should be remembered that this is a very modest selection, topics often overlap, and the articles and addresses were designed for different audiences.

There is a further reason for the placing of the first two chapters. 'My Parish Ministry,' part 1 of a two-part memoir of his days in Alyth and Beechgrove (Aberdeen), uniquely reveals the direction of TF's life and what drove him as a man. As an unpublished piece it deserves pride of place. 'The Place and Function of the Church in the World' also comes out of those early days: it was published on 21 January 1942 by the Presbytery of Meigle.

Inevitably some of TF's writings last better than others. This can be because some of them came at the request of particular bodies—like the Scottish Order of Christian Unity, which he helped to found and for which he wrote several pamphlets—or maybe because he was addressing particular issues with a practical concern that is perhaps seen differently years later. But behind all this there is a bigger issue. If God embraced the frailty of our human nature, we should not seek to turn our theologians into heroes who always wrote magnificent stuff that will stand every test that time can throw at it. That is unrealistic, contrary to the realist philosophy that TF embraced, and would hinder our learning from what has gone before. Chapter 2 in particular reflects the wartime situation, and chapter 7 the challenge of Marxism, which was soon to evaporate.

Apart from anything else, such writings reveal TF as a Christian leader seeking to show how theology related to the questions of his time in a profound way. In this respect he frequently showed prophetic insight, though he would not have called himself a prophet. Those who label him an ivory tower theologian simply fail to understand how he lived and worked. Commenting on the way the church develops a religious technology for mission in place of theology, he once wrote: "If theology without experience is irrelevant, and experience without theology is blind, the church without theology can be little more than a blind leader of the blind."[3]

1. My Parish Ministry

TF always underlined the importance of the time he spent in the parish—he says it was vital for his New College lectures. Nowadays it is much harder for a scholar to take this route into academic posts, partly because of the pressure for anyone at the start of an academic career to do research and publish as well as teach, partly because of the greater demands of parish and presbytery on a minister's time (particularly with linked parishes). On the other hand, to read of the attention that TF gave to his parish as well as to his research and publication, makes us realize that someone of his stature may be freer to choose his career path than lesser mortals! However, it is hardly conceivable today that a university principal would try to headhunt for a university chair of divinity someone from a parish who had not yet completed his doctorate.

---

3. T. F. Torrance, *God and Rationality* (London: Oxford University Press, 1971), 4.

Editor's Introduction

Some situations in life make us angry, as they made Jesus angry. While love and wrath may seem to be in tension, one of the tasks of theology is to see how they relate and what is God's own way of resolving them. This tension is exposed in the Gospels in the exorcisms of Jesus and his hostility to evil,[4] and it is fascinating to find that TF himself on one occasion engaged in what he described as a kind of exorcism, an exorcism by the word, which would certainly have fallen foul of fashionable non-assertive pastoral care—but it worked! A man surrendered his anger and bitterness against God and the church; his family and the community rejoiced at the change, which was lasting. The church worldwide is much more familiar with this dimension of evangelism than the mainstream Western church; for example, I recall finding that in one part of Tanzania exorcism was carried out by repeating (shouting, actually!) scriptures into the ears of the afflicted person.

TF used to visit all the members of his congregation as often as he could (not just once a year!), and felt this balanced his sermons, which he himself described as "rather theological." Later he would feel that lecturing on Christian dogmatics must be balanced by showing "something of the personal and pastoral thrust and power of the truths of the gospel" and would often pause in the middle of his lectures to give pastoral illustrations of what he was saying. As he mentions, "not a few" students in his classes were converted, and those of us who attended his classes in the 1960s can testify that this was still happening when we were students.

TF's style of preaching was expository; he mentions preaching a series on Romans and on Revelation. During the war, in Alyth, the latter series struck a chord, but he comments that after the war in Aberdeen they did not meet with the same response, so he "put them on one side." TF had hesitated to preach on Romans, fearing it was "too theological," but it was a lay elder who persuaded him, and again it was a series that struck deep into the lives of his hearers.

He does mention that preparing two sermons each week was hard work and that it took "most of each morning and afternoon." If this was literally true, his commitment to pastoral work does border on the

---

4. See also chapter 6.

miraculous, and it is perhaps a shame that he does not tell us how many hours sleep he used to get!

At this early stage he specifically mentions Galatians 2:20 in the KJV, "the life I now live, I live by the faith *of* the Son of God," rather than the more common translation "by faith *in* the Son of God." He was to justify this translation in his New College lectures, but even at this stage it is clear that he is stressing the active *faith of Christ* as part of the ground of our salvation.

He uses the expression "theological revival" (referring to his student days in New College under H. R. Mackintosh and Daniel Lamont), and shows his commitment to this aim, in particular through founding the Scottish Church Theology Society[5] and the *Scottish Journal of Theology*.

His war service clearly influenced him greatly; he specifically mentions the question of a dying soldier, "Is God really like Jesus?" TF was well able to be simple and direct when the occasion demanded. He would cite with approval a story about Karl Barth: the great man was once asked what was the most profound thing he had learned about Christian theology and replied, "Jesus loves me, this I know, for the Bible tells me so!"

2. The Place and Function of the Church in the World

The context of this address, published by the Presbytery of Meigle on 21 January 1942, is explained in a preface by the Moderator of Presbytery. It is a response to the Baillie Commission for *The Interpretation of God's Will in the Present Crisis* (which worked from 1940 and produced two reports).

TF's address was an uncompromising call for the church to evangelize the world and have an impact that would "turn the whole order of State and society upside down." This gave him the reputation of be-

---

5. The earliest remaining document of the Society, the 'Finance Book' (which I hold as current treasurer of the Society) has entries from 1943. The Society began with regional meetings, and organized conferences were launched after the war by J. K. S. Reid and Ian Fraser (while TF in his Memoirs says that Ian Henderson held things together during the war). TF was the 'ideas person,' and the Society is generally regarded as being founded by T. F. Torrance and J. K. S. Reid.

ing a political radical, which he says in chapter 1 he was not, but the address does make clear the way in which he believed the gospel was deeply relevant to the political and economic and social order. TF was not a follower of the John Baillie approach, with its emphasis on finding 'middle axioms' that Christians could share with others in order to support common action. His language was very different: "It is not the Church's business to be the bulwark of the old order; rather is it her business to throw the whole into ferment and upheaval."

Whereas TF described himself in his memoir as being in the Auld Kirk tradition, which generally had a high view of the place of the minister, he also makes it very clear in this address that he believed in the ministry of all members (as in Ephesians 4:12), as all are called to follow the pattern of our Lord, not just a few elders or Guild members: "But think of any average church in this country you care—is it not true that the people's main business is to gather together just in order to be ministered unto, instead of ministering themselves?" Such a view allowed him to appreciate any church whose members were committed to following Jesus.

This ability to span traditions, because of the one true Tradition of faith, is characteristic of TF, and nowhere is this better illustrated than by the invitation from the Student Christian Movement (SCM) in Oxford to him to be their President, while he was about to lead a mission for the Oxford Inter-Collegiate Christian Union (OICCU)! (SCM is strongly 'liberal', OICCU is strongly 'conservative'.)

TF could often be politically prescient. In this address he expresses a fear that after the inevitable increase of its power during wartime, the British State was heading for an unhealthy amount of power over the lives of citizens. While the danger of fascism, which he warned against, did not materialize, in other ways the British State now has a degree of control over its citizens far in excess of what was present before that war.

Clearly in this address TF is trying to keep a proper balance between calling the State to account and telling the State what to do. Unlike what was then the Church and Nation Committee of the Church of Scotland, he generally refrained from calling for specific political actions; a rare exception would come during his moderatorial year, when, during a visit to Dundee Presbytery, I recall him calling for the privatization of the Bank of England—a move which Prime Minister Gordon Brown took, in part, years later.

His main emphasis, however, was that the church must recover the gospel as the saving power of Christ and make this proclamation its primary task; its own organization or reorganization (which he wanted to see) is secondary; her primary task is *mission* and must be a passion! Mission is not just something the church does, it is how the church lives!

He has two complaints to make about the church of his day. First, her message has become "poisoned with modern thought"; second, she has inoculated society with such a mild form of Christianity that society is almost immune from the vital form. (As this was a common illustration used later by Billy Graham, one wonders where and by whom the point was first made.) TF had the right to make this first complaint because he thoroughly understood modern thought, and indeed made great use of the advances in scientific thought.

He was also an uncompromising believer in the importance of foreign mission. Before the 1939–45 war the Church of Scotland employed hundreds of missionaries to work overseas in various capacities. Today the Church of Scotland employs only a handful. While many reasons are adduced for this dramatic reduction, it is hard to avoid the conclusion that the Church today no longer believes in foreign mission. There are, of course, still a very large number of missionaries, in the usual sense of Christians sent by churches anywhere in the world to work for the gospel in a different place or sphere of service, but the vast majority are employed by younger and more vibrant churches. TF would I think salute the current vision of Chinese churches for 100,000 missionaries to evangelise the 'hard to reach' areas between China and Israel.[6]

3. The Place of the Humanity of Christ in the Sacramental Life of the Church

In this address TF introduces his plea that in Christian theology we should not think simply in terms of two dimensions of thought, divine and human (God and our human response), but work with a specific third dimension of thought, the dimension of the humanity of Jesus Christ the God-man, which he credits to Calvin and behind him to the

---

6. This represents just one thousandth part of the 100 million Christians estimated to live in China today. TF visited the land of his birth several times, and was one of the founders of Amity.

Greek Fathers. This is part and parcel of his 'Christian philosophy,' his conviction that we require a new logic that is appropriate for the revelation of God in the *Logos*.[7]

He also introduces us to two of his favourite characters from Scottish church history: Robert Bruce, minister of St Giles' in Edinburgh after John Knox, and John McLeod Campbell, minister of Rhu near Helensburgh in the nineteenth century. TF was Professor of Church History at New College for two years, from 1950 to 1952, before he moved to occupy the chair of Christian Dogmatics, and he welcomed the rehabilitation of McLeod Campbell, who had actually been condemned by the General Assembly for heresy because he insisted in judging the Westminster Confession by the Bible, not the Bible by the Confession.

TF was critical of an appeal to traditional forms of ministry *per se*,[8] and his interest in the Church Service Society was largely because it recovered aspects of Reformation practice in Scotland. He served as President of the Society from 1970 to 1972, and his attitude to the liturgical renewal that the Society represented was generally positive, to the extent that it was based on a proper Reformed understanding of Christ and the Sacraments. But he recognized that in some places it nourished what he provocatively called "an erotic hunger for symbolism" and he was always more concerned with underlying theology than with liturgical niceties.

It is significant that TF emphasized the humanity of Christ alongside his divinity, in a way that both followed Nicene Christology and sought to develop that Christology in a more dynamic direction. TF began teaching at New College in the John Baillie era, which represented the peak of 'liberal' theology in Scotland. Liberal theology had sought to recover the humanity of Jesus but, for TF, it had tried to do so apart from his divinity, which it did not believe in, and the result (paradoxically) was to emasculate the real humanity of Christ. TF wanted to see Christ's humanity built on a proper foundation.

In that context TF did not shirk controversy. Four years before this address was published, the American philosopher Brand Blanshard

---

7. He applauded the idea of "quantum logic" in science, and used it as an analogy for how we need a new way of thinking about God. See for example *God and Rationality*, 23f. or his plea for "a *four-dimensional logic* or a *logic of verbs*" in *Theological Science* (London: Oxford University Press, 1969), 209f.

8. See McGrath, *T. F. Torrance*, 99.

delivered the Gifford lectures at the University of St Andrews. *The Scotsman* noted that Blanshard had taken a swipe at Karl Barth, whom TF wanted to see welcomed in Scotland. Thereafter in April that year *The Scotsman* published no fewer than eight letters between Torrance, Blanchard, and one other minister, as TF sought to defend Barth against what he regarded as Blanchard's ill-informed criticism.[9]

4. The Meaning of Order

Order is often viewed in contrast to freedom, but with TF order is placed in opposition to sin, which is lawlessness. Creation then has a lost order, which is restored under the new covenant, an order "which comes from without and is planted within"—which means within the world and within humanity (in the incarnation), and also within the heart (through the Spirit). This "re-ordering in Jesus Christ" takes the form of service; however the church in its actual service and the ordering of its life still awaits full "redemption in the second advent of Christ" and so its actual order is provisional. This balance is in fact spelled out at some length in chapter 2 of this compilation.

God is the great householder who comes to give order to his creation. While TF uses the term *oikonomia*, from which the modern word 'economy' derives, he naturally explored the meaning of this for church order. I wish I had taken the opportunity during his lifetime to ask TF whether his wider views on economics, which I think were influenced by the Nobel prize-winning economist Friedrich Hayek, were connected with his theology in any way.

TF examines church order in terms of space: if the church on earth is the place of Christ, then one should have a high view of the church, its ministry, its Sacraments, and its unity. However, he refuses to tie down Christ to *our* forms, saying rather that *we* are tied by the exalted Christ to *his* place. He introduces again the idea of a "third order," not simply divine or human but that of the God-man.

The order of the church is not static, but dynamic, for this is the period of time for the preaching of the gospel. Historical succession in

9. This correspondence, edited by Iain and Morag Torrance, has recently been published in *Theology in Scotland* XVI (2009).

Editor's Introduction

the ordering of ministry bears witness to the binding of the church to Christ, but by itself does not secure that tie, which is the free gift of the eternal God, experienced in the Lord's Supper, which looks forward to our Lord's return. TF generally dislikes the term '*second* advent' (e.g., in his New College lectures he says that the NT uses the term *parousia* only in the singular, and that the distinction between two advents began with Justin Martyr and Hippolytus[10]) but here he uses it without hesitation.[11]

His discussion of the redemption of space and time was later to be expanded in his two books *Space, Time and Incarnation*, and *Space, Time and Resurrection*. The former does not deal with church order but the latter does make a few connections: on page 99, TF briefly discusses the service of the church within the conditions of fallen human existence, and why the NT commands us to "redeem the time;" on page 101, the risen Christ "knocks at the door of the Church" in the Lord's Supper; on page 119, he uses the additional words of Mark 16.19–20 to say how Christ today is active in the program of the church, although he does not opt for the other ending of verses 14–18 to discuss the healing ministry—instead, on page 149 he warns us that the church does not have any "appointed program of faith-healing."

5. Consecration and Ordination

In chapters 4 and 5, TF is marking out a Christian view of ministry and order as one that is both ecumenical and reformed; *ecumenical* in that it accepts the place of historical succession from the apostles and Jesus, but *reformed* in that it never regards such succession as 'guaranteeing validity' or 'endowing grace,' for it is the risen Christ who ordains and gives the Spirit—the church only acts in his name. Christ is really present in his church where we meet in his name, but that is because he fulfils what he promises, *not* because the church is faithful.

TF was once asked which modern theologian he respected and he confounded the enquirer by replying "Athanasius"! He could, of course, equally well have added "John Calvin." His writings not only reflect

---

10. T. F. Torrance, *Atonement: The Person and Work of Christ* (Milton Keynes, UK: Paternoster, 2009), 302

11. As he uses it also in a sermon on Matthew 25:1–3 in T. F. Torrance, *When Christ Comes and Comes Again* (London: Hodder and Stoughton, 1957), 37.

Calvin's approach to theology, but his language often reflects Calvin—as in his saying in this chapter that the risen Christ rules the church by the "sceptre of his Word."[12]

In a collection of his sermons published in 1957, TF warns against preaching "the Church instead of Christ in his Church, and so [giving] the congregation the traditions of men instead of Incarnation, Atonement, Resurrection, Ascension, and Advent. A sheep lost in a snowstorm may eke out its life a little longer by feeding upon its own wool, but the Church cannot live very long by feeding upon its own experience or conventions instead of the body and blood of Christ."[13]

TF is, of course, thoroughly reformed when he insists that there is no distinction in doctrine between a presbyter and a bishop (though see also chapter 9 for further discussion on the nature of eldership), but he reaches out to other churches by acknowledging the need for different functions, which may mean more responsibility being given to particular presbyters (as happens in practice in all Reformed churches).

In the chapter he refers to the idea of "bishop-in-Presbytery." Alister McGrath, in *T. F. Torrance: An Intellectual Biography*,[14] says that it was TF who developed this as a key idea (see his 1955 study *Royal Priesthood*), and it certainly travelled a long way in the Conversations leading to a proposal to unite the Church of Scotland with the Scottish Episcopal Church; the proposals were eventually voted down by Presbyteries when they were sent down from the Assembly to be considered by them under the Barrier Act. We also know from chapter 1 that he had read a book published in 1730 that contained a proposal to unite presbyterian and episcopal traditions, and (of course) TF had married an Anglican.

Looking at the consecration of priests in the Old Testament, TF discusses the importance of "filling the hands," and later argues that the early church custom of a newly ordained minister celebrating the Lord's Supper is a practice that should be followed today.[15]

---

12. Calvin, *Institutes* 3.20.42; 4.2.4.
13. Torrance, *When Christ Comes and Comes Again*, 8.
14. Edinburgh: T. & T. Clark, 1999, p. 96.
15. Colin Williamson in *Theology in Scotland* XVI (2009), tells us that this was done at his instigation in the Presbytery of Perth for a short while, but otherwise it

As stated earlier, TF holds together this high view of the ordination and function of a minister with a high view of the ministry of the body of Christ. *All* are baptized, therefore *all* share a priesthood in Christ, because baptism is our consecration to that priesthood. He says little about the nuts and bolts of church services, as he is always concerned to establish foundations—one thinks of Paul writing, "Christ did not send me to baptize, but to preach."[16] Ordination by the laying on of hands witnesses that ordination derives from the historical Jesus and that the church today is in historical succession to the apostles; but it is the risen Christ who ordains.

The laying on of hands is thus a custom that witnesses to a bond between the historical Jesus (who commissioned the apostles) and the risen Lord (who leads the church in its practice today). "The risen Lord sends us back to the historical Jesus." This bond on which TF insists is, of course, part of his wider theological concern to hold together the 'historical Jesus' and the 'risen Christ.' In turn, this is much more than an academic theological viewpoint, more than a disagreement with (say) Bultmann on New Testament interpretation; it is a deep conviction of life and soul that this is how things really are.[17]

He describes the apostles as "patriarchs of the new Israel." The Bible never uses the term 'new Israel'—although like 'second coming' it is an understandable way of speaking—and TF's phrase here may be not only surprising but liable to misinterpretation. In his New College lectures he prefers to speak of the church as the "reconstituted Israel of God,"[18] or "reborn"[19] but he does at least once there use the term "new Israel" of the church,[20] although he explains that this does *not* mean that

---

is rare today.

16. 1 Cor 1:17.

17. One of the best outlines of his approach to this question is in his "parable of the reporter" in T. F. Torrance, *Space, Time and Resurrection* (Edinburgh: Handsel, 1977), 161–66.

18. Torrance, *Atonement*, 415

19. T. F. Torrance, *Incarnation: The Person and Life of Christ* (Milton Keynes, UK: Paternoster, 2008), 50.

20. Torrance, *Incarnation*, 158.

the church has supplanted Israel, but rather than it has been ingrafted into Israel.

While TF does not spell it out here, his view of church order makes room for a freedom that could have allowed him to make a substantial contribution to dialogue between Reformed and Pentecostal churches, although his own inclination—reinforced by his marriage—was always to dialogue with Episcopal churches. Karl Barth once said that if he had started with Pentecost instead of Incarnation, his own theology would have taken a very different route.[21] No doubt that would have been true also of TF, but in practice neither of them did take that route, for reasons clear enough from their theological approach.

6. Service in Jesus Christ

TF had a view of practical theology that was unfashionable: rather than seeing it as a distinct subject on its own (as it has developed in most universities and colleges over the last century), he regarded systematic theology as inherently practical. Where there was a separate department of Practical Theology, he would always have hoped for an integral relation between the two subjects. It was therefore natural for him to speak about Christian service both in his lectures and his writings, without the kind of boundaries that one might find elsewhere. His whole discussion here is an important and neglected part of his thought.

"In the deacon's office the early Church saw most clearly the likeness of Jesus Christ as Servant of God." Jesus is both the Lord who commands, and the Servant who obeys.

TF understands service in a theological way, i.e., he understands it from its root in the life and work of Christ. It is the saving of creation. Although it would be a mistake to read back into TF all our modern ecological concern, yet there is a holism in his view of service that should help us to see and teach such ecological concern as a proper Christian activity, rather than as the church 'catching up' with modern concerns and trends.

The service of the church is neither a use of worldly power, so that the service arm of the church becomes simply a supplement to what the State may or may not do, nor a retreat into 'religious' concerns. Current

21. Mentioned by Roland Walls in one of his New College lectures.

talk in the UK of 'the big society' or 'the good society' conceals a plea by politicians for the voluntary sector to take over some functions currently undertaken by the State, mainly to save money, but perhaps with the recognition that sometimes at least, such voluntary service can provide something better. There may be an opportunity for the Christian church here to model new patterns of service without seeking power or influence through it.

TF points out how the church has found it hard to properly acknowledge the ministry of deacons. Yet ministers and deacons "are as necessary and as indispensable to one another as husband and wife, and father and mother, in the same family." This is an interesting statement, as it sheds light on TF's attempt, early in his life, to persuade the General Assembly that the way forward for women was to lift the diaconate to the same level as that of the ordained ministry.[22] Later TF realized that this approach was not going to be fruitful, and he became a supporter of moves to ordain women to the ministry of word and sacrament (see chapter 10).

In this chapter again we see TF cast in the role of reformer (as in chapter 2). "Three areas in particular call for drastic amendment and far-reaching reform . . ."

- *Intercession*, which can be seen as a battle between the forces of good and evil, and a participation in the intercession of Christ in heaven. Such intercession lies at the heart of the basic service of the people of God, and one regrets the modern trend within independent charismatic churches to understand 'worship' as simply praise. In his lectures on Christology and soteriology, TF

22. TF wrote two articles in Manse Mail, the in-house publication for ministers, about 'The Ministry of Men and Women in the Kirk.' In the first, published in May 1960, he wrote: "Woman have a diaconal, not a presbyteral, ministry in the Church . . . when a Church appoints women to presbyteral office or fails to commission women to proper diaconal office, it thereby calls in question its faithfulness to the apostolic foundation of the Church in Christ." He repeats the positive side of this in his second, published in February 1964, and continues, "It may also involve the setting apart of some women in a representative capacity to a particular ministry within the whole, appropriate to them and in accordance with the economic pattern of redemption and creation revealed in Christ. Women could thus minister as women, and men minister as men, within the one ministry in which they share in mutuality of authority and complementarity of function."

says that the bond of prayer between Father and Son lies at the heart of all Christ's atoning ministry.[23]

- *Witness and evangelism*: "It is a betrayal of *diakonia* to heal the hurt of God's people lightly, saying peace, peace, where there is no peace." There is no substitute for this inclusive understanding of *diakonia*, no way the church can slip round the call to evangelize. TF was prophetic in seeing that *diakonia* or any form of mission without evangelism was another unbalanced modern trend.

- *Reconciliation*. TF has three things in mind here, the joining of evangelism and practical service, the healing of divisions within congregations, and union between churches. He says that disunity is a scandal, and he himself was firmly behind moves to unite the Church of Scotland and the Episcopal Churches in Britain.

By *reform*, TF does not mean this or that plan of action, but a change of life and practice by church ministers and members that will lead to Christ actually doing 'kingdom stuff' in our midst. Of course, he holds a proper balance in speaking of what *God* does and what *we* must do, well expressed by the aphorism, "Without God we cannot, without us God will not."

7. The Church in the Last Quarter of the Twentieth Century

The first part of this closing address to the 1976 General Assembly is devoted to refuting any alliance of Christianity with Marxism. TF argues that the advance of science is destroying the intellectual foundations of Marxism and that the church should in any case welcome this advance, as it discloses the structures of our created world. Since this is so, he regards "with sorrow and shame" theologians and churchmen who claim that in the space age we can no longer believe in the incarnation or the bodily resurrection of Jesus.

Behind his concern with Marxism lay a positive conviction about the nature of the church. Speaking about the early church, TF says,

---

23. See Torrance, *Incarnation*, 118–21; Torrance, *Atonement*, chapter 9, esp. 274–76, 297.

"It was because the Church's message was free from ideological mixture, that it could create new situations in society and in the world in which the transforming power of the gospel left such an impact that all subsequent history has been affected." Years later, TF was to describe the Church and Nation Committee report to the General Assembly of 1982 as "a dark whirlpool of error,"[24] not so much because it discussed nationalism in a positive light (he voted yes in the referendum for a Scottish parliament) but because of the *way* it did so. It may seem that TF was confusing his legitimate concern that the high profile of the Church and Nation Committee led people to see its pronouncements as the message of the Church of Scotland, with an ill-founded view that identified Scottish nationalism with racism and even Nazism. The Scottish National Party, in line with thinkers like Jim Sillars and Neil McCormick, has been very careful to stand clear of ethnic nationalism. TF's statement here illustrates his passionate conviction that the church as the reconciled community embracing all nations must stand above all nationalism as such.[25]

TF picks up on the enduring interest in "spiritual realities" by men and women currently outside the church, claiming that human civilization is sick of materialism and secularism, and that from below is coming a longing for "otherworldly and divine resources." He was writing at a time when most Scots still acknowledged the church as a possible channel for such energy, and indeed when charismatic renewal was in full flow. He acknowledges the significance of what he calls "the tide of Pentecostalism."

Again he calls for reform. We must reach a deeper understanding, he says, of the essential mission of the church, away from our ecclesiastical pragmatism and legalism, and instead should bring "the great truths of Christ clothed with his gospel" to bear upon the heart and soul of our people.

The expression "our people" was commonly used by Church of Scotland leaders of his generation, and it was often ambiguous—does it mean church members, or does it mean the people of Scotland? Perhaps

24. See *Life and Work*, July 1982.

25. One of the best discussions of Nationalism and Christian faith is in W. F. Storrar, *Scottish Identity: A Christian Vision* (Edinburgh: Handsel, 1990), especially chapter 7.

there was a time when such ambiguity was of little practical consequence but in the following years the divide was to become so great that today the renewal of parish ministry is often tackled by 'Fresh Expressions' and other programmes. TF himself may have been ambivalent—on the one hand, he was critical of projects that seemed to him simply managerial, but at the same time he was a strong supporter of Billy Graham's mission in Scotland.[26]

The relation of TF to the Church of Scotland General Assembly was not a simple one. Of course, the Church of Scotland was proud of TF, proud of his achievements in dialogue between the churches, between theology and science, and of his reputation as a theologian of international repute. But in practice the Assembly seldom took him seriously: commissioners might be glad of his support on a particular issue, but they were usually reluctant to engage in the kind of theological journey he called for. I say that sadly as a participant in many Assemblies at which he spoke.[27] The Assembly is at its best when it engages in theological debate, but time after time I have seen pragmatism trump theology. There are two reasons for this: first, a remarkable number of ministers and elders seem to believe theology is unimportant, and second, where people hold very different theological views, 'practical' arguments offer a prospect of agreement on the way forward. Where TF himself was concerned, certainly "a prophet is not without honour save in his own country."

8. God, Destiny, and Suffering

It is talks like this—an address to the Edinburgh Medical Missionary Society—that reveal the practical features of TF's theology, and something of his inner motivation.

The content of the address arose from a recent visit to the Middle East as part of his moderatorial year. TF had first-hand experience of the region during his student days.[28] He speaks very carefully about the

---

26. TF spoke in favour of Billy Graham's visit at the General Assembly; incidentally his brother David decided against a programme of study under Karl Barth because D. P. Thomson challenged him to come and help him with the All-Scotland Crusade.

27. To be fair, TF did not find it easy to 'suffer fools gladly,' and this translated in later life into a tendency to 'lecture' the Assembly, which did not go down well.

28. There is a brief account by his brother David Torrance in the on-line Journal

sense of destiny that both Jews and Muslims feel in the Middle East; while land is immensely important to both, the Jewish sense of empire is restricted to one land, whereas for Muslims it is much wider.[29] Most people view the conflict in the Middle East primarily as a matter of justice.[30] TF, while careful to avoid taking sides, reminds us that theology and in particular eschatology defines the deeper context in which the future of the Middle East will be played out.

He does this with a typical theological question: The fundamental question we have to raise with both of them is "Who is God? Is he the living God who exercises active control over peoples and destinies of nations?" We say to the Jews, "Who is this God that you seem to have found again in the Six-Day War when you said 'The Lord of Hosts is among us; this is not our doing but the Lord's doing.' Who is that God of active providence, and how does he relate to the problems of suffering and pain and destiny? Or is God immutable and impassible?" He asks for a deep dialogue with Jews and with Arabs around the question of suffering.

As often, his talk is prescient. Back in 1977 TF was already identifying rising Islamic militancy as a force to be reckoned with. He asks for co-operation with the Orthodox in the Middle East, and says we should learn from their policy never to give up property in the Middle East! And he insists that Jews should become Jewish Christians not Gentile Christians, at a time when so-called messianic Jews were fewer in number and less well recognized than they are today.

In the last section of his address, TF returns to the scandal of Christian disunity, with the appalling example of the Holy Sepulcher in the Old

---

Participatio 1 (2009) 30–31, and a fuller account in his *Memoirs* held by Princeton University.

29. Since TF spoke, we have, of course, the 'benefit' of knowing more clearly how, for example, the leaders of Iran view Israel, namely as a people to be eliminated, because the reclaiming of Israel for Islam is for some Muslims a theological imperative to pave the way for the coming of the Mahdi. This has been referred to in recent times by Shi'ite Muslims such as President Ahmadinejad and the Ayatollah Khomeini, but in fact it is a much earlier theme—there is a thorough examination of the literature in Joan Peters, *From Time Immemorial* (New York: Harper and Row, 1984).

30. In this context, the question of Arab refugees from Israel, and Jewish refugees from Arab countries is an important issue that is seldom understood or taken seriously (Peters, *From Time Immemorial*, chapters 2 and 3).

City, where a Muslim has to keep the keys to avoid conflict between rival Christian claims to the place. How can we preach the gospel of Jesus Christ to both Arab and Jew, he asks, when our own house is so divided?

9. Eldership in the Reformed Church

TF argues cogently that contemporary Church of Scotland, and indeed wider Reformed understanding and practice, is confused and should be reformed in accordance with Scripture. The two mistakes we have inherited are:

(a) Calvin's calling the seven helpers in Acts 6 'deacons'—TF points out that *diakonia* describes the office of presbyter also, and that what the seven did was clearly to exercise a presbyteral ministry and not simply a diaconal one in the modern sense of the word.

(b) Making the modern office of 'elder' something different from the NT 'deacon,' for example 'ruling elder' as opposed to 'teaching elder.' In practice Reformed commentators on Philippians 1:1, which refers only to "bishops and deacons," have always included 'elders' under 'deacons' and not 'bishops' or presbyters.

TF does not recommend doing away with elders, who have performed a fine service for the church, but rather that the whole view of eldership should be raised to conform more closely to the NT 'deacon.' This is turn is part of his concern that *diakonia* should be a major characteristic of the ministry of both presbyters and deacons. There is no doubt that the importance of the diaconate for him remains a significant and neglected aspect of his thought.[31]

10. The Ministry of Women

The cover of the original booklet had a symbolic representation of the mural in the *Capella Greca* (painted within a century after the death and resurrection of Christ) depicting a celebration of the Eucharist. It

---

31. See again the fine article by TF, 'Service in Jesus Christ' (reprinted as chapter 6 above).

is known as the 'Catacomb of Priscilla,' the lady shown as one of seven presbyters seated in a semi-circle behind the holy table. TF also refers to this in chapter 9.

By this time (1992) TF had departed from his earlier argument that it would be adequate to raise the office of deaconess to equality with the office of minister (see footnote 22), and argues strongly on theological grounds that women and men should equally be eligible for ordination to the ministry of word and sacrament.

He pays particular attention to the high Anglican objections, based on the spurious idea that only a man can represent Christ at the Eucharist, and the booklet was published at the time when this was a major issue in the Anglican Church. The Movement for the Ordination of Women took a number of copies.

Today the question might well be, when will the Roman Catholic Church admit women to the priesthood? Like most changes in that communion, if and when it happens it will happen without much fanfare; all the theology is already in place (we are told), and the measure simply awaits the advent of a sympathetic pope.

11. Preaching Christ Today

This is one of the very clearest expositions of the way TF approached the New Testament and the preaching of the gospel. It features two of his favourite themes, modern science post-Einstein, and the gospel truth that we are saved by *the faith of* Christ, rather than by *our faith in* Christ. But it starts with one of the basic thrusts of his life and ministry, that preaching Christ is both an evangelical and a theological activity.

'Evangelical' has, of course, become something of a weasel word, a word that means very different things to different people. It is used to identify supporters and opponents, and even used to label particular churches: but there is a considerable distance between, say, an evangelical church in continental Europe, where 'evangelical' might mean 'not Roman Catholic,' and an evangelical church in California, where the word might mean charismatic, or dispensationalist, or whatever.

TF was nothing if not evangelical in the sense of seeking to be led by the gospel, wanting to proclaim Christ, desiring that Christ should be the pattern of life and thought. But chapter 1 illustrates how early in his life his theology, or maybe his willingness to serve a rival movement, fell foul of one grouping of 'conservative evangelicals,' though today he would be happily owned and quoted by many who might wear that label.

He has an interesting reference to anthropology and the Navarro Indians, which he uses to support his argument that New Testament scholars have been using the wrong presuppositions. TF, like all good preachers, 'poked around a lot in other people's backyards' when they were open to public view, using illustrations from widely different fields, and he was usually sufficiently well informed to get away with it, especially when it was in the field of science.[32]

Another example is more controversial. In support of his argument that Jesus used Hebrew not Aramaic, he refers to a passage in the Jerusalem Talmud where two rabbis are discussing the interpretation of a Hebrew word in Isaiah and call in a maid to help them, since they did not speak Hebrew. However, the conclusion may depend on whether these rabbis are Tannaitic (before 200CE) or Amoraic (later, which would favour TF's case), and there is still an ongoing scholarly debate about whether Jesus would have commonly used Hebrew or Aramaic, although the balance is probably shifting towards Hebrew.[33]

One helpful point to come out of this debate is that people in the Middle East then as now were likely to speak more than one language. Jesus may in fact have been familiar with Hebrew, Aramaic, and Greek, since Greek was commonly used in the area of the Decapolis which he visited more than once.

TF also refers appreciatively to his colleague James Stewart,[34] from whom he received warm and unstinting support. He did not always get support from colleagues, and occasionally must have felt a little like his favourite theologian Athanasius, once described as *Athanasius contra mundum*. Few Christian leaders function well alone: TF's parents,[35] his brothers and sisters, and his own wife and family all meant a lot to him;

---

32. See, for example, the testimony of Alister McGrath in *T. F. Torrance*, xii.

33. The publication of a Dead Sea Scroll called 'Some Precepts of the Torah' is an example of Hebrew being used in a more conversational form.

34. Professor of New Testament Language, Literature and Theology in New College for twenty years up to 1966.

35. Eerdmans published a marvelous booklet by his mother on bringing up a family, with a foreword by Ruth Graham.

they often consulted one another, and he valued the friendship likewise of former students.[36]

12. Legal and Evangelical Priests

This chapter was published in a Festschrift for Peter de Klerk in 1997 and was one of the last things that TF wrote for publication. By this time he had disposed of many of his books, and therefore borrowed a Latin folio volume contained Calvin's Commentary on Malachi from his nephew Robert Walker.

Each of Calvin's lectures on Malachi were preceded by a prayer, and it is these prayers which TF gathered together and incorporated into his article in illustration of Calvin's theology. For the most part he is content to use the translation of the 1843 publication of Calvin's commentaries, except where he deems the rendering to be inadequate or awkward, in which case he inserts his own. Inevitably there is repetition, and I have selected about half of the prayers, ones that best illustrate the subject of the chapter. The lectures on Malachi conclude Calvin's 'lectures' or homiletic and exegetical commentary on all the 'minor prophets.'

Those of an evangelical persuasion are often puzzled by the emphasis TF placed upon church order and on the ordained ministry as a priestly ministry, albeit subordinate to the priesthood of Christ and within the corporate participation of the whole church in that one priesthood. In chapter 5, where he spells out the role of the ordained presbyter, TF explains how there is no doctrinal distinction between a presbyter and a bishop. The other side to this argument, of course, is that the ordained minister has the full authority of a (New Testament) bishop!

Appealing for Christian liberty, Milton once famously complained, "New Presbyter is but old Priest writ large."[37] The centuries following the Reformation were, among many other things, a struggle for Christian liberty in an age accustomed to having a national church, even if now Protestant rather than Roman Catholic. This final chapter sheds some light on church order as understood by John Calvin, whom TF followed in so many ways. John Calvin took a high view of the church, its

---

36. This came across to me strongly when we organized an eightieth birthday celebration for him at Carberry Tower.

37. In a poem entitled *On the Forcers of Conscience under the Long Parliament*.

Sacraments, and its order; although expressed carefully in biblical and Reformed language, this language as described by TF includes expressions like "a fearsome tie between the offerings and the offerers," "immensely solemn consecration of priests for liturgical acts of worship . . . a terrifying experience."

Of course, in a commentary on Malachi, where slack and unfaithful priests are excoriated, Calvin was bound to use strong language. However, TF comments that in his later Commentaries Calvin used language, in speaking of ordained ministry and of worship, "such as he had not been in the habit of using before, but with no less an evangelical meaning."

TF further comments that Calvin distinguishes between the general priesthood of all church members and the priesthood of certain people within it, and also that Calvin regarded himself as a priest. Moreover, in speaking of our daily prayer as "offering Christ to the Father, Calvin uses language which might be regarded by some today as 'unreformed.'" However, this is helpful in showing how, provided our understanding of him is put in an evangelical instead of a legal framework, there is in Calvin's view more of a continuity between the medieval and the Reformed church than we might think. And given also the respect which Knox paid to Calvin, it becomes less surprising not only that what became the Church of Scotland always saw itself as in a true line of succession from the medieval church in Scotland, but that so many priests converted to the Reformed faith.

While the purpose of this paper is to show how Calvin distinguished between a legal and an evangelical priesthood, it is clear that Calvin never questioned the authority of the presbyter to rule in the church. His quarrel with the medieval priesthood was that its priests misrepresented Christ and his once for all priesthood and sacrifice.

Conclusion

I hope that these very varied articles by T. F. Torrance, spanning fifty years, may all be read with great profit to illustrate his views on what he might have called 'practical theology' and show how gospel, church, and ministry are each related to Jesus Christ and, therefore, to one another and to the world which God has redeemed and still upholds.

—Jock Stein

CHAPTER 1

My Parish Ministry: Alyth, 1940–43[1]

IN 1940 I WAS still at Oriel College, Oxford, working on my dissertation on *The Doctrine of Grace in the Apostolic Fathers,* when I began to think seriously of entering the parish ministry. I had earlier offered to serve as an Army Chaplain under the Royal Army Chaplains Department but was told that there was a two-year waiting list, and so I decided to get to work on my dissertation for the Basel doctorate, and to go up to Oxford. Professor Norman Porteous, my old Hebrew Teacher at New College, offered to write to his friend Dr. Marcus Tod, Vice-Provost of Oriel College, recommending me to him. I was accepted at once, and made arrangements to go up to Oxford. Rooms in the College were all occupied, and so Oriel gave me a room in one of their properties nearby, facing the High Street, and looking across to St. Mary's. I set to work at once and made good progress, especially in checking my research in secular Greek literature, mostly poetry, to examine the different ways in which the word *charis* is used in the New Testament for grace. The dissertation was becoming rather large, although it was by no means finished, but the linguistic section had been written up and checked, and with some minor corrections was approved by Dr. Marcus Tod. It was later to be cut down drastically in length.

---

1. This memoir was written down after TF had retired from New College at the end of September 1979. His son Thomas thinks it may have been written in the late 1980s or early 1990s.

I had quickly become caught up in the student life of the Oxford Inter-Collegiate Christian Union and the Student Christian Movement, where I met and became fast friends with Donald MacKinnon, then a don at Keble College. I was invited to lead a University Mission sponsored by the Oxford Inter-Collegiate Christian Union, with the blessing and the guidance of the Revd. Joe Fison, Chaplain of the Oxford Pastorate, and the Revd. Ian Thomson, Chaplain of Hertford College. The SCM in Oxford asked me to be their president even though they knew I was leading the OICCU Mission! But the Inter-Varsity Fellowship thought otherwise, for after one term my engagement in a student mission sponsored by the OICCU was abruptly terminated by the authorities of the Inter-Varsity Fellowship in London, as they did not approve of my form of theological evangelism or of my appreciation of Karl Barth, let alone my friendly relations with the SCM!! At the same time my calling and my commitment to enter the holy ministry in Scotland pressed heavily on me, especially since many Church of Scotland ministers had become army chaplains so that vacant parishes in Scotland were calling out for ministers. I had come to love Oxford, and the congregation of St. Columba's Church, in which the Provost and Vice-Provost of Oriel, Sir David Ross and Dr. Marcus Niebuhr Tod, were leading members, and I would have liked to stay longer in Oxford, possibly working for a D. Phil. on the Philosophy of Karl Jaspers of Basel about which I had talked with the Provost, W. D. Ross, who had never heard of Jaspers! That would have helped me to work out further my understanding of the epistemological and theological relations of Karl Barth's thought to that of German philosophy. However, that was not to be.

I agreed to let my name be put before the home ministry authorities of the Kirk at 121 George Street, Edinburgh—I think my father had a hand in that and James S. Stewart—and they put forward my name to two congregations urgently needing a minister, at Kinross and Alyth. In due course I was contacted by representatives from those churches, both of which seemed keen to have me. Kinross, on the other side of the Forth Estuary from Edinburgh, rather appealed to me as it was not far from Edinburgh and my parents there, and it would be easy for me to go frequently from there to the divinity library at New College in Edinburgh. However, when I met the deputations of elders, I was rather

My Parish Ministry: Alyth, 1940–43

drawn to those from Alyth in Perthshire. They were godly farmers, very friendly and intelligent people, elders of the Barony Parish Kirk in Alyth, and so I agreed to let my name go before them for consideration and selection. I was particularly impressed with Ritchie Smith, the Town Clerk of Alyth, Solomon Thompson and David Bell, well-to-do farmers—the latter, the son of an Edinburgh minister, had lost a leg in the First World War, and lived and farmed at Balloch near Alyth, close to the border between Perthshire and Angus; Balloch was once the residence of Lord Ogilvy, one of the Airlie family. Solomon (Sol) Thompson, with his brother David, were the sons of a mole-catcher, and became very successful farmers. David had died before I went to Alyth, but his widow lived at Airlie Brae. Solomon was one of the most go-ahead farmers in Perthshire; he had several large farms, in which he cultivated especially raspberries and potatoes. He lived humbly at a small farm steading called Mornity not far from Alyth station. The Interim Moderator of the Barony Kirk was the Revd. Robert Hastie, minister of St. Andrews Church in Blairgowrie, about five miles away from Alyth on the road to Perth.

David J. R. Bell, whose father had been minister of the Dean Church in Edinburgh, became a real friend, and used to have us frequently in his home, where we also met his mother-in-law Mrs. Ross, whose husband had been a minister of a Church in Clydebank during the First World War and in the 1920s. The Bells had three children, Margery, the oldest, Jo, who was later to marry David Grieve, one of my former students, a son Ross, and a younger daughter, Alison. David Bell had some rare books that must have been in his father's library—I recall particularly the *Syntagma Theologiae* by Amandus Polanus of Polansdorf, one of Karl Barth's favourite theologians. That work of Polanus was long used by Presbyteries in their training of ordinands for the ministry. It was many years before I was to acquire a copy for myself, which I picked up one day in Edinburgh. David Bell later donated his copy to New College Library. Another well-known farming family were the Mitchell brothers who had several farms, on some of which they bred Aberdeen Angus cattle. The wife of one brother was a close relative, a sister of Mrs. David Bell of the Balloch, whose widowed mother Mrs. Ross was then living with them there. The Mitchells lived on one of their own farms near

Kilry, where a neighbouring farm belonged to the Ramsay family. They were members of Kilry Church but frequently worshipped with us in the Barony Church on Sunday evenings. There were not a few Ramsays in the neighbourhood of Alyth, some of them descendants of Sir James Ramsay, Baronet of Bamff, and of the Revd. William Ramsay, minister of Alyth before the Disruption in 1843.

Alyth was a lovely old town with about three thousand inhabitants. It was situated near the border between Perth and Angus at the lower end of the foothills that ran down from the Grampians to the plain of Strathmore, near the defile through the lower hills that open the way to Kingoldrum, Lintrathen, and Kilry in Glen Isla. The Burgh of Alyth had been established at the foot of a hill which rose up three hundred feet behind it, with rough land on the Alyth side, but with a small farm called Balwhyme on the other side, belonging to the Lindsay family, but which had once belonged to the Vicars of Alyth before the Reformation, and then to John Ogilvy of Clova. A burn ran down from Bamff into Alyth through a lovely glen. Where it turned down into the town dividing upper Alyth from lower Alyth, there was a very old and picturesque bridge, beside which the Barony Parish Kirk was situated. The bridge was often visited by professional and amateur artists, one of which was my mother. Sometimes the burn was swollen in spate, and could even flow over into Alyth Square at the top of Airlie Street. The Town Council offices, with the ironmongers, flanked the western side of the Square, opposite Buick the butcher's shop. Airlie Street ran East from the Square, past the Post Office on one side and on the other side St. Ninian's Church and the Barony Church hall, which used to be the old United Presbyterian Church before it was united with the Free Church to form the Barony Parish Church. It stretched past the railway station to the War Memorial and Meigle Road. A small railway ran across the valley to Alyth Junction about seven miles away on the main line from Perth to Aberdeen. The little train from Alyth also ran on under the main line and across the Howe of Strathmore to Dundee, sixteen or seventeen miles away.

In due course I was invited to preach at St. Andrews Church in Blairgowrie to which the elders and a host of other members of the Barony Kirk came to hear me. I recall preaching a sermon on Herod and John the Baptist, a sermon with which I was rather familiar as I had preached it several times before, and so was rather at ease with it. That was in the morning, but in the afternoon I preached on St. John 3:7, "Ye must be born again," so that the people from Alyth would know that I was concerned to preach the gospel. The elders, deacons, and representatives of the Barony who met me afterwards were evidently pleased, and then at a meeting following the afternoon service they decided to ask their fellow-members in Alyth to call me. A formal meeting of the congregation was arranged in due course by the Interim Moderator, and before long I was invited to preach at the Barony Church when the whole congregation could hear and meet me. That took place, and they agreed unanimously to give me a call, which was then put forward to the Presbytery of Meigle by Mr. Hastie, at which it was formally endorsed, and a day was appointed for my ordination and induction on the 20th of March, 1940. My parents and I travelled up to Alyth a few days earlier on the 17th.

The Barony Kirk had a lovely manse in Cambridge Street at the West end of the town, which I had now to furnish and get ready. My parents helped out with finance, through borrowing from their Edinburgh bank, and my mother helped me to buy furniture and acquire the necessary kitchen equipment. The former minister, the Revd. Donald Ross, then minister of North Mayfield Church in Edinburgh, had left me a large book case, and a local joiner quickly made me another, so that I soon had a well-furnished study. The study, which was located upstairs, had a lovely view over some of the Thompson Farm buildings, and across the hamlet of New Alyth, to the other side of the Howe of Strathmore. We were fortunate to get a kitchen maid from a family in the town. My parents came to stay with me in the Manse—my mother was to stay on for a year or so, to get me settled.

The ordination service in the Barony Church on March 20th was very moving, when I was joined by several of my College friends, notably Ronald Selby Wright, George G. Campbell, John K. S. Reid, and John S. Ross. Principal W. A. Curtis of New College, and the Revd. J. M. B. Duncan of Tynecastle Parish Church, Edinburgh, also came to be with me. The Presbytery, or 'corporate Episcopate,' led by the Moderator, the Revd. Edward T. Hewitt of Airlie Parish, and the Revd. R. J. Wright of

Rattray East, a graduate of Oxford who had been at Brasenose College, officiated at the ordination, and my father, along with my Edinburgh friends, was invited to join the Presbyters in the laying on of hands. The Revd. Jacob Sibbald Clark, and the Revd. Henry Reid of St. Ninian's Episcopal Church, also took part. The elders of the Church were associated with the Presbytery in giving me the right hand of Fellowship. It was a very memorable and deeply moving occasion which I shall never forget.

Afterwards I wrote on a fly leaf of my pocket New Testament the words of our Lord to his disciples recorded in John 15:16: "Ye have not chosen me, but I have chosen you, and ordained you, that you should go and bring forth fruit, and that your fruit should remain: that whatsoever you shall ask of the Father in my name, he may give it to you." That was the copy of the New Testament, with Psalms attached, which I was to carry with me in my pastoral visitation round Alyth. Those words, which I associated with my ordination, have been a great source of strength to me throughout my ministry in parish and college alike.

The ordination service was followed in the traditional Scottish way by greetings from neighbouring churches and friends. And then in the evening there followed a 'Social Meeting,' with tea served in the Church Hall, which was chaired by the Revd. R. D. Hastie. After the singing of the 2nd Paraphrase, I was welcomed by the congregation and presented by Miss F. Findlay with ministerial Robes. The Choir then sang an Anthem, and presentations were made to Mr. and Mrs. Hastie by Messrs. Ritchie Smith and W. S. Kidd. Short addresses followed given by Principal Curtis, George Campbell, and my Father; then after a solo by Mr. Sydney Hynd, and an Organ Voluntary, more short addresses were given by my friends Jack Reid and John Ross, while cheerful thanks to all who had taken part were expressed by Messrs. Thompson, Symington, Murray and Hynd. So ended an extraordinary day, in which I was made vividly aware of the welcome by my colleagues in the ministry, and by the whole of the Barony Kirk family. That was the beginning of a long friendship, to which I owed a great deal.

On the following Sunday morning I was 'preached in,' as the custom was, by a senior friend, Professor Hugh Watt of New College,

Edinburgh, who held the Chair of Church History. I began my ministry of the gospel in Alyth by taking the evening service.

Soon afterwards I had a Kirk Session meeting with the elders. There were, if I remember correctly, at least fourteen of them at that time. The session clerk was John Black, a farmer; there was Ritchie Smith, the Town Clerk (who later became Session Clerk) and his solicitor colleague, Charles Anderson, James Ferguson, a draper and one of Alyth's most prominent citizens, John Welch, a very godly humble theological ploughman, his employer Solomon Thompson, David Bell, Jim Lindsay, and John Robertson (all farmers); Mr. Kidd who had a shoe shop, and another John Robertson, the Jeweller, who was always known locally as 'Watchie Robertson,' the Cochrane brothers who had a small soft-drinks factory, and William Williams, a gardener. We agreed to meet frequently to discuss the pastoral care of the congregation and to have prayer together. The elders supplied me with a list of all the members of the congregation, and their addresses, and I planned right away to visit them all as soon as I could. The old parish of Alyth had been divided into two after the Disruption of the Church of Scotland in the nineteenth century, giving the High Church Parish, and the Barony Church Parish. The minister of the High Church was Jacob Sibbald Clark, a graduate of St. Andrews—most of the members of the town and the countryside were members of his Kirk—my congregation numbered about 400, but it contained many of the most educated and go-ahead people. There were more people in both parishes who had not yet 'joined the Kirk,' as the expression was. The Barony Kirk was a union of the former Free Church and the united Presbyterian Church.

The Parish of Alyth had a distinguished Church history, dating back before the Reformation. An illuminating book about it, *The History of Alyth Parish Church*, had been published in 1933 by a former minister, the Revd. James Meikle, who had earlier published in 1918 *An Old Session Book: Being Studies in Alyth's Second Session Book* (1918), and a third very interesting work, *Places and Place-Names Round Alyth* in 1925. However, the most interesting and significant book for me was by the Revd. Thomas Ayton, 'Minister of the gospel at Alyth,' who published a very learned and remarkable volume book in 1730, entitled *The Original Constitution of the Christian Church: Wherein the Extremes on either Hand are Stated and Examined.* In it he put forward a proposal for the union of the Presbyterian and Episcopalian Churches, a way of thinking which I was later to develop and pursue, somewhat to the dismay of Professor Hugh Watt!

The old Parish Church in Alyth, which dated back to the thirteenth century, built in Norman style, had been enlarged after the Reformation, but had to be replaced in 1836—in any case it could no longer seat the population of Alyth. Some of the arches of the ancient Church remain, its ruins flanked by a piece of the wall on which there remain the arms of several local families, like the Rollos of the Balloch. A new Church with a high steeple and a loft was erected on a different site at the foot of Millbank in 1835. It was an imposing structure, which dominated the view of upper Alyth. After the division of the Parish of Alyth, it was known as the High Church. The Barony Church was a rather squat and not a very elegant building. It had been erected without a steeple in the middle of the nineteenth century for the congregation of the Free Church, situated on the north side of the Alyth burn across from the old Packhorse Bridge. There it was set back from the street at the end of a row of business buildings. It had a high pulpit, and a gallery that enabled it to seat about six hundred people. Perhaps what I most liked about it was the tolling of the church bell for morning and evening service. It was the congregation not the building that was so significant.

As I got to know the members of the Barony congregation I was impressed by the fact that they were rather go-ahead people who joined farm to farm and business to business, and were relatively prosperous. Why? I reflected on the dubious idea put forward by Max Weber that Calvinism lay at the root of capitalism! Louis Mumford the historian has shown that was not really the case, but had to do with the fact that Calvinist congregations developed in the prosperous City States that flourished during the renaissance of European thought and society. In Alyth I put down the robust go-ahead character of many of my congregation to the impact made on their forbears by one of my predecessors, who was a strong Calvinist, and taught them the Westminster Shorter Catechism. The effect of that, apart from its religious intention, was to stretch and train the intelligence of children and members of the Church, so that they proved to be very capable and go-ahead in their daily life, whether as farmers or as business people in the town. Another side-effect of that strict Calvinist outlook, however, was that members of the Free Kirk tended to marry Calvinists. About half of my elders were either childless or bachelors! But they belonged to a former generation—and things had now changed considerably, but, I fear, not always for the better!

In Alyth there was also a lovely small Scottish Episcopal Church, St. Ninian's, the minister of which was the Revd. Henry Reid, an Oxford and Oriel man, whose father had been Primate of the Scottish Episcopal Church. Henry, who lived near me in Cambridge Street, had lost a leg and did not manage to get about much, but we became very good friends. One of my first pastoral duties in Alyth was to visit an old lady over eighty years of age, Mrs. Gellatly, who called for me right away. She wanted to 'confess' her rather bigoted past. She told me that she had been the last person to agree to singing paraphrases and then hymns introduced by the Free Kirk, and always crossed over to the other side of the street when one of the 'Episcolopians' (as she called them!) came along! However, during the vacancy, Henry Reid had made a point of visiting her, had prayed with her, and she was rather ashamed at the way she had thought of him and Episcopalians and had behaved toward them. I visited Henry and told him about that and thanked him for being so kind and gracious to old Mrs. Gellatly. I was later to have a daughter or niece of hers as a member of my congregation in Aberdeen.

As soon as I could I set about visiting all the members of the congregation, accompanied by the elder of the district who introduced me. I made a point of reading a passage of the Holy Scripture and praying in each home, relating the intercession as far as I could to their family life and circumstances of which I learned from their elder. One of the first homes I visited was that of the Flemings at Aberbothrie, where Mrs. Fleming, a widow, was very ill, I think, with consumption. The farm was managed by her stalwart son Jim, who was later to become an elder of the Kirk. It took very many weeks for me to visit them all in that way, but I was determined to see them as soon as possible and as often as I could, and also to visit all the other homes within the bounds of the Barony Parish, whether they belonged to the Barony Kirk or not. In not a few cases I found that they had not had a pastoral visit from a minister for over twenty years, which rather shocked me. They were often in tears before I left. That was the case, for example, when I visited a farm with seven stalwart sons and their widowed mother who, though ninety years of age, danced a few steps of a jig to show me how fit she still was. She certainly ruled the roost! During those pastoral visits I used to recall the statement of John Calvin that the gospel should be preached *privatim et domatim,* privately and from house to house, and made that a major part of my ministry. I found that after I had visited people two or three times and read the Bible to them and prayed with them, they often opened their hearts to me. I learned more of the needs of people's lives and souls in that way than I could have done otherwise, and it helped to make my preaching of the gospel and exposition of the Bible as personally relevant to them as possible. I recall on one occasion, for example, a lady member of the congregation hesitatingly told me that she had a vision of angels, but had never dared tell any minister about it before in case it was dismissed. When I told her that I believed her, and spoke a little of the ministry of angels, she was overjoyed in a way that deepened her faith and her own reading of the Holy Scriptures.

I must record another pastoral experience, which left me with a vivid recollection. I learned of a former deacon of the Barony Kirk who had for some reason quarreled with the minister and had become very bitter and hostile to the Faith. When I said I would visit him, I was urged not to do so, but of course I went. When I knocked at his door it was opened by his daughter who was half-blind and unkempt, and told her who I was and that I had come to visit her father. She told me he would not see me—he heard and shouted at me from within telling me to go away. But I insisted, and when I went in I found him lying on his bed, which was rather filthy—he was clearly very ill. When he knew who I was and why I had come he shouted fiercely at me, but I told him I was a messenger from the Lord and had come to read the Bible and pray with him. In spite of his foul-mouthed objections I began to read the 51st Psalm, but he kept shouting at me all the way through. When I had finished he told me that now I could go, but I said that I would now pray, at which he objected vehemently. I prayed for him and his daughter, and asked the Lord to forgive his sins. In spite of his attempts to stop me I kept on and prayed through the 51st Psalm applying it directly to him,

My Parish Ministry: Alyth, 1940–43

and at length he grew quiet. When I opened my eyes, he was quite calm, an entirely different person. I realized that it was a kind of exorcism, and now the poor man was restored to his right mind, and at peace with God. When I went away to the war, I asked my brother-in-law, Kenneth MacKenzie, who had come to take services in Alyth for a few weeks before he left as a missionary for Central Africa, to visit the old man, which he did and found him quite changed as I related. He had not long to live and died soon afterwards. What impressed me was the wonderful power of the Word of God, which I read in that ancient Psalm, and the power of the gospel of the Lord Jesus. The congregation soon knew what had happened, and welcomed my pastoral visits even more than before. That was an unusual incident and an extreme case, but it reminded me of what happened in the mission field when my father prayed and spoke to people, which sometimes provoked bitter, even demonic, opposition, but when again and again the grace of the Lord Jesus triumphed over opposition and when even the most hostile were saved.

I look back upon my house to house visitation in Alyth as the most rewarding and fruitful aspects of my ministry. I used to visit all the members of my congregation and parish like that as often as I could, not just once a year, and continued that practice when later I went to Aberdeen. It served to complement my rather theological sermons. I myself learned so much by way of the relevance and healing power of the Word of God, that it had a decided impact on my theology—again and again when I was lecturing about some aspect of the gospel or evangelical truth in Edinburgh, I recalled pastoral visits in Alyth where its deep significance had become clear to me, and I realized its spiritual power. As I could not separate my preaching in Alyth from my house to house visitation of the congregation, so I was never able to separate lecturing in my Christian Dogmatics class in New College from showing something of the personal and pastoral thrust and power of the truths of the gospel. Not a few students in my classes were converted, such as Lloyd Ogilvy, who after his ministry in Holywood Presbyterian Church in Los Angeles, became Chaplain to the US Senate in Washington, where as he told me it is a personal form of ministry that really counts.

Like most parishes, even in the early months of the war, Alyth was to have its casualties. I recall vividly when news came of the death of the son of the Revd. Donald Ross, the minister of North Mayfield Church in Edinburgh, my predecessor in the Barony Kirk. Fl/Lt. James Ross was a fighter pilot who lost his life on patrol over the Channel—he was a close friend of Adam Lindsay who had trained with him at Edinburgh University and the RAF. Adam was later to die of a brain tumour after the war. They were both well-known and loved in Alyth, and young Ross's death came as a particular shock to the community. Jim Lindsay, Adam's brother, had been called up in the navy and had a harrowing time in the submarines. Of our Alyth young men, I think, those that served in the Merchant Navy suffered most. Mrs. Mackay, one of my members who was a widow, lost three of her sons in the war—one of them, she told me, had left a note for her with their solicitor, to be handed to her when he did not return. He had a premonition of his death. He was killed when his ship was hit by German bombers in the harbour of Algiers. Mrs. Mackay's eldest son, who was Town Clerk of Fraserburgh, miraculously survived heavy bombing by German planes sent to destroy a factory located there making parts for Rolls Royce aero engines.

There were two doctors in Alyth, one of whom was a member of my congregation with whom I was not able to cooperate very much. He was a dour and rather abrupt widower, with a daughter and two sons who were not too fond of him. When speaking to the younger son one day (a year or so later) about the fatherhood of God, he told me that he could not think of God as 'Father' due to the way his own earthly father had behaved. One day about that time that doctor was called to visit old Mrs. Gellatly, who was ill. She told me that when he entered the bedroom where she was lying, he stood at the end of the bed, and said abruptly, "You are full of cancer and are going to die," and left. She was so incensed that she said to herself, "I am not going to die!" The doctor's behaviour made her determined to prove him wrong, and gave her such determination that she lived on to the ripe age of eighty-seven! Little did he know how much he had helped her! There was another doctor in Coupar Angus several miles away, a very kindly person of evangelical beliefs, with whom I got on well, and whom I used to call to visit some of the sick people in my congregation. Once after visiting two godly maiden sisters in Toutie Street (a few doors away from no. 16, the house with the ancient Hebrew inscription on it), whom I had got to know

My Parish Ministry: Alyth, 1940–43

quite well as deeply religious folk, I found one of them rather distressed and religiously confused—quite unlike herself. I asked Dr. MacPherson, the Coupar Angus doctor, to visit her, as I could see something was wrong which was physical rather than psychological. He came and after examining her told me she needed the minister rather than the doctor. I went back to see her, and was convinced that there really was something physically wrong, and reported to the doctor that she really needed him more than me. He returned and gave me the same verdict. Then I asked if he could have her sent to a hospital in Perth, which he agreed to do. There they found she had a poisoned kidney, and when that was cured she was right as rain. That was the kind of doctor/minister way we sought to care for people's needs, bodily and spiritual. He was happily a spiritual physician who had engaged in the evangelistic campaigns of the Revd. D. P. Thomson of Dunfermline, and we cooperated rather well. The minister friend of Dr. MacPherson in Coupar Angus was the Revd. Fred Levison who had been one year ahead of me at New College, but whom I had got to know well.

I found many new houses built in what I called upper Alyth and along the Meethill Road. In one of them I met a fine middle-aged couple who had recently arrived in Alyth. They told me that when they retired, and wondered where they would live, in Crieff or Alyth, they decided to pay a visit to the cemeteries in each place to see whether people had lived longer in Crieff or Alyth! When they found that Alyth seemed to favour longevity, they bought a house in Alyth and settled down very happily. They were now members of the Barony Kirk.

There was a fine nursing home not far from them, several hundred yards further along the Meethill road beyond the Lands of Loyal Hotel, out toward Balloch. There the road turned left past Barry Hill and on up the Glen to Craigisla. The matron and staff at the nursing home were very fine helpful people, who were much appreciated by patients and their families. They cared for people who were not ill enough to be sent to one of the large hospitals in Dundee or Perth, or the Cottage Hospital in Meigle, and catered for confinements as well, although many of the straightforward deliveries took place in the homes. My pastoral visits to the staff as well as the patients were always welcome there.

Old Mrs. Gellatly had two notorious grandsons who were plumbers, looked after by their sister. The Gellatly brothers were members of the Home Guard, and were crack shots. The elder had won a prize for shooting at Bisley. But they were irredeemable poachers, and were far from being what Scots spoke of as 'kirk-greedy.'

There was an elementary school in Alyth which children attended until they were of age to enter the high school at Blairgowrie. The school master was a member of the High Church Parish, but he welcomed me very much, and I used to give some religious instruction to the older pupils. On July 3 the annual School service was held in the Barony Church, which I took. During the year I held a regular Bible class for young people, which met in the manse, at which I was able to give more gospel instruction than in the School. The schoolmaster joined with some of my Barony Kirk members in a group that met from time to time in the manse for biblical study and discussion. This helped to overcome the tension between the two Alyth congregations that had grown up over the years before I came. The minister of the High Parish Church regarded himself as belonging to the 'Auld Kirk' and looked down on the Free Church, but I told him my own tradition was also that of the Auld Kirk. Both kirks have now at last joined rightly together, but that was long after I had left.

Alyth boasted a small police force, a sergeant and a rather flamboyant constable who had been a sergeant himself but had been demoted after he was caught once or twice poaching deer! No one blamed him, for good meat of any kind was difficult to get during the war. I was never able to help the local police in ministerial ways, but the sergeant's daughter and son used to attend my Bible class, which met weekly in the Manse. The son, John Murrie, who had been a regular member of my Bible class, was later to join the RAF and then train as a minister after the war, when he became one of my students in Edinburgh. He proved to be a very fine minister of the gospel, first as a Chaplain in the RAF and then as a parish minister at Kirkliston near Edinburgh. His sister Helen was ordained an elder when the eldership was opened to women.

I ought to mention that when Robert Hastie, the minister of St. Andrew's Church, Blairgowrie, knew that I was very interested in John Calvin, he generously gave me his complete set of Calvin's *Commentaries*,

Institutes, and *Treatises,* which proved a godsend to me in my preparation for the two sermons I had to preach each Sunday, morning and evening, and for my continuing theological study and writing. I also had a complete set of Alexander MacLaren's fine Biblical Expositions, and of Joseph Parker's sermons, which helped me in my sermon preparation, especially the former. To write two sermons each week was often hard going! I later gave them away to one of my nephews, Jamie Walker, to help him in his sermon preparation. The subjects for my sermons week by week reflected very much my regular pastoral concern, and seemed to select themselves in answer to concerns in the congregation, and the country's engagement in the war, when the needs of the sons, and sometimes daughters, of Alyth people, called for special response in congregational worship and prayer. Many of the young men were away at the war, in one or other of the services, the navy and merchant navy, and the army and air force. I did preach a series of sermons on the Book of Revelation, seventeen in all. They were expository and hortatory in character, designed to strengthen the faith of the congregation by spelling out the implications of St. John's apocalyptic visions for people's outlook upon the war, and the struggle in which the country was engaged with the evil forces of tyranny and oppression. How were we, in the light of the gospel and divine revelation, to regard what was happening and, not least, our prayers and expectations for victory? I believe those sermons met a real need, for they struck deeply into people's anxieties, sorrows, and concerns, and helped to strengthen faith and kindle the hope that we have in the sovereign rule of our Lord and Saviour. Later on in 1959 in response to repeated requests, I prepared them for publication under the title *The Apocalypse Today.* When after the end of the war I left Alyth for Aberdeen I sought to repeat the sermons in Beechgrove Church, but they did not meet with the same response, and so I put them to one side.

I also preached another series of sermons, in exposition of the Epistle to the Romans, on which I embarked at the instigation of John Welch. When he asked me one day why I had not preached on Romans, I told him it was a very theological epistle, and might be too difficult for the congregation. His rejoinder, however, was that the congregation needed some teaching on justification by grace. I could not but agree to that, and set about preparing sermons on the Epistle. My third sermon on the Epistle was devoted to the significance of justification by grace alone, the personal and practical implications for faith and Christian life. I tried to spell out, if I remember correctly, a statement of Kierkegaard which had impressed me deeply: "That before God we are always in the wrong: *Dass wir vor Gott allerzeit unrecht haben.*" At the end of the service, when I came from out the vestry, I found a number of people grouped round the person of Jim Ferguson, one of my fine godly elders, who was clearly very agitated. When I asked him what was the matter he said something to this effect: "Do you mean to say that although I have been an elder for forty years, that does not count at all for my salvation?" I said as gently as I could, "It is not what we are or do, but what Christ alone has done and continues to do for us as our Lord and Saviour, that counts. It is by his grace alone that we are put in the right with God, and by his grace alone that we are saved, and live day by day as Christians." I noticed John Welch, standing near us—and I felt at once that it was partly for his friend Jim's sake that he wanted me to expound St. Paul's doctrine of justification by grace alone. He himself, I recalled, had steeped himself in Luther's *Commentary on the Epistle to the Galatians* in which Luther had expounded justification by grace alone—*justificatio sola gratia*. I tried to explain to Jim Ferguson that it is not what we do but only what God in the Lord Jesus has done and does do for us, that is the ground, and the sole ground, of our salvation, and of our life as followers of the Lord Jesus. He was and remained very upset. When I talked to John Welch, afterwards, as we walked home, he told me that Jim Ferguson and he had been converted under D. L. Moody forty years ago when he visited Dundee, but he felt that they had been losing something of their early evangelical convictions—confirming what I had felt at the church door, that it was partly for Jim Ferguson's sake that he wanted me to preach on justification by grace alone.

Jim was so hurt that I made a point of visiting him as soon as I could in his home to talk about it, but he was quite adamant, even though we met and talked about it again and again. I prayed with him and for him, but found that the truth of salvation by grace alone had cut deeply into his soul. It was his sheer godliness as a loyal Church member and elder that was at stake. I was deeply distressed, for Jim became ill, deteriorated steadily, and died—although there was no medical reason for that. That incident taught me as never before what Luther used to say, that people could react to justification like a cow staring at a new gate—something I recalled in my farming parish. Luther also used to say about justification by grace alone that it roused bitter opposition and causes tumults.

My evening services in the Barony Kirk were rather less formal than the morning service, and so for several weeks one winter I came down from the pulpit and faced the congregation in front of the choir. There I conducted the service in a less formal way and gave brief expositions of the First Epistle of St. John, and showed its evangelical and practical application to daily belief and life. I encouraged several of my elders to read the chapter for the evening, and to read a brief prayer, which I wrote out for them. It was very much an informal family form of service. I had my brief address on each chapter typed out and made copies available to those who attended the service, and encouraged questions and discussion. It helped to open up even more the conversation I had with people in their own homes when I made my pastoral rounds. It also deepened my own understanding of and love for that Epistle.

Soon after my arrival in Alyth, I also got to know the Revd. Dr. John McConnachie, of St John's Church, Dundee, well-known for his books on Karl Barth, a friend of my old teacher H. R. Mackintosh. He asked me to join the Angus Theological Club in Dundee, which I attended as often as I could and greatly enjoyed. It was partly through his encouragement that I wrote the book *Calvin's Doctrine of Man,* in which I had hoped to do something to reconcile the thought of Emil Brunner and Karl Barth, in their disagreement over the interpretation of Calvin, especially over the problem of *Anknüpfungspunkt* or point of contact between God and man! I had now the works of Calvin (or most of them, that had been translated into English) in my Alyth study and read them all carefully. Probably, however, my continuing theological activity had the effect of making my sermons more theological than they would have been—but that often proved a point of contact with the members of the congregation, who asked me when I visited them to explain some of the things I had been trying to say. It was that combination of theological study with what I learned from people's hearts face to face with Christ in their homes that taught me a great deal which I was to recall and use when the time came for me to teach Christian Dogmatics in Edinburgh.

The effect of my friendship with Dr. John McConnachie and of my membership in the Angus Theological Club helped to keep my theological thinking alert, and to encourage my reading of theology and some philosophy. In 1941 I penned an article on "Theology and the Common Man" for the Church of Scotland Record, *Life and Work;* and several articles for *The British Weekly*, the editor of which was the son of a former minister of the old United Presbyterian Church in Alyth, before its union with the Free Church: for example, "We need a decisive Theology before we can restate the Creed," and "The importance of Fences in Religion." I also reviewed for *The British Weekly* Norman Kemp Smith's *The Philosophy of David Hume*, and a new edition of *Essays on the Intellectual Powers of Man*, by Thomas Reid.

I had been asked by J. H. Oldham to write a paper for a high-powered theological group called 'The Moot' which met in the Athenaeum in London. It was entitled "Christian Thinking Today." In it I replied to a paper by H. A. Hodges, an Oxford Philosopher, an authority on the philosophy of Wilhelm Dilthey, in criticism of Karl Barth, and supported my argument by extensive references to modern German Philosophy. That was never published. However, three of my addresses on "The Modern Theological Debate" were printed for private circulation for the Theological Students Prayer Union of the Inter-Varsity Fellowship of Evangelical Unions; and an essay on "Reason in Christian Theology," which was published in *Evangelical Theology*, in 1942.

The Presbytery of Meigle used to meet once a month, not always in Meigle, but usually in Blairgowrie. The Presbytery Clerk at that time was Mr. Morrison, the minister of Ardler. Once at a special session arranged by the Presbytery of Meigle in Blairgowrie I gave an address on "The Place and Function of the Church in the World," which the Presbytery on a motion by Ritchie Smith our Barony Church Presbytery elder agreed to have printed and distributed. The Moderator of the Presbytery, the Revd. D. F. MacKenzie, wrote a foreword to it and it was printed by John Lunan in his Alyth Printing Works.

In it I called for a much more vigorous stand by the Church, recovering her distinctive commitment to the proclamation and teaching of the gospel in the world. I called for the recovery of the gospel as the New Testament proclaims it, the saving power of Jesus Christ, and to make that proclamation her foremost task. The Church being the body of Christ must refuse to become merged in ordinary social life and culture. I claimed that the trouble with us today was that the Church's message had become poisoned with modern thought and had therefore little to say to the modern world. The Church had inoculated society with such a mild form of Christianity that now it was almost immune to the vital form. The Church had no right to identify herself with the social order here and now or with any political regime, far less with the 'status quo.' The Church can only be the Christian Church when she is ever on the move, always campaigning, always militant, aggressive, revolutionary. It is the business of the Church to evangelize the world, and if she does not actually Christianize the world, she must at least have such a powerful impact upon it as to turn the whole order of State and society, national and international, upside down. I went on to spell out a little how the Church can affect society and State. By throwing the social environment into ferment and upheaval, by an aggressive evangelism with the faith that rebels against all wrong and evil, and by a new machinery through which her voice will be heard in the councils of the nation as never before, the Church will press toward a new order. Whenever there is evil in the industrial and economic order, in the political or international sphere, so in the social fabric of ordinary life, the Church must press home the claims of the Christian gospel and ethic. I went on to spell out how this would affect the Foreign Mission question. If the Church does recover the New Testament vision, she will see that the great task of the Church is the redemption of the world and not a comfortable life in little, religious churches and communities. The Church simply cannot keep alive unless her eyes are upon the farthest horizons of the world, unless she keeps herself in line with the master-passion and the world-outlook of Christ who was the propitiation not for our sins only but for the sins of the world. It is for that reason that mission work does not arise from arrogance in the Christian Church—mission is its cause and its life. "The Church exists by mission, as fire exists by burning." Where there is no mission, there is no Church.

Because in that address I tried to spell out something of the evangelical mission of the Church in the world, and the implications of the gospel for change and development in social and business relations, I got the reputation of being something of a political radical, which I was not! I was delighted that John Lunan in Alyth agreed to publish, and hoped it would have some impact on his nephew John Lunan, who was later to become a minister in Glasgow.

In the following year a rather different address I had given in Oxford, on "Kierkegaard and the Knowledge of God," was published in *The Presbyter*, while a review I had written of Leonard Hodgson's book *Towards a Christian Philosophy*, was published in *The Evangelical Quarterly*, vol. 15. At the same time I was still working on my Basel Thesis, when I sent a copy to Professor Karl Ludwig Schmidt in Basel, one of the Professors appointed to examine it. He told me to cut it down, and remove philosophical discussion and extraneous references to modern thinkers like Kierkegaard. And so I cut it down drastically to a quarter of its size, ready for printing and submission after the war.

I had not forgotten the theological revival that we had experienced in New College in 1935 and 1936 under the teaching of H. R. Mackintosh and Daniel Lamont, and particularly the impact made on us by the work of Karl Barth. The influence of Barth had been deepened through his Gifford Lectures delivered in Aberdeen in 1937 and 1938. They were translated by James Haire and Ian Henderson, and published under the title "The Knowledge and the Service of God according to the Teaching of the Reformation," recalling the *Scottish Confession of 1560*. It had the effect of provoking quite a lot of opposition from the liberalizing ministers and theologians like the Baillie brothers and their friend Andrew Walton, but it also had the effect of strengthening and forwarding theological revival, which I had committed myself to deepening and developing. In pursuit of that purpose I formed plans to establish a Theological Society in the Church of Scotland and a Theological Journal. That was something I set about doing from Alyth. I gathered a group of former New College men who had been influenced by Mackintosh and Barth; we were joined by George S. Hendry, an Aberdeen graduate of an earlier vintage. The main members of our group were my brother-in-law R. S. Wallace, Jack K. S. Reid, Ian Henderson, James S. McEwen, and later R. G. Smith. Our one Glasgow graduate was Alastair Rennie. We met during holidays to study theology together.

On one particular occasion that I recall vividly, we met in Aviemore, and studied Barth's *Kirchliche Dogmatik,* 1.2. Nearby there was a regular gathering of theologians and philosophers, which earlier had included H. R. Mackintosh as well as A. B. Macaulay. One day Macaulay visited our boarding house and found *Kirchliche Dogmatik* open on a table in the drawing room, and asked who we might be. From that moment he took me to his heart, and later asked several of us to join The Creed Association, started by him and Mackintosh some years earlier, with a view to preparing a new Creed for modern use. Several of us, particularly Ronnie Wallace and I, and later Jack Reid, took an active part in the meetings of the Creed Association—it fell into line with our aim to promote and develop theological renewal in the Kirk. The larger group that we had formed met regularly at Crieff, and came to be called the Scottish Church Theology Society. It was given the blessing of the General Assembly when I was away on war service. Another person who joined our group at some time was John Heron of Kirkintilloch, a graduate of Trinity College, Glasgow. When I was away Ian Henderson nursed the Theological Society, and handed over care of it to me when I returned, but by then he had really lost interest in it.

When Dr. George MacLeod of the Iona Community heard I was planning to publish a theological Journal, he wrote suggesting that we might cooperate, and told me that he had become interested in another journal that was being launched. I was not very taken with the idea, but in Edinburgh one day I tried to find out something about this journal or magazine, and discovered it had to do with promoting weird anthroposophical ideas about mind and matter! I wrote to tell George MacLeod that I would be unable to take up his suggestion, and added that the publication he had in mind was not really concerned with Christian theology. We had some correspondence about that, and George, who had long tried in vain to recruit me (and Ronnie Selby Wright) for membership in the Iona Community, became rather sharp, and wrote that there was "a great gulf fixed between me and him!" I recall that he ended that letter by telling me to stand on my head, drink a glass of water, and have an apoplectic fit!! Ronnie who was always a good friend of George's was both amused and horrified.

My parents, who had come to stay with me for a while in Alyth, and especially my Mother, were a great help to me. I also had visits from my sister Mary and her husband Ronnie Wallace, the minister of Crosshill in Ayrshire, who preached two sermons, which were greatly appreciated by the Barony folk. My father, who had preaching engagements in different parts of the country, was constantly preparing new expositions of holy Scripture, following up his 1938 volume, *Expository Studies in St. John's gospel*, which kept him ministerially alive. He was more often in Edinburgh than in Alyth at that time. My mother and father, of course, had their home in Edinburgh to look after. There my sisters, Grace and Margaret lived as school-teachers, and were preparing to be missionaries in Central Africa. Grace married the Revd. Dr. R. B. W. Walker, a physician as well as a minister, and Margaret married the Revd. Kenneth Mackenzie. At that time my parents' home was in Chalmers Crescent, Edinburgh. They used to take in boarders, mostly students, to help augment their meagre missionary pension. My father was still a missionary at heart, and was very restless when he was not preaching the gospel, or winning souls for Christ. My Alyth people enjoyed having him in the pulpit, in spite of his habit of preaching long expository sermons for forty minutes or more.

It was especially in my first year at Alyth that my mother and father came to stay with me in the Barony Manse, helping me to settle in. My mother was a wonderful pastoral help to many of the women in the congregation. She was also a very wise and spiritual guide to me in the pastoral problems I encountered, as well as in theological and biblical discussions in which we often engaged during the preparation of my sermons. I found it hard work to prepare two sermons each week—it took most of each morning and afternoon. I wrote out all my sermons (as Mackintosh told us), but sometimes in the evening service I preached only from notes, which my mother preferred! She was much appreciated by the Woman's Guild who met regularly at their 'Working Party', where her spiritual addresses were greatly enjoyed. I found the quarterly seasons of Holy Communion always very wonderful and rewarding. In our Scottish tradition what became known as 'action sermons', sermons preached at Holy Communion on the thankful celebration of the Eucharist (or *actio gratiarum*), had often initiated seasons of evangelical revival, like the notable one in the seventeenth century at Shotts Kirk where my forbears are buried. I came to understand why that was so, for it is at Holy Communion above all that we see Christ face to face and handle things unseen and feed upon his body and blood by faith. It is there in the real presence of Christ that we grasp something of the wonder of the Saviour's love and redeeming sacrifice, and understand that it is not *our* faith in Christ that counts but *his* vicarious life and sacrifice, his redeeming life and death that count. It is at Holy Communion when the bread and wine are put into our hands, that we know it is not our believing that counts but he in whom we believe, not what we do but what the Saviour has done for us and what he means to us. It is at Holy Communion, in short, that we really understand best the gospel of salvation by grace alone. Thus it was at Holy Communion that I found it easiest to proclaim and make clear to people what the unconditional grace of God's saving love really is. As so often in our Scottish tradition, it was the teaching of St. Paul in Galatians 2:20, that meant so much: "I am crucified with Christ: nevertheless I live; yet not I, but Christ lives in me: and the life which I now live, I live by the faith of the Son of God who loved me and gave himself for me." That is to say, it is not ultimately our believing in Christ that counts, but his vicarious life and faith—the "I yet not I, but Christ" applies even to our believing. What a strength to faith that is—and that is what I tried to show to my people as we met for Holy Communion in the Barony Kirk, which we celebrated, as the custom then was (only too infrequently), four times a year.

The correlation of Holy Communion with pastoral visitation was a very enriching experience. At first I hesitated to hold private communion services with people in their homes, but came to feel it wrong that they should be denied the wonderful experience of Holy Communion, and so more and more, especially after my return from war service, I gave much more attention to the celebration of the Lord's Supper with the housebound. When possible I tried to get the district elder to accompany me, but that was not always very possible. I felt that in my little way I was following the practice and example of the apostles who, we are told by St. Luke, broke bread from house to house.

When I was well settled in the manse and parish my mother returned to Edinburgh, and I had to be more concerned with the role of women in Church life, and in particular with the local branch of the Woman's Guild. Two of the leading women vied with one another in wanting to be its local President, a role that is normally undertaken by the minister's wife. And so, to break the impasse, I boldly announced that I would be President! The good women met once a month or so in the Church Hall when they knitted and sewed clothes for the needy and for the mission field. When they met in their Working Party, I used to read aloud to them one of the Pollyanna books, to their amusement! After a year they agreed to have Miss Watson, who came from a ministerial family, to be their President, and so made their own arrangements quite happily. She was certainly very capable. Those women were a wonderful group of people deeply committed in the Lord's Service.

In response to a request of the General Assembly to all Churches to express their congregational opinion on the eligibility of women for eldership, the Kirk Session had decided to send each member a voting paper on which they might give their opinion and return it to the minister and Kirk Session. That was not actually to elect women as yet but to find out whether the members of the Barony would be favourable or not to the election of women as elders. There was not a little dissent from women as well as from men in Alyth (as well as throughout the Church of Scotland) and it was not until 1966 that the General Assembly eventually decreed that women could be elected as elders in the same way and on the same terms as men. In their actual appointment in any congregation the agreement of its Kirk Session was required.

When my mother was with me in Alyth she did her best to find a resident housekeeper for me who would also do the cooking, one, however, who would fit in with Manse life and duties. She was not successful in getting the kind of person she would have liked. However, my congregation found one for me. She was Mrs. Bella Edwards, the widowed daughter-in-law of one of my members, and she certainly coped very well. My mother was pleased with her, and it was a great boon to her, as it relieved her of the many household tasks she had been undertaking, and she could have some time for reading. I noticed that she kept a copy of Calvin's *Institutes* by her bed—rather heavy reading in bed! She was to stay on in the Manse until October or November when she returned to Edinburgh. My brother David remained with me for a year and a half, and he and I found Mrs. Edwards very efficient and helpful. We got on well together. This meant that we no longer needed Lucy Christie as a housemaid, but she was to return after the war when I got married and was a real help to my wife, while Bella Edwards went to work in the High Manse as a housekeeper to Sibbald Clark.

After I had been a year or so in Alyth I became engaged to a young school-teacher, Barbara Patterson, who came from North Berwick. I had first met her there at the Church of Scotland Seaside Mission which I helped the Revd. MacKenzie Grieve to inaugurate, and which proved to be so successful that similar seaside services during the summer were started at other holiday resorts. When she was a student in Edinburgh first in Arts and then at Moray House where she trained as a teacher, Barbara Patterson had been a keen member of the Christian Union Edinburgh and knew my sisters well. She visited me in Alyth a number of times when my mother was with me, but more and more I felt I would not like to have her as a mother of my children, and came to realize that she would not really make a minister's wife. Eventually when I went away to serve with the Armed Forces, I was convinced that I should ask her to agree to a termination of our relations, and our engagement was broken off quite amicably. But I learned not a little from that experience. My father had a similar experience as a young man, and my two brothers were likewise mistakenly to be engaged to someone for a while, before they met the women who were to become their wives and the mothers of their children.

I had not been long in Alyth when someone, perhaps Miss Janet Lunan who lived in Cambridge Street across from the Manse, asked me if I knew J. M. Barry's play *What Every Man Should Know*, for it concerned people some of whom, like the Lunans, had relatives in Kirriemuir, where Barry came from. (I think they also felt that I needed a wife!) Barry's writing taught me a lot about people in Kirriemuir over the border of Perthshire in Angus, and also about the character, way of life and thought of Alyth people, for they were very similar. *What Every Man Should Know* was a lesson to me in more ways than one, and stood me in good stead when I got married!

Gospel, Church, and Ministry

Very soon after settling in as the minister I found myself regularly invited to the home of Solomon Thompson and his wife Nan for Sunday supper after the evening service. They were a wonderful couple with three children: Gordon the oldest who suffered from a foot deformity, and was rather a harum-scarum but a most likeable fellow, Edith the daughter who was later to marry a farmer near Blairgowrie, and David the youngest who inherited his father's farming instincts and abilities. He later emigrated to Australia. On those Sunday evening occasions at Mornity, Sol and Nan Thompson usually had one or two of their friends present, especially Sol's good friend William Muir, a farmer several miles away at Eassie, and sometimes also David Bell of the Balloch. They regularly brought up questions arising out of my sermons, which they wanted to discuss. That was of considerable help to me, as I learned what and how to preach, and communicate the truth of the gospel in ways that would be more readily grasped by people. As a result of that weekly discussion and following upon questions raised after several of my expositions on the Sermon on the Mount, when I tried to spell out in practical ways its relevance for daily life and work, I organized a monthly study group in the manse on the Sermon on the Mount. We discussed, for example, the implications of our Lord's teaching for the kind of questions on social and financial issues often raised by trade unions. As a result Sol Thompson decided to raise the salaries of his farm workers to a level that proved to be above that which the Government proposed after the war. Sol Thompson was taken by surprise one day when in came one of his workers, John Welch the ploughman, who wanted to return some of his weekly wage as he said it was too much! That was an unheard of event! But as it happened Sol Thompson's farm hands worked so well and contentedly, that it had the effect of increasing the prosperity both of the farmer himself and his workers. In addition to his growing of raspberries he was a grower and dealer in seed-potatoes, which were dispatched all over the country, particularly, I recall to Lincolnshire, which was a rather lucrative business. What Sol did set a good example to other farmers and employers in the neighbourhood.

John Welch was one of the finest and most remarkable people I have ever known. He had been converted long ago when attending a revivalist meeting by D. L. Moody in Dundee, and became deeply con-

My Parish Ministry: Alyth, 1940-43

cerned to develop his grasp of biblical and theological truth. Somehow he had acquired a copy of Luther's *Commentary on the Epistle to the Galatians*, and devoured it, and studied it so carefully that he became in his own way a real lay theologian. He would often come to see me in the Manse, when we would talk about biblical and Reformation doctrine, and the spiritual needs of people in the Parish. I learned a lot from him not only in understanding the gospel but in the way in which I might best communicate the gospel message to people personally in my pastoral visits. He would also put me in touch with people who did not go to Church, but needed a minister. He was greatly loved in Alyth and was himself, in fact, an unassuming lay pastor to whom people went for spiritual counsel. One of the people he put me in touch with was Bill White, known in Alyth as 'London Bill.' He was a veteran of the Boer War who had been a rather wild fellow in his earlier days, and never came to Church. I used to visit him and pray with him in his home. An excuse he used to give for not coming the Kirk was that he did not have the clothes for it. But one Monday after David Bell whom he admired had come to Church in his informal or casual farming clothes, I went to Bill and told him that his excuse would no longer carry any weight with me! But it was of no avail—and so I made sure his own place of abode became a place of prayer. John Welch was his real pastor.

One evening I had a visit from Mr. Willie Kidd the shoemaker who wanted to talk to me about some delicate matter. He was very nervous and clearly felt awkward. He told he was not a Free Mason but had been asked by Free Masons to find out whether I would agree to let them have a service in the Barony Church! After a few moments of silence, I said: "Mr. Kidd, if they were to hold a service in the Kirk, I would have to reconsecrate it afterwards!" He was very pleased and more or less leapt with joy. I heard no more about it! But Willie Kidd and his wife became very good friends. She suffered very badly from rheumatoid arthritis, which gave her a great deal of pain, and she could hardly move about. I was often summoned to have afternoon tea with them, when I read passages from the Psalms or the Gospels and prayed. When I got to know them well they helped me considerably in my pastoral duties, letting me know of people who needed the minister. They lived a few yards away from the Barony Kirk, and let me know of another old lady who was bedridden nearby, to whom I ministered again and again until she was taken home to be with her Lord and Saviour. She was the mother, or mother-in-law, of Mr. Robertson, the watchmaker and jeweller. Mrs. Bella Edwards who was to become my housekeeper was one of their relations by marriage.

Not far away from where the Kidds and Robertsons lived on the other side of the Alyth Burn there was a Council housing scheme, which I used to visit. Most of the people officially belonged to the High Kirk and so were Sibbald Clark's people, but, I am afraid he was not very attentive in his pastoral care. I had two maiden lady parishioners there, both of whom suffered incessantly from tinnitus, which was very wearing. I tried to find out from my doctor friends what might help them, and relayed to them what I learned. Near them was a family that rather horrified me, for the father had incestuous relations with two of his daughters and had children by them. I was asked by a neighbour of theirs to visit them, but, I am afraid, I made very little headway, and I never spoke to Sibbald Clark about them. I was very, very sorry for the girls and their babies, and rather angry with their poor mother who had not been able to prevent that from taking place.

When I was taken around the Barony Parish by my elders to meet people in their district, they drove me in their cars. When I had learned where they lived I cycled round everywhere to their homes. I could not afford to get a car yet, but I hoped to be able to do so before too long, as it was very necessary for a rural parish. My stipend was only £404 a year, out of which I had to pay back what I had borrowed from the bank and from my parents to buy furniture, carpets and equipment for the manse, as well as to pay the wages of Lucy Christie, the house maid which the congregation found for me. She was the sister of one of my members whose first child I baptized—the custom was that the first child that a new minister baptized should be called after him! And so Lucy Christie's little niece had to have 'Torrance' as a middle name.

After a while I did manage to get hold of a car in Edinburgh, a second hand Austin Ten, which was a great boon, both for my parish visitation and for the benefit of my parents when they came from Edinburgh and returned there. Under the instruction of Bobby Walker, my brother-in-law to be, I had learned to how drive on the baby Austin that my sister Grace had acquired. The Austin Ten was more suitable, but I had then to buy petrol, and maintain it, which was rather costly. Petrol was rationed, but my farmer friends were generous with their rations, as they were indeed for almost everything else we needed.

When many of the children in the cities and towns were evacuated to the country to escape bombing, my brother James went to stay with my brother-in-law, Ronald S. Wallace, the minister of Cross Hill Parish in Ayrshire, and Garrick Academy at Maybole. David my younger brother came to stay with me. Like James, he had been a pupil at the Royal High School in Edinburgh, but then he came to Alyth where there was only a primary school. And so he cycled every day to attend Blairgowrie High School. After a year and a half he returned to Edinburgh and his old school where he took his 'Highers' for entrance to the University at Edinburgh. There he studied classics and philosophy along with my brother James who was a year ahead of him, until they were both called up for war service, James into the RAF and David into the Royal Scots.

In the year and a half when he was in Alyth, David was a great help to me in my work with the young people whom we used to take camping and fishing up the Glen. Once when James as well as David was staying with me we took a group of teenagers, about fifteen in all, on a camping holiday at the top of the Glen, beyond the Tulcan Shooting Lodge owned by the Earl of Airlie. There the road ended, and so we borrowed some ponies from the gamekeeper to help us transport our tents and baggage five miles further up the Glen to a convenient site where the Canness and Canlogan burns joined to form the River Isla. There we set up camp for two weeks or so, lived on trout and rabbit and roamed over the heather-clad hills. We had camp prayers each night.

After twelve or more days in Cannes we came down five miles and went up Glen Brichtie. One evening at dusk we heard German bombers flying high above us on their way across Scotland to bomb the shipyards and installations at Clydebank. One airman who had seen our camp fire, decided to drop his bombs on us instead! But as he circled round James and I threw the tea and all the water we had over the camp fire to try and put it out, and then held a blanket over it, so that he could not be guided by its light. He failed to spot us again, and dropped his bombs over the hill to our left towards Glenshee instead. Later I learned that the bombs they dropped left fifteen craters in hillside—they must have been rather large bombs. *[Editor: His brother, David Torrance, remembers six bombs going off, not fifteen.]* We were very thankful that they were not offloaded on to us! Those bombers that managed to fly across Scotland over to the West coast created fearful damage and havoc at Clydebank on Clydeside.

After we returned from our camp one of the young farmer lads was visiting his aunt at another farm when she asked what he thought of the new minister—and he gave a very amusing answer. On our first morning at the camp David and I rose early and caught the trout for breakfast, but I fried them on a pan that was too hot, so that the fish all curled-up to the disgust of the boys. Later when asked by his aunt, Mrs. Whammond, another farmer's wife, what he thought of me, young Will Lindsay (the son of a sheep farmer in Glen Prosen, and the nephew of Jim and Lena Lindsay) said in broad Scots, "An affa' coorse frier o' troots!" That was long remembered and is sometimes repeated to me when I am back in Alyth! Years later, after the war, when I married Will to his wife in Kirriemuir, and presided at the reception afterwards, I told the guests about that incident, and then unfolded a present I had bought in Dundee—a large frying pan, the biggest I could get! And as I presented it to his wife, I told her that if she was to be a good wife to Will she should learn how to use the underside of the frying pan on him! The company, who all knew Will Lindsay's mischievous character, were hugely delighted. He told the wedding guests that I had got my own back on him!

I usually took Monday off work, when I played golf at the Alyth golf course, and occasionally played tennis with some of the young people, one of whom, Norman Lindsay, played as a junior at Wimbledon. In the winter I managed to get a little skiing, which rather startled some of my old ladies when they found the minister in strange garb skiing along the High Street and down Toutie Street! It was with work in the garden, however, that I had most of my physical exercise. It was a lovely garden, with several fruit trees, one that produced a mass of Victoria plums, which the town youngsters used to plunder. Once I caught two of them and brought them into the manse dining room and set before them two plates piled up with plums, and would not let them go till they had eaten the lot. The word was soon passed round about the minister's strange generosity!

The farmers here were very helpful—Jim Lindsay used to send us milk, and some game, sometimes venison, but mostly rabbit. I recall being regaled with lovely oatcakes, honey, and rich cream at evening meals with them. Sol Thompson kept us supplied with potatoes and got two of his farm-hands to plant two rows of raspberry bushes at one end of the garden, and had ground prepared for potatoes which he had planted for me. In the middle of the garden there was a large lawn surrounded by lovely flowering plants and shrubs. In one corner a family of hedgehogs flourished. William Williams the gardener used to help me keep things in order. My father loved gardening, and when he stayed at the manse did a lot to improve it. My brother David was very keen that we should keep bees and was given two hives by Sol Thompson who bought five and gave three of them to his son Gordon. We kept the bees in the garden in a sheltered place behind a clump of myrtle bushes.

I found bee keeping very interesting and enjoyed it but I had a lot to learn about them. One day during the summer I took them up to the heather (which I continued to do each year), and set the hives down near a stream and a good stretch of heather—but the jolting of the car and trailer carrying the hives over rough hill roads made them rather angry. Once when I opened the hives I found myself being attacked and stung with so many bees in my hair that I rushed to the burn and kept my head under water as long as I could to calm them down or drown them. But the rich brown heather honey had a lovely taste, and it was a delight to be able to give some away to sick or elderly members. One of my great delights was to cycle, or later to motor, up the Glens—Isla, Prosen, and Clova—and enjoy the gorgeous mountain scenery, and also, especially when my brother David or one of the Lindsay or Thompson boys was with me, to fish for trout at Tullymurdoch or in the river Isla. They were rarely over half a pound in weight in the upper reaches, but made fine eating. I found fishing trout in mountain streams, with the scent of the heather in my nostrils and the music of the rushing water in my ears, very relaxing, and conducive to spiritual and theological meditation. The Tulchan Lodge at the top of Glenisla was a favourite visiting place of ours where we were always warmly welcomed by the gamekeepers. I recall that there were some Landseer wall paintings in the lodge, and scrawled on one of the walls the names of the Mitford girls, one of whom, it was said, had been a girl friend of Hitler!

Alyth now began to have a taste of war as enemy planes flew over us in bombing raids, and the sirens rent the air with their warning. I was asked to join the ARP, Air Raid Precautions, in which I engaged one night a week. Unlike my friend Jim McEwen, the minister of Rathen East, near Fraserburgh, in Aberdeenshire, I did not join the home guard! But, as I knew German, I was asked to take services for German Internees, some of whom were prisoners of war. There were not very many of them, but I took services for them and preached the gospel, in which I made use of and adapted some of the published sermons of Emil Brunner. They were more helpful to me in that ministry than Karl Barth's sermons.

Some months after I had become the minister of the Barony Kirk, the war department established a camp in the parish for many hundreds of Poles who had been recruited and were being trained for war service. Not all of them came from Poland, some even came from Brazil, and many were clearly a rather rough lot, but there were also not a few from Poland itself. The two Churches in Alyth combined to minister to help them through establishing canteens and cultivating friendly relations with people round about. They were not easy to help or cope with—some were very crude and demanding, but there were not a few highly educated people among them. Before long I found that several of the private soldiers were actually doctors, but they were not allowed to practise as doctors for they were Jews. The Pole who acted as their camp doctor was a veterinary surgeon—they preferred to have him rather than a Jewish doctor. The Jewish doctors were private soldiers and had been highly educated, and soon made themselves known to me, especially as I spoke German as well as English, and often came to the manse, to borrow books or play chess. The anti-Semitism among the Poles deeply shocked me. Those Polish doctors were later to be pulled out by the War Department and set to medical service, one or two of them in one or other of the Medical Schools in Scotland.

There was another problem we had to face, the relations of the Polish soldiers to the girls and women in Alyth whom they frequently

My Parish Ministry: Alyth, 1940-43

beguiled or seduced. I was horrified when I over-heard two of the Poles in the Canteen discussing in German the fact that the Alyth women with whom they were having affairs did not want sex more than once a week. I didn't know that sort of thing went on. It was particularly disturbing when some of these women were married and had husbands who were away at war. I felt I had to give some attention, if only in a back-handed or oblique way, to the improper way the wives of some of our members were apparently behaving. I could see that a few of the women in the congregation were rather disturbed by some of the things I had been saying about the husbands at war being stabbed in the back by the behaviour of their wives at home. My mother thought one of these sermons was rather "stingy and heart-searching," as she said in a letter to my sister Grace—but I did not feel I could be easy on them or turn a blind eye to what seemed to be happening. Several of the Polish soldiers actually married Alyth girls—I think particularly of a Polish sergeant who married Jean the daughter of Jim and Lena Lindsay. She had a child by him, and later, after he had died during the war, emigrated to Rhodesia where she joined two of her brothers, Norman and Rennie, who had established farms there. Leon and David Lindsay had preferred to remain at home on farms in Scotland.

After three years I felt I had to offer myself to serve as a chaplain in the Army, and went to the Church of Scotland Headquarters at 121, George Street, Edinburgh, to make inquiries how best I might do that. There I ran into the Very Revd. Dr. Charles Warr, minister of St. Giles' Cathedral, acting as head of the Church of Scotland Huts and Canteens. Earlier during the war they had sent Professor Edgar Dickie of St Andrews to serve as a minister with the Scottish troops in Europe. He told me that they were urgently needing a minister to take the place of the Revd. George Campbell, a College friend of mine, who had been serving in the Church of Scotland Huts and Canteens in the Middle East Forces, and was now returning home. He asked me whether I would join the C. of S. Huts and Canteens in Egypt and Palestine, instead of the Royal Army Chaplaincy Department. That certainly appealed to me, as I knew the Middle East. When I learned that they would take me right away, I agreed, and duly 'signed on' with the Huts and Canteens. I found out what would be needed of me by way of dress and equipment, for which they made arrangements right away. I also spoke to the officials at the Home Board of the Kirk to tell them of my decision, so that they could make the necessary arrangements for absence. And then I visited my parents at Chalmers Crescent in Edinburgh and told them of my decision and of the steps I had taken. My father had hoped that my ministry in Alyth would "keep me out of the hands of the military," (!) but that was not to be. I felt it was my moral and spiritual duty, to offer myself for service in the armed forces of the Crown in one way or another—the solders also needed the gospel ministered to them, and when more than on active service. I think they were pleased that it was with the specific work of the Church of Scotland, rather than with the military chaplaincy, that I was now to serve.

My next task was to tell my people in Alyth, the Kirk Session and the Congregation, and also of course the Presbytery of Meigle. They applauded my decision and gave me the warmest support. I told them that I had visited those responsible for the Maintenance of the Ministry of the Church in Edinburgh, and had their agreement and promise to put into effect arrangements for the ministry of the gospel in Barony Parish and Kirk during my absence. Mr. McLeod the minister of Ruthven five miles away from Alyth on the road to Kirriemuir was appointed Interim Moderator, and was put in charge of the pastoral care of the Barony Parish. Steps were taken to find a locum and/or supply preachers for the Barony Kirk until I returned. Several of my own family and friends stepped in and helped, particularly the Revd. Kenneth Mackenzie who married my younger sister Margaret, but they were soon to sail to Central Africa as missionaries.

Various members of my congregation in Alyth helped me to get equipped in preparation for life with the army. Willie Muir, who had been an officer in the First World War, presented me with the kind of equipment they reckoned I would need, particularly a waterproof sleeping bag, the sort of thing that he himself had used. I sold the Austin car which was a mistake, as cars, I was to find, were rather difficult and expensive to acquire after the war. I paid a last visit to my elderly and infirm members; one of whom who had not long to live, a retired gamekeeper at New Alyth, insisted on giving me a splendid telescope which he had used for many years, but which I had to leave behind at home.

In Edinburgh I was given a Military Document or Pass in which I was given the honorary status of Captain, which was also designed by the War Office to ensure my treatment as a Captain should I be taken a prisoner of war.

Then I left Alyth to be with my parents in Edinburgh, to complete arrangements for my travel made by the officials of the Church of Scotland Huts and Canteens in Edinburgh. Eventually the summons came to board a troopship that was to take me to Algiers, from where I had to make my way to Cairo, and the Church of Scotland Centre there. It was some time in June before I was able to embark on the ship sailing, if I remember rightly, from the Clyde, with many thousands of soldiers and officers from the Highland as well as other Divisions in North Africa, in preparation for the invasion of Sicily and Italy. For many days and nights we had to face the dangers of the Atlantic, constantly under threat from enemy submarines, particularly as we ploughed across the Bay of Biscay. We then slipped into the Mediterranean, sailed past Gibraltar, and on to Algiers where I arrived at the end of June. Before leaving Alyth I had prepared a list of all the homes and addresses of my congregation to take with me, and promised to write to them, which I managed to do from time to time. Many of my Barony folk wrote back to me during the next two years, so that I learned how they were and was able to pray for them with knowledge.

Alyth, 1945-47

I returned to Alyth as soon as possible after V. E. Day plus one, but had to kick my heels in Naples for several weeks before I could get a berth on a troop ship to take me back to the UK, where we disembarked on the Thames. On arrival in London I was astonished to find that Churchill had been defeated at the polls and that Clement Atlee now formed a Labour government. I could understand that swing to the left in view of the socialist propaganda that had been spreading throughout the armed forces, including the little red books of Lenin. I spent a day or two in London, and recall particularly the visit I paid to the Church of St. Martin in the Fields in Trafalgar Square, where I knelt for a long time in prayer, in thankful wonder that the Lord had spared my life, and recommitted myself to him for whatever he would have me do. After spending a few days with my parents in Edinburgh, I took the train for Alyth. The congregation gave me a very warm welcome home. They had learned not a little of my life and activity from my own letters from the Middle East and Italy but also through copies of the newspaper of the Tenth Indian Division in which I had served during the Italian campaign, which somehow had found their way to people in Alyth. In a special number of the Congregational Quarterly issued by the Kirk, they printed a letter someone had sent to the Kirk about my service in the Tenth Indian Division in Italy, to which was added an appreciative letter from the Commanding Officer, General Denis Reid. The congregation also learned something of my life and activity in Italy from reports sent to the daughter of Mr. Mackintosh the Schoolmaster, by his daughter's fiancé who had been with me in the Tenth Indian Division in Italy. Though we did not often manage to meet, he relayed to me also news of Alyth, which I was always eager to receive.

My first happy duty on return to Alyth was to visit all the members of the Kirk in their homes: naturally I had a special concern for families who had lost loved ones in the war. We now had a lot to talk about, and I was eager to learn from them something of the change that had been taking place in the life and belief of people, although I soon realized that the socialization and secularization of life and thought which had become rampant during the war years, had not yet afflicted Alyth people very much. In any case, I was still committed to the preaching and teaching of the gospel, but with a deeper concern to overcome the tendency to damage the relation between belief in Christ and belief in God which had resulted from a resort to natural theology fostered by liberal theologians and ministers. I was haunted by the question of a mortally wounded young solder, half an hour before he died, about whether God was *really* like Jesus. I was all the more concerned to encourage theological change throughout the Kirk, and to help restore in it the centrality of the crucified and risen Lord Jesus Christ. This also had the effect of deepening my concern for more liturgical worship, and for more attention to the celebration of Holy Communion. In a lax or dying church it is the evangelical and sacramental liturgy that keeps alive and deepens the beliefs and spiritual life of people. I had

My Parish Ministry: Alyth, 1940–43

brought back with me a lovely sisteenth-century Communion Chalice given me in Jerusalem by the minister of St. Andrews, which I had often used when celebrating the Lord's Supper with the troops. Now I had less compunction than before in taking Holy Communion to people in their homes especially after its celebration in the Kirk. It also meant much more to me in my own personal ministry and pastoral care of others.

I was then alone in the Manse and sought to find domestic help. Mrs. Bella Edwards told me that she had been acting as the Housekeeper to Sibbald Clark in the manse of the High Kirk, and regretted that she could not come back to the Barony manse. At first I tried an ex-army batman, an old de-mobbed soldier in Murrayfield in Edinburgh whose advertisement for a job I had read in *The Scotsman*. I had become used to having a batman in the armed services, and thought that I might try that at home. But he proved useless. And I did not like his passion for the football pools, and the betting literature that started to flow into the manse through the post! And so I paid him off. Then someone in Alyth put me in touch with a Dundee ex-service woman, who had served in the Woman's Auxiliary Air Force (WAAF). I do not now remember what her cooking and housework were like, but when she began to intrude into my personal affairs, I felt I had to send her away. I talked to Mrs. Smith, the widow of the Chemist who lived not far away in Cambridge Street about her, and asked her if she would be so kind as to dismiss the WAAF for me! That she did, and I was greatly relieved. Then I looked after myself. I did not have much housework to do, and used to go to a small Cafe not far away (round the corner of Cambridge Street) to have lunch, and fixed my own breakfast and supper. But I was often asked to have a meal with people during my pastoral visits, and got on very nicely. I had a lot of quiet time in the Manse for study and sermon preparation, which suited me.

One day to my surprise there turned up an old army friend, Alastair Bruce who had been an officer, a fighting patrol leader, in the Gerwahl Regiment in the Tenth Indian Division in Italy. There he had became rather hyper-manic and was sent off to the base Psychiatric Hospital at Assisi, and after a while was discharged, somewhat better. He dropped in on me at the end of one week when I still had another sermon to complete. He was clearly on a hyper-manic wave, but I packed him off to have a look at Blairgowrie while I completed my arrangements for the Lord's Day. There he ran into a sergeant whom he had met in Italy, who kept him out late after visiting several pubs! When I got up in the morning I found beer cans lying about the kitchen floor, and a red flannel shirt hanging out of his bedroom window, evidently to get rid of some fleas he had picked up in the pub! After breakfast, I told him that I had some duties at the Barony Kirk before the service, and would have to go off early, and told him where it was located. Alastair found his way there a little later. He introduced himself to Sol Thompson at the door as 'General Bruce,' and as a friend of mine, and was shown to the manse pew! He spent several hilarious days in Alyth, and then returned to London where he took lessons in football refereeing, before returning to his home in Buenos Aires where his father, Dr. D. W. Bruce, was our Church of Scotland minister. Alastair's hope in becoming a football referee was to continue something of the excitement he had during the war! But one day, he wrote to say, that after he had awarded a penalty against the home side, they shot at him with revolvers! He said he would not have minded so much if he could have carried a revolver himself as well! But that was out of question, and so he gave up that ploy. I never heard from him again, but he was long remembered by some people in Alyth!

Sol and Nan Thompson and family had moved from Mornity to Kinpurnie beyond Meigle and near Newtyle. It was not far away from Willie Muir's home at Eassie. It was a spacious farmhouse with a lovely garden—but I missed the homeliness of Mornity in Alyth. The Lindsays had sold Balwhyme on Alyth Hill to Sydney Hind, who was a scholarly rather than a farming type; he was a splendid member of the Barony congregation. I believe that he had once hoped to enter the ministry, but turned back to farming. Young Jim Lindsay had been demobbed, but was far from well, for his fearful experiences in submarine warfare left their mark upon him, and he was sent away to a Psychiatric unit near Perth, where he was diagnosed as schizophrenic. When I visited him I felt that his problems were not psycho-physical but more personal and spiritual, and that it was really quiet, rest, and a strengthened Christian trust and belief that would help him. I told Dr. Sleigh in Alyth what I thought. He agreed and, with the agreement of Jim's parents, had him

My Parish Ministry: Alyth, 1940–43

recalled from the Hospital. Jim and Lena Lindsay then took him away to the farm of a friend of theirs in a remote part of Argyllshire, where he ruminated for three months, and was completely restored. He needed to be on his own, and I think his parents realised that. And so they bought Balwhyme back from Sydney Hind, and handed it over to Jim to farm. That was just what he needed. Jim's younger brother Leon worked at a farm on the other side of the strath. Some years later, when I was in Edinburgh, he had an altercation over some problem in the Church that he attended; the dispute was with the minister of Montrose, the Clerk of the Presbytery of Angus and Mearns, a legal type who was later to be Principal Clerk of the General Assembly. I felt Leon was in the right and supported him. To express his gratitude Leon brought me in Edinburgh a huge salmon that he had caught!

I had not long returned to Alyth when I had some pressure put on me by Sir David Ross, the Provost of Oriel College in Oxford, backed up by Dr. Marcus Niebuhr Todd, the Vice-Provost, to consider going to be minister of St. Columba's Church of Scotland in Oxford. That certainly appealed to me, but I could not consider it, for after being two years away from the Barony Church in Alyth, I felt I should, and indeed, wanted to, remain longer with my people there. They had been so good to me when I was away, and I did not wish to let them down by saddling them with a vacancy so soon after my return.

I threw myself into my ministerial duties in preaching, parish visitation, and teaching the young people in my Bible class, several of whom were now school teachers. However, at the same time I found myself getting heavily involved in scholarly and writing activity, as in the publication of an article for *The Presbyter*, a magazine, which I had a hand in founding in Oxford. It offered a somewhat dynamic view of the atoning work of Christ, entitled "*In Hoc Signo Vinces*," which met with a warm reception from Principal D. S. Cairns, the father of Professor David Cairns.

Now that I was back in Scotland and Alyth, I was free to take up again some of my theological interests, regarding the Scottish Church Theological Society, and what came soon to be called *The Scottish Journal of Theology*. The Revd. Ian Henderson had moved from Fraserburgh to Kilmany, the parish made famous by the ministry of Thomas Chalmers,

63

and we arranged to meet in Dundee. I will never forget the meeting we had. I thanked him for helping to keep my projects alive when I was away, but he told me that frankly he wanted to be dissociated from me and my theological outlook and interests! He wanted to be a Professor, and that meant that he had to distance himself from Karl Barth, and me, for no 'Barthian' would have a chance of a chair in Scotland! I knew that there was some truth in what he said, for Professor John Baillie, who was bitterly opposed to Barth, had blocked any academic appointment for George Hendry, the very able Minister of Bridge of Allan, who was later snapped up by Princeton!

About the same time I received a letter from Principal Sir Hector Hetherington of Glasgow University, asking me to consider going to the chair of Divinity in the University of Glasgow. That appealed to me, and several of my teachers and friends, among whom was Professor Karl Barth of the University of Basel, Professor Oscar Cullmann, and Professor William Manson, wrote recommending that. However, I wrote to Sir Hector recommending George Hendry. Actually Professor Gervase Riddell, who held the former Church chair of Theology at Trinity College, Glasgow, was appointed to the Divinity chair, and then Ian Henderson, to my surprise, who was now openly a follower of Rudolf Bultmann, was appointed to succeed him in Trinity College! He was joined later by Ronald Gregor Smith, another follower of Bultmann, and a rather secularizing thinker. When they began to lecture in Glasgow, I remember hearing Professor Pitt Watson saying one day at a meeting of the Creed Association, "They have taken away my Lord and I know not where they have laid him!"

My principal literary activity at this time was to get my Basel dissertation finally ready for submission: forty printed copies of it had to be sent to the University at Basel. It was a severely cut-down version of my dissertation on *The Doctrine of Grace in the Apostolic Fathers*. Oliver & Boyd Ltd, the Edinburgh Publishers, prepared for me forty copies in paperback, which I sent off to Basel early in 1946. They held back the hardback copy until after I had taken my doctorate, so that it was not published until 1947. When I approached Oliver & Boyd in connection with the printing of my thesis, I asked them if they would consider publishing *The Scottish Journal of Theology*, plans for which were now being completed. I recall having discussed that with Ainslie and Tom Thin, and with Douglas Grant. I had hoped to raise funds from Sir James Lithgow the Glasgow ship-builder, but he was rather canny. On the recommendation of Ronnie Wright, however, we were promised a supply of paper by Dr. (later Sir) Patrick Russell of Markinch and St. Andrews, from his paper works. I also told Oliver & Boyd that we had been organizing support for the project in Scotland, not least with the help of the Revd. T. M. Murchison, the minister of St. Columba's in Glasgow, the Kirk's Gaelic expert, who was later to become Moderator of the General Assembly. Oliver & Boyd gave it their blessing and in due course it began to be published in 1948, with J. K. S. Reid and myself as Editors.

Meantime, I had already managed to launch the Scottish Church Theology Society, which was designed along with the support of *The Scottish Journal of Theology* to contribute to the theological renewal of the Kirk. During those preparations I had made several trips to St. Mary's College, St. Andrews, and New College, Edinburgh, to consult books, and was able to spend time visiting my parents. On one of those occasions I met Margaret Edith Spear from Combe Down, Bath, Somerset, who had come north to visit my sister Margaret on her first furlough from Central Africa. They had been friends ever since they met in the Edinburgh Christian Union or Evangelical Association, as it was then called, in the session 1938/39, when she was studying at Atholl Crescent Domestic Science College, later to become Queen Margaret University. When I first met Margaret Spear I knew at once, without a shadow of a doubt, that we were meant by the Lord for one another. And so I planned to visit her in Somerset, when I went south on my way to face the ordeal of the theological *rigorosum* at the University of Basel prescribed for doctoral candidates. I was given leave by the Presbytery of Meigle and the Barony Kirk for several weeks in order to spend the summer Semester at Basel. I left for Basel via Bath in order to visit Margaret at the Spear home in Combe Down, near Bath, where she lived with her brother Dick. Their father had died the previous year, and their mother some years earlier. On the 24th of May, Margaret and I became engaged to be married—the most memorable day of my life. Shortly afterwards, overwhelmed with joy and thankfulness, I set off for Basel. Unfortunately a Post Office strike in Britain took place, and letters from Margaret were slow in reaching me.

I spent a few weeks in Basel in order to refresh my knowledge of and use of German for the doctoral examination, and attended the lectures of Karl Ludwig Schmidt, and of Emil Brunner who was lecturing there when Karl Barth was away in Bonn. The doctoral examination (or inquisition!) was conducted by Professors Karl Ludwig Schmidt, Oscar Cullmann, and Fritz Lieb. It was a rather gruelling three hours they inflicted on me, and I was relieved to be awarded the *Dr. Theol. magna cum laude*. Karl Barth's younger son, Christoph, and Karl Ludwig Schmidt's son, Martin, were the two other *doctorandi*. Christoph like me was passed *magna cum laude*, and Martin *insigni cum laude*. When Karl Barth heard of the result he wrote from Bonn to tell me that had he been there he would have awarded me *summa cum laude*. But I was quite happy with what I was given. Professor Schmidt was evidently determined that his son Martin would do better than either Christoph Barth or myself!

On my return to Combe Down, Bath, Margaret and I arranged our wedding for October 2, in the Parish Church of Combe Down, which her family attended, and then returned to Edinburgh and Alyth. When the great moment came my parents and brothers and sisters, and my friend Jack Reid, all went to Combe Down for the occasion. Margaret's brothers George and Dick and her sister Mary, and her Aunts, with family friends in Combe Down, all joined us at the service which was taken beautifully by the Revd. Ben Turnock. Afterwards the reception was held at Forte's in Bath. Margaret and I drove away in a car loaned by Dick Spear, my wife's younger brother, for the honeymoon in Cornwall and Devon. On the way back to The Brow, the lovely Spear home in Combe Down, a drunken driver nearly crashed into us! Then we set out for East Linton [in Devon] and nearly had another accident when a cow suddenly jumped down from a bank in front of the car! During the first week of our honeymoon we stayed at East Linton, and spent much of the time visiting Cloud Farm on Exmoor and riding over the hills made famous in the book *Lorna Doon*. Margaret had often been on holiday at Cloud Farm and was very familiar with the countryside. She rode on her favourite white horse called 'Tommy'! Then we motored on

My Parish Ministry: Alyth, 1940-43

to Cornwall where we stayed at St Mawes on the sea coast. One of my vivid memories there when attending the Parish Church, was to see inscribed on a grave stone, "This man died, because his physician erred!" My Alyth farmer friends had supplied us with ample petrol coupons for that unforgettable fortnight. Although Margaret was very familiar with Devon and Cornwall, I had never been there before. The days passed all too quickly. We returned to Combe Down, and then took the train back to Edinburgh and Alyth.

Margaret loved the manse and the garden. Lucy Christie returned to the manse as the resident housemaid. It was a great handicap not having a car—how I regretted having sold my Austin Ten when I went off to the forces! In a pastoral charge like the Barony Parish, a car was very necessary, not only for our life in Alyth but also for my pastoral activities, particularly in visiting the rural areas. The Kirk took Margaret to its heart. During the weeks that followed we walked around together to visit many homes in the congregation, not only in the town itself but in some of the farms nearby. Those pastoral visits to members of the Barony congregation by both of us in which we read passages of the Bible and prayed together were, I believe, particularly helpful to people. Walking about Alyth at this time was very hard on Margaret as she was pregnant. On some of our visits we were fetched by members of the congregation in their cars, as to Kinpurnie and the Balloch. Once or twice we must have borrowed a car when I took Margaret up Glen Isla to see the heather covered hills and to do some fishing—she caught a lovely trout with her first cast over a pool on the Canlochan, an upper branch of the Isla! Everywhere the good folk of the Barony Kirk, and of the Town, took very warmly to Margaret and did everything they could to make us comfortable in the manse, and loaded us with food, milk, butter, vegetables, and fruit, and other goodies which had become very scarce.

We were soon to have visitors. Our first was the Revd. Ronnie Selby Wright, widely known as 'the Radio Padre,' now minister of the Canongate in Edinburgh, who spent two days with us in November. Bobby Walker and my brother David came toward the end of December. Another visitor was the Revd John H. G. Ross who had served with the Church of Scotland Huts and Canteens in the Middle East and Italy and had become its General Secretary at the Church Offices in George Street, Edinburgh. Both of them had been present at my ordination in 1940. My parents and brothers visited us also, and James and David helped me with the bees about which they knew a good deal. Once when merging two swarms, the queen bee of one swarm disappeared, but, to Margaret's horror I found it in my arm pit when we went to bed!

Another visitor we had in February was Tommy Stewart now demobbed from the American Army, and on his way back home to Auburn, New York. He was later to become a student of mine at New College, Edinburgh, and to be the minister of a Church on Long Island and then of a large Church in Rochester, New York. Tommy returned to Alyth again in April for a week. Then another of my good friends came to stay with us for a while, Dr. Christoph Barth from Basel who was to become godfather to our son Thomas. I recall particularly one sunny day when we had a picnic at Reekie Linn, a lovely waterfall on the river Isla. Still another visitor was Professor Charles E. Raven of Cambridge, theologian and botanist, who had once made a study of the plant life in the Glens right up to the Glas Maol in the Grampians. He told us that at the back of the pool in the Canlochan, the pool where Margaret had caught her trout, there was a rare plant preserved by the waterfall, which prevented the deer from getting at it.

In 1945/46 the War Department had established a camp in the parish for German prisoners of war, waiting for repatriation. I did what I could for them, both in pastoral care and in taking services for them, when I preached the Word of God to them in German, as I had done for the Polish troops when they were quartered in the parish. I found them very responsive to the preaching of the gospel, and to what personal ways I was able to witness to Christ as their and our Lord and Saviour. One of the prisoners was evidently an ordinand whom I invited to the manse, and to whom I loaned some theological books to read and study. I do not know what became of him. But I learned years later that the well-known theologian Jürgen Moltmann had a similar experience in a Prisoner of War Camp in Ayrshire, when through the visits of a Church of Scotland minister he had become a Christian.

In January 1947 Margaret's brothers, George and Richard Spear, motored up from Somerset to see us in Alyth. It was great fun having

My Parish Ministry: Alyth, 1940-43

them. We showed them the beauties of that part of Perthshire, and made a special point of travelling up Glen Isla about twenty miles to the Tulchan Lodge situated near the confluence of the Canness and Canlochan streams which joined together to form the River Isla. There we were warmly welcomed by the head gamekeeper Sandy Alexander (known to the locals as 'Sandy Eck'). They were busy shooting deer to help augment the country's meat supplies. The snow had begun to fall, when I set out with a rifle they loaned me to see if I could bring one back for them. It took me some climbing over valley and ridge until I came near enough to a herd. I managed to shoot a hind, and then went back to the lodge to let the gamekeepers know. I showed two of them where the deer lay, and they brought it back to the lodge. But I got a sharp but friendly word from Sandy Eck for having taken two shots to kill it. They gave us a haunch of venison to take back to the Manse, and, I seem to remember that George and Dick were able to take some venison back to Bath as well. At this point I must record another incident when I did a little hunting for Sandy Alexander. I stalked a hind across a gully and shot it through the neck. I thought I had killed it with a single shot, but when I went over to get it, the deer gave me such a look as it expired that I could never bring myself to hunt deer again.

George and Dick stayed with us for a few days, when they met some of our good friends, like the Thompsons and Bells. But the weather was deteriorating rapidly, and they set off for the south.

I must not forget the visit of Gordon Hewitt of the Lutterworth Press, who had come to talk about books. He was later to publish my work on Calvin, and two volumes about Ecumenical Issues.

That year, 1946/7, was a very hard winter for the parish when sickness took a severe toll—the congregation lost six children through meningitis. Then in the new year we suffered the severest winter people could remember. We were snowed up for many weeks, and the ground was frozen hard to a depth of several feet, so that we had to melt snow to get water. One day I got out my skis and set off to get some milk from a dairy farm, if I remember aright, at Bankhead, near Barry Hill, not far from the road up to Craigisla. The snow had drifted unbelievably, and even covered trees by the road. My skis kept catching on hidden obstacles and I fell over again and again, so that much of the milk I was carrying in a haversack on my back was spilt. But I did manage to bring enough home for our needs. The farmers were all very badly hit, and helicopters had to drop, near the farmyards, bales of hay and straw for the cattle.

Normal pastoral visitation of the parish was out of the question, so that Margaret and I lived a very quiet life in the Manse. It also provided me with time to gather together and organize the results of my research in the *Commentaries* and *Institutes* of John Calvin for the book which I was to call *Calvin's Doctrine of Man*. My intention in writing it was to offer something by way of healing the breach between Karl Barth and Emil Brunner in their disagreement over the relation between grace and nature, and by avoiding traditional Calvinism to present my account of Calvin's own thought as far as possible in his own words. In working at this, I had been encouraged by the Revd. Dr. McConnachie of Dundee, in what he called my *Calvinforschung*. It was eventually published by the Lutterworth Press in 1949, dedicated "To my Father and Mother, My First and Best Teachers in Theology." In 1947 I was also to publish a review of Emil Brunner, *Revelation and Reason*, in *The Record*, a review of C. Van Til's book, *The New Modernism: An Appraisal of the Theology of Barth and Brunner*, in *The Evangelical Quarterly*, vol. 19. I also wrote the chapter "The Word of God and the Nature of Man" for the book edited by F. W. Camfield, *Reformation Old and New, Festschrift for Karl Barth*, published by the Lutterworth Press in the same year.

After the weeks of storm and snow we had the pleasure of a visit from my mother with my sister Grace and her husband Bobby Walker who were back on furlough from Livingstonia in Central Africa. Bobby's brother Bernard came with them also. Then in May my parents returned for several days. It was a busy time for Margaret at that stage in her pregnancy, but she coped beautifully with it all.

1947 was an *annus mirabilis* for us. At 10.30 on the night of July 3, with Dr. MacPherson and a nurse in attendance in the manse, Margaret gave birth to Thomas, our first-born son! It was a wonderful occasion, which altered our lives and way of living in a blessed way. I had a pressing duty in the Church earlier that evening, but returned in time to hear the cry of the newborn baby. I was overcome with thanksgiving to the Lord

My Parish Ministry: Alyth, 1940–43

for his love and mercy. Thomas was a very good intelligent baby who from the beginning seemed to resonate with me as well as his mother.

Three or four days later we had a visit from a deputation of elders from Beechgrove Church in Aberdeen who wanted to discuss with me the possibility of my becoming their minister. It was Professor James S. Stewart of New College, a former minister of Beechgrove Church, who had recommended me to them. I believe they had already heard me preach and had attended services in the Barony Kirk. Beechgrove Church certainly appealed to me, for its first minister was Hugh Ross Mackintosh, who had been my Professor of Christian Dogmatics in New College, while James S. Stewart, who had also been one of my teachers in Edinburgh, had been its third minister following A. J. Gossip who became Professor of Homiletics in Trinity College, Glasgow. I was frankly not keen to leave Alyth, nor was Margaret, for she and I both loved it and were very happy there. I told the Beechgrove elders that I was not very keen to move, and gave as an additional reason that I had already started *The Scottish Journal of Theology,* soon to be published in Edinburgh, and was engaged in other theological and literary activities. I recall that they promised me a stipend of £700, and said that they would give me additional help with secretarial assistance in view of my theological and publishing commitments. I was also in touch with James S. Stewart who pressed me to consider the move to Beechgrove, if the congregation would call me. After consideration, Margaret and I agreed to let matters go ahead. In due course I was invited to take services and preach in Beechgrove Church on September 28th, when the congregation decided to call me.

By this time we had at last acquired a car, a red Morris Eight sold to us by David Bell. It was a Godsend, especially at that time, but we were to enjoy it for some years to come, all through our time in Aberdeen, until we moved back to Edinburgh, when I was appointed to New College in 1950.

Soon after Thomas' birth my father and mother came up from Edinburgh to stay with us and see their grandson. It was wonderful having them in the manse. I think James and David came up as well— they probably brought my parents up by car. For several years James and David had helped to 'rogue' and then 'inspect' the potato crops for Sol

Thompson, to help them pay their way through the University, and so knew many people in Alyth.

Before long, however, Margaret and I motored south with baby Thomas to Combe Down, Somerset, to show him to members of the Spear family. We stayed at the Brow with Dick and were well looked after by his housekeeper. On our return we had a visit from two of my cousins, Annie Thomson from London and Nina Smith from Dumfries, both of whom had been brought up in Shotts—their mothers were my father's sisters.

After several weeks Margaret took ill and had to go off to the Cottage Hospital in Meigle. In the second week of August we had a visit in Alyth from my old army friend—Gerald Bishop from Sanderstead. It was good to see him again and to introduce Margaret and now little Thomas to him. Gerald then left us earlier than he or we had anticipated. By this time I had to look after Thomas in the Manse, and take him each day to see Margaret and be nursed by her. At night I recall dressing and settling Thomas in bed in our spare room, while I slept next to him, but kept on waking up all through the night to see if he was alright. He for his part seemed happy when he saw me—I shall never forget the intelligent look of recognition in his eyes when he did that. Margaret was far from well, but they were very kind to her in Meigle Hospital, and before very long she was able to return home to the manse in Alyth.

Then toward the end of the summer my cousin Annie Thomson came back again. She had been working privately as a special nurse for many years in London, and would later help at the birth of Princess Margaret's two children. She was eager to help us with little Thomas, but had not been able to come earlier. My parents came back again to be with us during our last few weeks in Alyth, and also for the baptism. That took place on October 5, when my father baptized him "Thomas Spear Torrance," when he used some water from the River Jordan, which he had once brought home from the Holy Land for just such an occasion. It was a lovely thought. I was glad that our eldest child had been born in Alyth, and was baptized in the Barony Kirk, for Alyth and the Barony Kirk had a very special place in our affection and life.

My days in Alyth were rapidly drawing to a close. Before I left I paid visits to a number of aged and infirm members of the congregation and to pray with them. And I made a particular point of calling on 'London Bill,' who had yet, as I said, to make his peace with God. I told him that when I was away he must look on John Welch as his pastor—he would be better for him than any minister.

Early in November Margaret, Thomas, and I moved to Aberdeen, and settled in the manse at 39 Forrest Road. My father, and my sister Grace and her husband, and my other brother-in-law, Ronald S. Wallace, travelled from Edinburgh and Glasgow to be with us. The Induction took place on November 12th, when the Presbytery of Aberdeen assembled in Beechgrove Church and formally introduced me as the new minister of Beechgrove Parish Church. Several of my friends, Professor David Cairns and Professor Archie Hunter in particular, took part, and gave me a very warm welcome. Archie Hunter had been Interim Moderator of Beechgrove during the Vacancy. A group of my Alyth friends and elders came to Aberdeen as well to be with us for that solemn occasion, and to thank me for my ministry of the gospel in Alyth. I was very moved.

CHAPTER 2

The Church in the World

By the Rev. Thomas F. Torrance B.D., Barony Parish Church, Alyth

The following address was delivered on 21st January, 1942, by Mr. TORRANCE to a special meeting of the Presbytery of Meigle convened for the purpose of discussing the spiritual issues involved in the present world situation, particularly with reference to the Report of the General Assembly Commission for the. Interpretation of God's Will in the Present Crisis and the Supplementary Report of the Foreign Mission. Committee.

In the course of the discussion it was realized that the number and importance of the questions involved called for fuller and more detailed consideration, and it was resolved to adjourn the meeting till 11th February. It was also felt that it would be most helpful if Mr. Torrance's inspiriting and suggestive address could be before all members of the Presbytery when preparing for the adjourned meeting, and an offer to have it printed for circulation, and a number of copies sent to each congregation within the bounds, was gratefully accepted, in the hope that it will rouse general interest in the vital issues raised and perhaps be used in conjunction with the above-mentioned Reports and the Questionnaire prepared by the Commission, in study groups wherever it is possible for such to be formed, with a view to these sending to the Presbytery through their respective ministers, opinions and suggestions to supplement those of the Presbytery itself.

In name and by authority of the Presbytery,

D. F. MACKENZIE, Moderator
Manse of Clunie, 26th January 1942

The Place and Function of the Church in the World

WHEN WE THINK OF the relation of the Church, and her task, to the world, society, culture, or civilization, there are always two points to be kept in mind:

A. The Church is something quite distinct, and cannot be identified with society, or with civilization. She has a unique message, which never can be naturalized; she has a unique function, which cannot be merged with anything else.

B. The Church does, however, have a worldly form, and is bound to keep in touch with the State and society. Here she must look to her methods and to her organization, for she must have some outward form through which she can translate her message to society; and through which she can have a purchase upon the State.

What About the Present Situation of the Church in Relation to These Two Cardinal Points?

A. The Church has tended to identify herself with society, and her distinctiveness tends to be lost in the midst of modern culture and civilization. Of course, much of our Western culture has been 'Christianized' and we have produced the phenomenon of 'Christendom,' which does not come under the purview of the New Testament. But the tragedy of the moment is that the Church has identified Christianity with Christendom. Thus the distinctive function and message of the Church have been swallowed up in the breadth of modern life; the Church is dying with sheer broadmindedness. The loss of this distinctiveness is evident in the general equation: "To be good" = "To be a Christian," which is simply not true, but universally held! We have compromised the Church standard of life, until now a Christian life is hardly distinguishable from good citizenship or public-spiritedness, or philanthropy, or humanitarianism. Thus the supernatural element in the Church, the Kingdom of God, has been naturalized, or humanized; and the Christian message has been whittled down to the meagre ideals of civilization. The "Christ" of so much of our Christianity is a pale, ghostly, anaemic figure, not the strong Son of God. That is why the Church is so impotent and weak in the face of the present situation. She has become so much a part of ordinary society that she finds herself unable to raise society. She has so compromised her message with the ideas of the modern world, that she is now not in a proper position to stand over against the world and deliver the pure Word of God with passion and conviction, and with power.

B. The Church has allowed her worldly form to become terribly outmoded; she has failed to keep pace with the tempo of modern times. Think of her many organizations, especially her financial affairs, which are often quite out of date. How many good businessmen with good business brains are in the Church, but fail to use them for God's work, and use them only for their own profit-making? Think of education, where the Church has been so slow to move with the times and has allowed a great deal of it to become so thoroughly secularized that the country is in danger of turning pagan. Think of the antiquated means, and hopelessly slow means, the Church has of forming her authoritative voice, and for communicating that to the people, the State, and the government. The Church has in fact fallen so far behind in these things, that at the moment, when she finds herself in danger of being swamped, she is striving to preserve what might well be described as an anachronism, which is daily lagging farther and farther behind.

If this diagnosis be correct, it means that where the Church should keep pace with the State and with civilization, she is falling behind; and where the Church should always be ahead of State and society, she has tended to become identified with the 'status quo.' The modern democratic State and the orders of life it entails arose largely as a result of the impact of Christianity, but now the Church has become tame and languid, apparently content to take her cue from the State, if not from the Conservative party. Indeed this has been so much the case in recent times that many look to the Church for a defence of the old order of things, social and political. But it is not the Church's business to be the bulwark of the old order; rather is it her business to throw the whole into ferment and upheaval. Of course, in one sense the Church must be conservative, because it is her business to uphold the eternal ordinances of God, but just because these ordinances are continually infringed by the ordinances of men, the conservatism of the Church must be identical with revolutionism. That is why a real era of disquietude entered this world with the coming of Christianity; the Church is called upon to play the part of leaven, in society, in the State, in the whole world, causing fermentation, destroying the stabilization of orders fashioned to suit human selfishness. Now, however, the Church has apparently lost sight of this aggressive function given her by the Christ who came to cast fire on the earth, and instead she has identified herself rather with the loaf than with the leaven. Does that not amount to a deplorable betrayal of the mission and function of the Church of Jesus Christ? We have allowed evil to take the initiative and are on the defensive, having forgotten that the Church is the army of God created for offensive action. If Christianity looks toward a new creation, she cannot but be fundamentally destructive and revolutionary over against the "fashion of this world." Just because the Church belongs to this new creation; she cannot help but be radical in this "present evil world."

In our own country the situation has been rendered very acute by the war. That is due not only to the tremendous changes in social life that are transforming the face of the country, but to the fact that the country has now reached one of these great turning points in her constitutional history, which is bound to have the most far-reaching repercussions upon the Church. Look at it this way: Every state just because it must maintain right by might, because it must maintain order in the last analysis by the power of the sword, is always on the point of developing into an authoritarian power, that is, into a fascist state. In our own country two major factors have contributed to inhibit that development: the Church, and private economic power. Strange as it may seem, it has been the lot of the great industrialists and financiers (that is, the capitalists), who by holding in their hands the economic control of the country (even for private ends), have stood in the way of the evolution of the State toward total power, therefore, toward totalitarianism. This check upon the State by the industrialists has helped to keep it democratic. But now, according to the demands of total war, the State has had to assume economic control, or is in the process of doing so, and it is not likely that it will relinquish this power after the war is over. That means that the church alone stands between the State and authoritarianism. Can the Church as she is today fulfil that role? Has she the machinery, modern and effective machinery, to attempt it? What about her propaganda, her communication with the government, not to speak of her faith? At the present moment the Church is to a great extent lost in the world, she has become merged with society, identified with the 'status quo.' Therefore from a government that is minded to change the 'status quo,' the Church can only expect opposition. And so far from having any real power to inhibit the evolution of the State toward total power, neither has she at the moment a message distinctive and revolutionary enough to proclaim, nor is she in is position to have a say in the new order which the Government hopes to put upon the face of the country. There are already on the horizon all sorts of evidences of a coming struggle between Church and State. The most ominous of these is in the handling of the country's youth organizations, and in the pressing question of education. At this critical juncture the country will be made or marred according as the Church is able to interject with power her voice into the counsels of State. The State can produce the technique: the Church alone can offer the message that can save the situation, for she is called to be the salt of the earth. The technique being evolved by the State is total, which will inevitably yield the fruit of totalitarianism, unless the Church is prepared to make a vigorous stand.

What Must the Church Do to Face This Emergency?

(A) The first thing she must do is to recover her distinctiveness, which she has definitely lost. That is to say, she must recover the gospel as the New Testament proclaims it, the saving power of Jesus Christ, and make that proclamation her foremost task. The Church is the body of Christ, and as such must refuse to become merged in ordinary social life and culture. She must show that there is a world of difference between being Christian and just being nice and gentlemanly. That difference will only be evinced with the recapture of the New Testament evangel, with all its supernatural power and character; and only then will she be able to make the impact upon the world that she wishes. Once again the Church must become militant, aggressive. Away with all comfortable, complacent 'Christianity' and stick-in-the-mud Churchmanship! Let the Church remember that she is committed to everlasting war; that her function in the world toward society and the State is to throw them into upheaval, to disturb them, and into that fermentation to interject the living Word of God whose impact upon society and State will mean a better order and shape for things in the future. But the Church must be prepared to take offensive action! The most sacred emblems of our faith are broken bread and poured out wine—the emblems of violent death. Do these emblems genuinely represent our type of Christianity today: a Christianity characterized by passion, and tears, and blood; a Christianity characterized by sacrifice, and devotion to the point of martyrdom? Only a Church inhabited with this Christian spirit can conquer.

The trouble with us today is not only that the Church's message has become poisoned with modern thought and has therefore little to say to the modern world, but that she has inoculated society with such a mild form of Christianity that now it is almost quite immune from the vital form. We have domesticated the Kingdom of God, and made the Church something puny and tame, and anaemic and impotent. Over against all this the Church must learn again from the New Testament that she has no right to settle down here; she is born from above; she is only here as an outpost from heaven. She has no right to identify herself with the social order here or with any political system, far less with the 'status quo.' She dare not think of herself as at home even in civilized and (as we say) 'Christian' Britain. The Church can only be the Christian Church when she is always on the move, always campaigning, always militant, aggressive, disruptive, revolutionary—what else can she be in this "this present evil world"? It is the business of the Church to evangelize the world, and if she does not actually Christianize the world, she must at least have such a powerful impact upon it as to turn the whole order of State and society, national and international, upside down. If she does not succeed in Christianizing the State, she must at least rub salt into it (even to the point of its nipping!) until it is kept from putrefying. The leaven must be thoroughly kneaded into the dough to produce proper fermentation. Without this thorough-going fermentation, the Church will have no power to alter the face of society, to bring industry into line with the Christian ethic, to influence the orders of the State in such a way that they do not become fascist.

(B) The Church must be prepared for a thorough overhaul of her whole shape and form, for a radical alteration in her organizations and methods. That is perhaps most imperative in her financial business, and in her immediate relations with social questions such as education and industry. While the pace of modern life is quickening with such enormous bounds so that all branches of it, industry, business, even farming, are rapidly falling into line with modern development and science, the Church cannot afford to be a single step behind. Of course, she has already taken some significant steps. She uses the wireless and newsprint, but her use of these is still deplorably impotent compared to what it might be. If the Church were really concerned about her evangelistic mission, what would she not do, what could she not do, if she chose to make full use of all the machinery of modern propaganda? It is especially important that this demand that the Church keep pace with the increasing tempo of modern times be brought speedily home to the individual kirks and presbyteries. So often it is true that anything that works down from 121 George Street is hopeless by the time it reaches the country kirk, and there is little wonder it is ill received. These motions for reform must begin from the kirks themselves, from the local presbyteries. We here in the country must be prepared to dispense with the idea that what was good enough for our fathers and grandfathers is good enough for us. They lived in a time in which things moved, and they moved with them; they would be the last to stick in the mud were they living today. The tempo of the times demands not only that we make these alterations, if the Church is to have anything like adequate machinery for her impact upon the country, but that we make them speedily. We must simply leap ahead, not only because we are so far behind already, but because the country is itself leaping ahead. We are confronted with a quite unparalleled situation in the whole of our history. The Church must be prepared to act accordingly. If need be she must be ruthless with many of her customs; for she must be willing to make such changes in her organization as will in some real measure correspond with the altering face of the whole country.

Think of what we would be able to do, for example, if every kirk in every presbytery had a really business-like way of tackling the financial calls of the Church and her missions? There would be no more need for these dribbling 'ad hoc' remedies that are shoved upon us from time to time, of which we are all now so sick, because they do not really strike at the heart of the practical difficulty; nor are they at all properly commensurate with modern finance. This Presbytery, without any delay and without any external boosting from headquarters, ought to institute an inquiry into such business here within her bounds, and learn what changes can be made, and actually introduced to remedy the situation.

How Is This to Affect Society and State?

By throwing the social environment into ferment and upheaval, by her aggressive evangelism with its faith that rebels against all wrong and evil, and by a new machinery through which her voice will be heard in the councils of the nation as never before, the Church will press toward a new order. She must do that: it is part of the duty of Christians to the State and to their fellow men. Wherever there is evil in the industrial or the economic order, in the political or international sphere, or in the social fabric of ordinary life, the Church must press home the claims of the Christian gospel and ethic. The goodwill necessary for a new order in which men can live together in a measure of security and peace will only come from the Church. Nothing will more easily betray the task of the Church after this war than the setting up of cheap programmes of social activity, and a whole apparatus of sterile social technique—but they will never solve the problem. Evil can flourish and gain its end better under a good order than under a thoroughly wicked and anarchic order. Everything depends on the potency of the Church's witness and the dynamic of her life. Therefore she must never identify herself with any particular social or political programme or with any new order. If that new order is to be alive itself and kept quickened, the Church must always be protesting, and throwing ferment into it all, for there will always be evil in the world until the creation of "the new heaven and the new earth." Thus, however much a new order may partake of, and be improved by, the Christian ethic, it can never be thought of as an approximation to the body of Christ, which is the Church. After all a new order can only give fresh disposition to the forces of evil. It will only change for a while the fashion of this world, and the inherent evil will be bound to break forth again and again, until God has made himself a new heaven and a new earth. Nevertheless, by pressing her witness, the Church can help to bring about a new order in which there is the real possibility of peace and brotherly relations on the basis of the Christian ethic, and she will keep that new order from decay if she continually presses it toward new reform, and refuses to identify herself with it.

One of the greatest tragedies that ever happened in the religious and social history of this country was during and after the last war, when the Church deluded the people into thinking that the Kingdom of God would gradually develop upon the earth, produced out of the kingdoms of the world by the efforts of the world plus divine aid, and that there would come a time when the Church would be at home in this world, identified with a better order. People were thoroughly disillusioned, and they have left the kirk by the tens of thousands. The Church herself is largely to blame, because she did not have a right understanding of her place and function in the world; because she failed to grasp the supernatural nature of her New Testament faith and vision. It was surely just because the Church was so closely allied to the State in Germany that the country once the most Protestant and vigorous in Christian faith has now become so thoroughly pagan. We now know that it is not Prussianism that has made Germany bad. Prussia with all its genius for organization and discipline supplied the technique and gave systematic expression to a soul (Kultur) in Germany which ever since the Renaissance has been pressing through the teaching of the Reformation until at last it came to the surface, first in the poets and philosophers, and then in a national movement. The Church alone had the power to curb that development, but by lowering her standards, and amalgamating the faith of the gospel with a spurious natural theology, she made room for a thoroughgoing attempt to follow the basic impulses of human nature (such as the will to power). We must take to heart that lesson. By recovering her original vision and task the Church in this country must create such a soul that it will give Christian substance to a new order; but by refusing to identify herself with that new order, she will always be in a position to curb it, to throw it into ferment, and keep it from reverting to type, from becoming a monster (i.e., "Leviathan"). That is possible only if the Church realizes again her supernatural mission, her otherworldly character, her Christian distinctiveness, and fulfils her function with all the passion and conviction of which she is capable.

How Is This to Affect the Foreign Mission Question?

In this way: if the Church does recover the New Testament vision, she will see that the great task of the Church is the redemption of the world, and not a comfortable life in little religious churches and communities. The Church simply cannot keep alive unless her eyes are upon the farthest horizons of the world, unless she keeps herself in line with the master-passion and world-outlook of Christ who was the propitiation not for our sins only but for the sins of the whole world. It is for that reason that mission work does not arise from any arrogance in the Christian Church: mission is its cause and its life. The Church exists by mission, just as fire exists by burning. Where there is no mission, there is no Church. Of course, it is ultimately a secondary question whether we mean by mission Foreign Missions or preaching the gospel at home. Mission, gospel preaching, is the spreading of the fire that Christ cast upon the earth. He who does not propagate this fire shows that he is not burning. He who burns propagates the fire (Brunner). But to burn, the fire must have fuel to burn—that is why it must always be reaching out and out and out.

Jesus Christ came, he said, not to be ministered unto but to minister and to give his life a ransom for many. If the Church claims to follow this Christ, she most learn that she cannot claim to be Christian until her major effort is engaged in ministering to others after the pattern of her Lord. But think of any average church in this country you care—is it not true that the people's main business is to gather together just in order to be ministered unto, instead of ministering themselves? Is it not true that what ministrations individual churches do carry out are left to the minister himself, or to a few of the elders or members of the Guild or the Work Party? And the bulk of the folk thinks it can commute military service in the Kingdom of God by dropping a few pennies into the plate each week! Thus the vitality of the Church is sapped by in-breeding, by in-growing. It is a major disaster that the Church has become introvert (i.e., turned in upon itself) when it ought to be extrovert (i.e., turned out toward the world). The Church has become static and self-regarding, instead of an army of conquest The major task of the Church in all ages is world mission. If the master-passion of Jesus was the redemption of the world, how is it at all possible for us to call our churches 'Christian' whose major purpose is certainly very far different from the passion of Christ? Our major emphasis is upon ourselves—and in so doing we have brought about in the Church a complete reversal of the will and command of Christ; we have betrayed the supreme purpose of the Cross. The Church of today appears simply not to believe that by losing her life for Christ's sake and the gospel's, she will find it, that the Church exists only by mission. Instead the Church tries miserably to cultivate her own strength, and becomes self-centred and soft, and impotent over against the ills of the world. The Church needs to be turned inside out; her whole effort and life must face outwards, and only inwards so far as it is necessary in her effort to evangelize the world. Only if the Church determines to put this first and foremost in her life and work, and in the life and work of every single individual country church, will she begin to have the blessing she craves from God. Instead of trying to cherish a tiny quiver of flame, shielding it from all the draughts and winds that blow, let her fling it out into the storms of the world where it is meant to be, and it will become a raging fire radiating heat and light. If the Church exists by mission, just as fire exists by burning, then the Church at home will never be healthy and strong until she is bent upon consuming the world with the fire of the Cross.

CHAPTER 3

The Humanity of Christ in the Sacramental Life of the Church[1]

IT BELONGS TO THE very essence of the New Testament gospel that it is not concerned only with two dimensions of thought, with God and man, but with a third dimension in Jesus Christ in whom God and man are one and in whom there is a new creation. That is all-important, for example, in our understanding of eschatology. People like Bultmann and Dodd, Niebuhr and Tillich, think mainly in two dimensions—of the act of God and the act of man, of eternity and time, and of the tension between the two. But when we think of eschatology in terms of the tension between eternity and time, time is always the loser, and in the last resort temporal relations become irrelevant or merely symbolic. That is true in varying degrees of all the four thinkers I have mentioned: in the last resort they all have a docetic attitude toward history. The witness of the New Testament, however, teaches us to think of the Incarnation not only as the assumption of our humanity in union with God but as the assumption of our frail temporal life in union with the eternal life of God. In Jesus Christ crucified and risen our time is redeemed and joined together in an abiding union with eternity: that is *the time of the new creation* which is the very substance of Christian eschatology; it is the time of the new man, which has its abiding reality in the time of the risen Jesus.

---

1. Published in the Church Service Society annual, issue 26, 1956; the full title is "The Place of the Humanity of Christ in the Sacramental Life of the Church."

We have to think of the doctrine of the Sacraments in the same way. We are not concerned in the Sacraments only with two dimensions, with the act of God and the act of human response; we are concerned above all with the third dimension in the crucified and risen Jesus Christ, and therefore with the new humanity in Christ who is God and man, in which we are by grace given to share. It is his new humanity, risen from the dead and eternally in union with God, that is the *substance* or the *matter* of the Sacraments (as Calvin used to put it), and indeed of the whole Christian life in time and eternity. Jesus Christ is the *new Adam* and it is in him, in our sharing of the humanity of the new Adam, that our salvation and our new life consist.

This is the teaching that we in the Reformed Churches owe to John Calvin who recovered it for us out of the New Testament. In this, Calvin owed a great deal to the Greek Fathers, notably to Irenaeus, Athanasius, and Cyril of Jerusalem. There was a tendency among the theologians of the Early Church to divide into two camps—those of the Antiochian school, who stressed the historical humanity of Jesus, and those of the Alexandrian school, who stressed the eternal nature of Christ as divine Logos; but there was a third 'school,' running from Irenaeus to Athanasius, which stressed the vicarious humanity of Jesus along with its stress upon the deity and Lordship of Christ. That is where Calvin derived his theological ancestry when he thought of the Incarnation and reconciliation in Christ not only as the mighty act of God on our behalf, but as the atoning obedience of Jesus, the Servant of the Lord and our High Priest. Calvin was, in fact, the first theologian to work out fully the place of the human obedience of Christ in a doctrine of atonement. He did not, of course, neglect the fact that it was *God* in Christ who reconciled the world to himself: but in unity with that he was the first great theologian since the Early Church to give a full and satisfactory account of the saving significance of the humanity of Jesus, and of the life of the Church as union with Christ through the power of the Spirit sharing in his new humanity.

The fruits of the atoning work of Christ, Calvin could sum up in the words of John 5:26: "As the Father hath life in himself, so hath he given to the Son to have life in Himself." This life, which the Son has residing in his humanity, he communicates to us through Word and Sacrament, so that we are given to share in the durable and incorruptible life of the Son of God, who has taken our humanity upon himself for ever.

We may note, for our purpose here, three main respects in which the doctrine of the vicarious and saving humanity of Christ was so important for Calvin.

(a) In regard to the Priesthood of Christ. Only with a proper stress upon the humanity of Jesus can an adequate conception of the Mediatorship of Christ be attained and false notions of human mediation and priesthood be abolished. If what Christ did for us he did as pure act of God, then there must of necessity be a human priesthood to respond to it and convey it to man. But if Christ acted not only as God but as man, and has once and for all offered man's sacrifice, man's response to God, then our sacrifice is already made and our response is already offered, and there is no need for human mediation or a human priesthood. This does not mean that we do not have to worship God in sacrifice and oblation, but it does mean that our sacrifice is one of praise and thanksgiving for what is offered on our behalf, and that whatever we offer, even by way of thanksgiving, praise, and prayer, and when we offer ourselves in living sacrifice, we offer only "by the hand of Christ," as John Knox put it. Thus the stress upon the saving, vicarious humanity of Jesus determines the whole nature of the Church's life of prayer and worship.

(b) In regard to Baptism. If the whole course of Christ's obedience on earth was part of his atoning work, then the "whole course of his life lived out for us from infancy to maturity, from the cradle to the cross, was sanctifying and redeeming in its effect." And so Calvin, following Irenaeus and others, held that our birth is sanctified by the birth of Jesus, our infancy by his infancy, our youth by his youth, and our manhood by his manhood. He took upon himself the whole course of our human life to redeem and sanctify it. It becomes immediately clear that the Sacrament of Baptism has very definite relation to the birth of Jesus Christ from above by the Holy Spirit, and is concerned with his growth in wisdom and grace into the full stature of manhood before God and people. The Baptism of infants is thus grounded upon their sharing in the birth of the human Jesus who was born an infant for them, and who already gave new birth to their humanity in himself, as well as upon his

death and resurrection for them. At the same time, Baptism is grounded upon the whole life of Jesus, and is our sacramental initiation into the life of the new Adam who was born at Bethlehem that we might be born again in him, and who was raised from the dead for our justification.

(c) In regard to the Lord's Supper. As members of the new Adam or the new Man we are nourished by the life residing in Christ. And so one of the aspects of the Lord's Supper that Calvin stressed is that in it we are continually being nourished with "the vivifying flesh" of Jesus Christ who gives us to participate in the eternal life that abides in him. This teaching is very fully and clearly expounded in several sections of the *Institutes* (4.17.7–12), which have had the profoundest influence upon our Scottish tradition.

All these three aspects of Calvin's teaching were taken over by our Reformers in Scotland, and in some respects they enjoyed a fuller and purer exposition in Scotland than anywhere on the Continent. John Knox's emphasis upon the priesthood of the man Jesus, for example, was of great significance, apparent not only in his debates with the Abbot of Crossraguell but in the *Declaration of the True Nature of Prayer,* one of the richest documents for the understanding of the Scottish Reformation. Here the linking together of prayer and the Lord's Supper, on the ground of "the perpetual prayer" of Christ—recorded in the seventeenth chapter of John—is of primary significance for the true understanding of the Sacrament. As Christ is the only high priest, "He is the right hand by whom we offer anything unto the Father." It is by Christ that our prayer at the Eucharist is offered, or to put it otherwise: Christ's high-priestly prayer (which we are given to overhear in John 17) is behind our prayer at the Eucharist when we spread forth the bread and wine and pray in Christ's name. It is in prayer and intercession at the Lord's Supper that John Knox saw the true 'priestly character' of our ministry, involving not only the prayer of thanksgiving, but also of intercession in Christ.

Along with this, particularly in relation to Baptism and the Lord's Supper, belongs what the *Scots Confession* called "that most blessed conjunction, union and society which the elect have with their Head Jesus Christ." All our standards and catechisms contain this doctrine of union with Christ, but it is principally in the earlier ones that it is expressed most fully, and nowhere better or more beautifully than in the Catechisms of John Craig. It was this, too, that formed such a powerful ingredient in the celebrated *Sermons on the Sacrament* of Robert Bruce. It was in fact this doctrine that contributed so much to the depth and to the wealth of our Scottish conception of the Church, and of the ministry of the Word and Sacraments, and it is still at this point that the Church of Scotland stands decidedly nearer to the teaching of John Calvin than any of our sister Reformed Churches on the Continent.

But, strange to say, it is precisely at this point that so many ministers today are baffled in their understanding of the New Testament doctrine of the Sacraments. Why should that be the case? In the last edition of Robert Bruce's sermons issued in 1900 Professor Laidlaw wrote of Bruce as follows: "The author's formal standard was the *Scots Confession* of 1560. But the possible exaggerations in Calvin's sacramental ideas, just hinted at in that Confession, are avoided by Bruce. He had evidently taken his stand on the more generally accepted Reformed view which had already appeared in the Second Helvetic Confession (1566), in the XXXIX Articles (1563), and which was yet to be more clearly stated, immediately after his time, in the Westminster standards." That is a most revealing statement. It is probably true that Bruce's views were influenced by Bullinger's sermons on the Lord's Supper as well as by the *Thirty-Nine Articles* of the Church of England and to a certain extent also by the growing emphasis upon forensic notions of salvation emanating from the Low Countries; but why should Laidlaw have followed these aberrations against Calvin and the *Scots Confession*?

Professor David Cairns has drawn my attention to another significant passage from the pen of William Cunningham in which he has this to say of John Calvin: "We cannot deny that he made an effort to bring out something like a real influence exerted by Christ's human nature upon the souls of believers, in connection with the dispensation of the Lord's Supper—an effort which was, of course, entirely unsuccessful, and resulted only in what was about as unintelligible as Luther's consubstantiation. This is, perhaps, the greatest blot in the history of Calvin's labours as a public instructor." (*The Reformers and the Theology of the Reformation*, 240).

That was, of course, a ghastly failure on the part of the great Cunningham to understand Calvin, but behind it lies a severely forensic interpretation of the *Westminster Confession of Faith* in terms of the rationalistic Calvinism of the Synod of Dort. That needs a little explanation.

Following hard upon the Reformation in France and the Netherlands came a formidable counter-attack on the part of the Roman Church; but a Protestant champion arose in Du Moulin, who had achieved fame as an exponent and teacher of Aristotelian logic, and who had published a standard text-book on the subject. He challenged his Roman opponents to debate after debate in public, in which the disputants argued with one another exclusively in series of syllogisms. Du Moulin, who was undoubtedly a master in such logical disputation, overpowered his opponents and became the most formidable Calvinist theologian in what is now known as France, Belgium, and Holland, exercising a very wide influence. During the controversies with the Arminians it was the teaching of Du Moulin which came to be generally adopted by Calvinists, but it was a strange form of Calvinism in which the biblical teaching of the Reformer had been cast back into the rigid mould of Aristotle from which he had, by the mercy of God, been emancipated after his education in the Sorbonne. It was this perverted, rationalistic brand of Calvinism that dominated the Synod of Dort, which sent a gold medal to Du Moulin in recognition of his great services. From the Low Countries the same brand of Calvinism came into Scotland and it was revived by many of the theologians of the Disruption and is still maintained in all its rationalistic and rigid intransigence in the Western Isles; but the almost exclusively forensic conceptions of justification and salvation through the death of Christ have generally prevailed, or provoked Pelagian reactions which only too readily fell in with the rising subjectivism of the nineteenth century.

In this connection it is most instructive to look again at the contribution of John McLeod Campbell, one of the most remarkable and godly theologians in the history of the Kirk in Scotland. As I see it, McLeod Campbell, reacting against the logical determinism of hyper-Calvinism, on the one hand, and against the superficial subjectivism of his day, on the other hand, sought to reformulate the doctrine of the atonement along the lines of Calvin's Christology and its emphasis upon the obedience and priesthood of Jesus. His great work, *The Nature of the Atonement*, published first in 1855, is a moving and deeply devotional work, but it fell down rather badly both in its failure to appreciate the element of judgment in atonement and also in a fundamentally Pelagian element in its conception of the vicarious penitence and priesthood of Christ. But McLeod Campbell did wrestle very seriously, as no one else in his generation, with the saving significance of the human obedience of Jesus as the *Amen* of truth to the divine will. Does the fact that we have allowed the centenary of the publication of McLeod Campbell's great book to pass unmarked indicate that the Church still fails to appreciate the place of the humanity of Christ expounded in different ways by Athanasius, John Calvin, and McLeod Campbell?

After McLeod Campbell's great attempt and failure to find a way between the extremes of logical determinism and Pelagian subjectivism, Scottish Theology began to fall more and more apart and was characterized by a radical dichotomy. On the one hand, there persisted in even more extreme, though also in modified evangelical forms, the forensic conception of salvation in which the whole focus of attention was directed upon the work of Christ in his actual death, and not upon "the constitution of his Person" as also of the substance of redemption; but on the other hand there arose out of the Pietist subjectivism of the nineteenth century and its idealist conception of history, largely under the influence of Schleiermacher and Ritschl, the liberal conception of the Jesus of history, which in accord with the romantic outlook of the late nineteenth and early twentieth centuries eliminated the elements of judgment and transcendence from the Gospel witness to Jesus Christ. It is now clear that both the forensic conception of Christ and the liberal reconstruction of Jesus failed signally to give any adequate account of the humanity of Christ in soteriological terms. The forensic theology knocked out the whole conception of union with Christ, which had long been such a powerful ingredient in the Scottish Church. That has left our life of prayer and devotion throughout the Church fearfully impoverished. The liberal theology, for all its fixation upon the historical Jesus, cast everything into an idealist mould which damaged and mutilated the realism of the teaching and message of Jesus, removed him from the wounded conscience and tears of sinners, and paved the way for the Marxist revolt against all vague idealistic religion in favour of a kingdom of God translated into the flesh and blood of the common life.

What we are concerned with here, however, is the fact that both forensic and liberal theologies, in their different ways, by failing to grasp the place occupied in the New Testament gospel by the full humanity of the crucified and risen Jesus Christ, failed to give to our people an adequate understanding of Word and Sacrament, and of our participation through them in the life of Jesus Christ as the new Adam or the new Man. That is why so many of our people, even of our ministers and theologians, are baffled by the Sacraments, because they do not fit into their meagre conceptions of the person of Christ and of our union with Christ through the power of his Spirit; and that is why the life of prayer both in the home and in the prayer-meeting of the Church is at such a low ebb. Would to God we could recover the teaching of John Knox about the true nature of prayer and of the ministry as stewardship in the holy mysteries of God!

The theme we have been discussing is of primary relevance to the Liturgical Movement today. So much of this has its origins in the desire of the nineteenth century for a romantic repristination of the glories of the past and lacks, just as much as the forensic and liberal theologies, an adequate theology of the saving humanity of Christ Jesus. So long as that is the case it may have a vogue and a fashion, and may satisfy the superficial and often erotic hunger for symbolism, but it cannot do anything to meet the great pastoral needs of the flock of Christ. They need to be nourished (in Calvin's startling language) with "the vivifying flesh of Christ," and need to be led in worship which not only draws out their soul in ardent prayer and devotion, but builds them up in the new humanity of the risen and triumphant Lord, and then sends them back to live it out in the common life of home and work. If the Liturgical Movement is to have an adequate theological foundation and is to have a continuously invigorating and evangelical impact upon the life of the Church it must find it where, in their different ways, Cyril of Jerusalem, John Calvin, and John Knox found it—in the saving humanity and royal priesthood of Jesus.

CHAPTER 4

The Meaning of Order[1]

ORDER IS THE CO-ORDINATING of the life of the Church in its fellowship, worship, and mission in the service of the glory of God. The order of the Church's ministry is the ordering of its life and work through participation in the obedience of Christ. Let us elucidate that in a number of paragraphs.

(1) In the biblical revelation the whole concept of order is viewed over against disorder and chaos. Apart from the ordering of God's creative Word the world is without form or void, but into the ordered cosmos there has broken the disorder of sin. It belongs to the very nature of sin to divide, to disrupt, to be anarchic—sin is lawlessness, *anomia*. The opposite of all that is order, harmony, communion. When God made the world, he made it in order and everything was set in its due proportion. But through the lawlessness of sin the world fell out of proportion, out of order, and was threatened with sheer chaos. Were it not for the persistent fact of God's purpose of love the world would destroy itself; but in his covenant mercy God holds the world together in spite of its chaos, and to that end he has promulgated his law which restrains and contains disorder and chaos, and reduces it to a measure of proportion, even while it is in the grip of *anomia*, or lawlessness. But God's covenant contains the promise of a new order, of a new creation when all things will be restored to their obedience and perfection in the

---

1. In the *Church Quarterly Review* 160 (Jan 1959) 21–36, also published in *Conflict and Agreement*, vol. 2 (London: Lutterworth, 1960), 13–30.

divine will. Meantime wherever there is *anomia* it is met by the divine *nomos*, and there is conflict between disorder and order.

(2) The biblical revelation does not work with a concept of natural law, that is, of an order immanent in natural processes capable of being brought to its self-expression. There is an order of creation (*ordo creationis*) but that is not discernible by observing the creation (*cursus naturae*) but only by observing the creative will of God. This creative will of God will restore to creation its lost order, and restore to creation its true form and harmony in the Word of God. That is shadowed forth in the divine law promulgated in the Old Testament, the revealed law of God, but as yet that law set over against the lawlessness of the world is revealed mainly in its negative aspect of judgment upon disorder, and of restraint upon lawlessness. It is through the judgment of disorder that order is maintained, and laws are formed to make life in the disordered world possible at all. But the ultimate function of that law is to point beyond itself to the new law, the new order of the new covenant. Under the old covenant there was a divine form of administration or economy given in the law of Moses; but that points ahead to the new covenant when the covenant will of God will bring and manifest a new form of administration or economy. This will be inserted into the world and written into its inner being—the new law to be inscribed upon the heart through the Spirit. As such it is a new order that comes from without and is planted within.

(3) That new order, the new economy, or rather the eternal economy of God for his creation, came into the world in Jesus Christ. In the Incarnation the Word of God entered into his own disordered world; the light shone into the darkness; the divine economy entered within historical and creaturely existence. In other words, the covenant will of God broke into our world and is completely fulfilled in Jesus Christ both from the side of God and from the side of man. That is the economy of which St. Paul speaks, when he describes its work as that of gathering up all things into Christ the head, things visible and invisible, and their ordering in the eternal purpose of the divine love and fellowship. *Oikonomia* describes literally the ordering of a house, household administration. God is the great householder who has come to take control of his own house and family and order it according to his love.

He does that in and through the Incarnation, in which his *Oikonomia* is not imposed upon the world from without but enters into it and operates from within it. *Oikonomia* represents the great condescension of the divine will to work out his purpose of love without violence within the alienated will of man, to work out his divine economy within the disordered existence of the world. Now the *mode of that economic condescension* is the way of Jesus Christ the servant, the way of obedience even to the death of the cross, and it is through that mode of economic condescension that he is exalted to be the head of all things, and especially the head of the Church, his body.

(4) In Jesus Christ, therefore, in his Incarnation and in the whole course of his obedience, there has taken place in the divine economy a restoration of alienated man to fellowship with God, a conversion of rebellious humanity to the obedience and love of God. In other words, in the whole human life of Jesus the order of creation has been restored; in the midst of our disordered, sin-disrupted existence, there has been lived a human life in perfect order and proportion to the will of God. The covenant purpose of God in creation has been fulfilled and more than fulfilled. Here we have the divine economy entering into our creaturely and human existence and ordering it from within against our human nature, that is against the consequences of sin in all its disorder, chaos, and lawlessness entrenched in fallen human nature. This is the order of redemption, which reaches back to the original order of creation and far transcends it in the amazing purpose of the divine love, as the order, of the new creation. Here in the new humanity in Jesus Christ nothing is out of order, or out of proportion. Everything has its proper order, proper time, proper place, proper sequence, and proper end. From beginning to end the whole life of Jesus in obedience to the Father is directed to his praise and glory, so that the new order of creation established and revealed in the humanity of Christ can be spoken of as the praise of creation for the Creator.

(5) Order in the new creation is to be regarded as a third dimension. We are not concerned here simply with the will of God and the obedience of man, with the law of God, and the conformity of man to that divine law, but with a *third dimension* with a divinely provided fulfilment of the divine law. In the Old Testament we have a situation in

which God gathers his children into covenant relation with himself, and within that covenant he declares: "I will be your God, and you will be my children . . . I am holy, therefore be ye holy. I am God; walk before me and be perfect." But God knows that his children are unable to be holy or obedient or perfect before him; they are unable to fulfil the requirements of his covenant will, so that within the covenant and as part of its covenant mercies he graciously provides a way of response to his will, a way of obedient conformity to his covenant which he is pleased to accept as from his people in the covenant. That was provided in Israel's cult or *leitourgia*. But that cultic pattern of response had to be acted out in obedience, while it pointed beyond itself to God's promise of a way of obedient fulfilment of it in the actual existence and life of his people. That was the theme in the 'Servant Songs,' which was fulfilled at last in Jesus Christ who in his obedient humanity is our God-given way of response to the divine will. God's covenant will is fulfilled for us on our behalf, and in our stead, and through our participation in the obedient humanity of Christ we are given to share in the fulfilled economy of the new covenant, indeed of the new creation. That then is the third dimension. We are not simply concerned even in the Christian Church with the will of God in love and grace and then with the obedience of man in love and fellowship. We are concerned with these two but with the two as fulfilled and completed in Jesus Christ in the obedient ordering and perfection of his human life as an oblation of all praise and thanksgiving to God the Creator and Father, and therefore of our sharing in his obedience through the power of the Spirit. Thus order in the New Testament refers to the concrete ordering of our human life and being in the obedient humanity of Jesus Christ. All order in the Christian Church is a participation in his obedient humanity—whether that order be an ordering of its daily life, daily worship, daily fellowship, or daily mission. The whole of the Church's life is ordered through participation in the ordered life of Jesus Christ, the new Adam, the head of the new creation.

(6) The form that this re-ordering in Jesus Christ takes is the form of a servant. It was through his obedience within our disobedient humanity that he restored us to order and peace in God. But in that he the obedient Servant is given to be the head of all creation, all

creation is now re-ordered in obedience to him, for he gives it to share in his obedience to God. Because Christ is the head of creation, chaotic lawless creation is restored to order in him, and because he restored order through obedience to the Father he restores order to the creation through bringing creation into obedience to himself, by granting it through the Spirit to share in his own obedience. Thus as Jesus was obedient in the Father, who sent him to fulfil his will, so the Church is ordered in its obedience to Christ who sent it to fulfil his will. The obedience of the Church to Christ is not simply an imitation of his obedience but a fulfilling of God's will through participation in Christ's obedience.

(7) It is through the Spirit that the Church is given to share in Christ's obedience, and so to be ordered in and by and through his obedient humanity. Christ is the law of the Church's life, the law according to which its life and work are to be ordered, but that law is fulfilled not simply by external obedience and conformity but by inner and outer sharing in his life, so that *through the Spirit* the Church is in-the-law to Christ (*ennomos Christou*), conformable to him through communion with him. It is the Spirit who is the law of the Church's ordered life; not the Spirit as a new law of nature, not the Spirit as the soul of the Church, not the Spirit as a new immanent norm in the development of the Church through history, but the Spirit who gives the Church to share in the obedience of Christ the head of the body and who is other than the Church, its Lord and King but who in economic condescension has come to be obedient to the Father from within the Church, that the Church may share in an obedience not its own, and in an order that is new to it, indeed against its own nature; an order from beyond the Church's own being but in which it is given to participate by the Spirit.

(8) This being so, *actual order* as we see and have it in the historical Church on earth is essentially ambiguous. Its basic order is the obedient new humanity in Christ. The Church shares in that through the Spirit, so that its life is ordered through the communion of the Spirit. But the Church that shares in that order of the new creation is the Church that is sent by Christ out into history, to live its life in the physical and temporal existence that awaits redemption in the second advent of Christ. The Church in the midst of the old creation and all its disorder shares in the new creation and its new order. By sheer participation in the empirical

life of this fallen world, which comes under the divine judgment and therefore the divine law, the Church participates in worldly forms and laws and cannot escape from them. It is sent to have its mission right there under law, but under law to share in the new order in-the-law to Christ through the Spirit. Just as the Son of God himself condescended to be made under the law and through obedience to fulfil the will of God, and as such was exalted above all, so the Church which is given to share through the Spirit in the new humanity of Christ is sent into history to live out its new life in the form of a servant under the law— not to be fettered by the law, not to be schematized according to the forms and patterns of this age, that is, not to be legalized in its life, but to use the patterns and forms of the law of this age in the service of its new life in the risen and ascended Lord. Thus all order in the historical Church is essentially ambiguous because it is order in the overlap of the two ages, this present age that passes away and the new age which through the Spirit already overlaps it in Christ.

Another way of putting that is to say that all order in the historical Church is essentially eschatological. By 'eschatological' here two things are meant: (a) that order carries within it the tension between the new and the old; and (b) the tension between the present (including the past) and the future. True order in the Church of Christ is order that points above and beyond its historical forms to its new order in the risen Christ, and points beyond its present forms to the future manifestation of its order in the new creation. All order in the Church is thus ambivalent and provisional: it is order that visibly reflects its life hid with Christ in God, and order that exercises a provisional service in time, until Christ comes again. The outward order is like the scaffolding of a building that is to be torn down and cast away when the building itself is complete. In history God has given the Church its historical order and structure which participates in the forms of this passing world, but when the building of the Church as an habitation of God is complete, and its new order is revealed in the advent of Christ, the historical forms of order and structure will be cast away. Or to put it another way: all order is at once juridical and spiritual. It is at once participant in *nomos* and participant in *Pneuma*, that is, in Christ through the *Pneuma*. The validity of orders in the Church partakes of that ambivalence. Validity is at once a juridical term relative to the particular nomistic structure of a Church, relative to the law of a Church, but validity is also a spiritual term referring to the sharing of the Church in the authority of Christ through his Spirit, a sharing in the *exousia* of the Son of man. It is that essential ambiguity in validity that makes it such a difficult term, and forgetfulness of it that causes persistent confusion.

Now in the light of all these eight heads we have to think of the order of the Church's ministry with reference to its actual life in the space and time of this world. The ordering of the Church's life through sharing in, and therefore according to, the obedient humanity of Christ, is an ordering within the physical and temporal life of this world. Order has therefore to be thought out in terms of space and time.

1. Order in regard to Space

Because the Church is the body of Christ, it has a physical and spiritual life in which the physical and the spiritual are not to be separated, though they may be distinguished, from one another. The Church as body of Christ in history has therefore space. It has its place in this world, the place that it has been given by Christ and into which he has sent it. It is in its place in the physical world that its life is to be ordered. Let us look at that in this way. Jesus Christ, the man Jesus, is the place in this physical world where God and man meet and where they have communion with one another. The temple in the Old Testament was the place where God put his name, where he kept tryst with his covenanted people, and where they kept covenant with him. Jesus Christ is that temple on earth and among men where God has put his name, and where he has appointed us to meet him. It is the place where heaven and earth meet, the place of reconciliation. Jesus Christ is himself God's mercy-seat, God's place in this world where he is really present to us in our place. But Jesus Christ ascended, and he is in heaven—that is, he has a heavenly place far beyond anything that we can understand and far beyond our reach, but Jesus Christ through his Spirit has also bestowed his presence upon us in the Church, so that the Church on earth is the place of Christ.

The place of the Church in history is the place where Christ's presence is to be found. That is his real presence. It is, of course, above all in the Sacrament of the Lord's Supper, in the midst of the Church on earth, that we are given the real presence of Christ. That is the place of Christ in the place of the Church on earth. That is the place where heaven bends down to earth, and where man on earth is made to sit in heavenly places in Christ. Here we are concerned with two places, as it were: the heavenly place of Christ and the spatial place of the Church. The place of the Church is to be defined with regard to that heavenly place of real presence of Christ, on the one hand, and with regard to its participation in the spatial context of the physical world, on the other. The Church's life, worship, fellowship, and ministry are all ordered in regard to that twofold place, heavenly and earthly place. No adequate understanding of the order of the Church can neglect that twofold involvement in space enshrined so clearly in the Sacrament.

Order will concern the indicating or defining of the place on earth where the heavenly place of Christ makes contact with it, but that earthly place cannot be so delimited and defined as thereby to define and delimit also the heavenly place of Christ. Christ the risen and ascended Lord is in a place that is beyond definition and delimitation. It is through the sovereign Spirit that he graciously condescends to be really present in the appointed space of the Church and to make that his place on earth. But he does not thereby bind himself to that place on earth; rather does he bind us through that place to his own real presence, to his heavenly place, and so from that appointed place on earth he exalts us to sit with him in heavenly places.

All this means that the Church's *order* in space is concerned with the ordering of its physical fellowship and worship in the Spirit. Order serves the proclamation of the word and the Eucharistic fellowship on earth, but orders it in such a way that it makes room in it all, makes a place in it all, for the sovereign presence of the Spirit, for the heavenly place of Christ—that is, for his real presence. The Christian Church as the body of Christ on earth knows nothing of a spaceless ordering of its life.

2. Order in regard to Time

Because the Church is the body of Christ, it has a temporal and eternal life in which the temporal and the eternal are not to be separated, although they may be distinguished from one another. The Church as the body of Christ in history therefore has time as an essential ingredient of its reality. It has its time in this world, the time that it has been given by Christ and into which he has sent it. It is in the time-form of this world, in historical existence that its life is to be ordered—to be ordered as Christ's body in time. Now Jesus Christ in his historical life is the area in the time of this creaturely world where God and man, eternity and time, meet and have communion with each other. Israel through its history was the area within world-history into which God intervened with his redeeming purpose, in order to work into our time and from within our time toward that area in the fullness of time when God would become man and gather man into the life of God, when the eternal would come into the passage of time, and gather time into union with the eternal. In Israel God bound our time into covenant relation with himself, but all that is completely fulfilled in Jesus Christ where time is not only the sphere of the eternal event, but time is sanctified, redeemed, reconciled, and given new reality in union with eternity, once and for all.

In Jesus Christ, therefore, the eternal Son of God has lived his life within our time; he became time and has in himself elevated time into abiding communion with the eternal God. In Jesus Christ God has recreated time, redeemed it from its vanity, from its guilt and irreversibility, its decay and corruption, and given it a new reality in the new humanity of the incarnate Son. But Jesus Christ has ascended and he is in heaven, in eternity—that is, he has an eternal time far beyond anything that we can understand, or can measure by the kind of time we have in this passing age. It is not a timeless time, or a timeless eternity, but eternal time in which our time, redeemed new time, is eternally real in union with eternity itself. That is the new time of the Kingdom manifested in the forty days of the risen Jesus Christ upon the earth, and within the lapses of our temporal history; but now that Jesus Christ has ascended, he has withdrawn that new time of his new humanity from sight, from the visible succession of passing time on the plane of history.

And yet Jesus Christ bestows himself upon us in time, and in such a way that our faith and worship are not timeless, any more than they are spaceless. It is within our passing time that he has time for us, that he makes time for us, makes time for communion, for faith, for worship, for growth, for development, for advance. It is in the Church in history that Christ has time for us, for by the very act of his ascension he waits for us and makes time for us, in which we can hear the gospel, time in which we can repent, time for decision and faith, time in which we can preach the gospel to all nations.

This was a frequent element in the teaching of the historical Jesus, in his parables of the householder or the king who went into the far country and waited till the right time to return, but in that period of waiting he gave his servants time, and then returned to call them to account for the time he had given them—the word sometimes used to describe that is *chronizein*, but it has also associated with it the word *chorein*, to make room, that is room for freedom to believe, freedom to decide, and freedom to be obedient (within time) until the return of the householder or king. It is in that light that we are to understand Christ's ascension, and the fact that by the very act of ascension, and his heavenly waiting until the right time for him to return, Jesus Christ establishes the Church in history with temporal form within the passage of time where it has time to work, and time to obey him. It is in that time that the Church has time to exist and carry out its mission, within the succession of history where there is time between revelation and decision, time between decision and act, time between present and future, time for the gospel. Thus the existence of the Church as bound up with its mission is inseparable from time. The Church as the body of Christ in history is the area within the time-form of this world where God and man meet in the gospel, and where man is reconciled to God and united to him in Jesus Christ.

But it is *in Jesus Christ* that God gives the Church that time, and that place in time—and that means in the historical Jesus, and in the risen and ascended Jesus. Just as Jesus Christ is the place where heaven and earth meet, and God and man are reconciled, and the only place where that takes place, so Jesus Christ is the one place within time and the only place within time where God has provided time for the reconciliation of man, and man finds time for forgiveness and redemption. Jesus Christ is himself the fullness of time. Therefore the order of the Church in time means the ordering of the Church's life and mission in relation to the time of Jesus Christ, the historical Christ, and the risen and ascended Christ. In all Church order we are concerned with *the time of Jesus on earth* when God's Son condescended to enter within our fallen time in order to redeem it, but also with the *time of Jesus ascended into eternity* who yet bestows himself upon us in time through his Spirit. The time of the Church will therefore be defined by the relation of the Church in history to the historical Jesus Christ, and to the ascended and advent Jesus Christ; the Church's life, worship, fellowship, and ministry are all ordered with regard to that twofold time, heavenly and earthly, historical and eternal time. No adequate understanding of the order of the Church can overlook that twofold involvement in time.

Look at it like this. On the one hand, Christ by his ascension has withdrawn himself from the visible passage of time on the plane of this earth in order to send us back to the one time in all history where in the fullness of time the Son of God became incarnate—that is the time of the whole historical life of Jesus, culminating in the 'hour' of his death and breaking out into the new time of the resurrection. The Church is for ever bound to the historical Jesus, for the truth and the life of God have become historical fact in Jesus and are now historically communicated and transmitted. The Church exists in that history stemming from the historical Jesus, and lives by the word historically communicated through the apostles. Therefore all the life and ministry of the Church has to be ordered in time, according to the nature of that divine event in time, the time of the historical Jesus. By withdrawing himself from the visible succession of history, and by refusing to abrogate our existence in time by sheer immediacy, Jesus Christ gives us time, enables us to take time with the historical Jesus and the historical word communicated by and from Jesus. Thus, far from abrogating our existence in the on-going time of this world, by his ascension Jesus Christ sends us into the time of this empirical world, and commands us within it to focus our attention on the time of the historical Jesus, to be bound by it, and to be obedient to it; for it is by that time and through it that Jesus continues to rule the Church and order it according to his word in actual history. Hence throughout all its life on earth, throughout all its continuity in history, the Church lives its life in historical attachment to the fullness of time in Jesus, and in historical continuity with it. It is out of that one time in Jesus that the Church lives from age to age, and from it that the Church derives its own time in history. It cannot in any circumstances detach itself from the historical Jesus, or depreciate its historical attachment to him in the fullness of time, for it is precisely by its being bound and obedient to the historical Jesus Christ in the tradition of the apostolic Church that Christ continues to rule over the Church by his word and Spirit, making it his own body and servant in history.

Church order is therefore the ordering of the Church's life in history in relation to that one time in all history, the time of Jesus; for that is the only place in time where eternity and time have really met, and where they are for ever joined, and it is in and through that union of eternity and time in Jesus that the Church lives its life on the plane of history. On the other hand, it is in that time of the historical Jesus that the Church, from age to age, still meets with the eternal God and is gathered up 'into' eternal time. It is only within the time of the historical Jesus that the new time of the risen Jesus breaks in upon the Church in history, and gives it to share and abide in the new time of the new creation. It is in the historical Jesus that the new time overlaps with the old time in our history, and only there, so that it is as the Church lives there in that overlap of the two times, that it is given to share in new time above and beyond the time of this passing age on the mere plane of earthly history. The Church continues to live within the time of this on-going world, but it finds its life above and beyond it in the risen and ascended Lord, not in some timeless eternity, but in one who has himself descended into our time, redeemed it and gathered it up in himself into union with eternity. The Church is therefore bound to the succession of time by relation to the historical Jesus, but it is precisely in the historical Jesus that it knows its true life to be hid with Christ in God, and to be found beyond the passing and successive forms of this age. This does not mean the abrogation of the Church's historical existence, but it does mean that the historical existence of the Church, its continuity within the succession of time on earth, is determined by relation to the new time of the risen Lord. Hence the Church within the succession of time on earth is given a new orientation within the limitations of time; so that instead of being fettered by the bonds of time, bound by the sheer irreversibility of time that is laden with guilt, instead of being determined by the temporal processes of this world, the Church within time has freedom to meet with eternity, to rise above its past and to live a new life from age to age in Christ.

It may help us to understand that by thinking a little naively of the 'two times' of the Church, as horizontal time on the plane of history in which it is bound to, and ordered in relation to, the time of the historical Jesus, and as vertical time in the Spirit in which the Church shares with Christ the time of his new humanity. If the Church had only horizontal time, then the Church would only be a construct of historical succession, having only its temporal origin in Jesus but actually being fettered and determined by its place within the temporal process. Then the Church would not be free to have real meeting with the risen Lord; it would be enslaved to history, enslaved to its own past and all the errors and sins of its past; it would not be free from all the limitations and determinisms of history. But the Church within history is the Church of Jesus Christ in whom the eternal has broken into our sin-determined and guilt-fettered time, and brought freedom and redemption from bondage. Jesus Christ is the area in our fallen time where the eternal has broken through the limitations of this passing age to which we are in bondage, and where God acts freely upon men through his word and Spirit, confronting them with his own person and enabling them to respond freely in spite of all the downward drag of sin, in spite of all the piled-up determinisms of our guilty past, in spite of our bondage in the time of this world. The Church is therefore the place within time where that free meeting with the eternal is possible, where within time men are delivered from the tyrant forces of bondage and are made free for God, so that real meeting in faith and love is not only possible but actual.

In the light of all that, then, the order of the Church's ministry in time is to be regarded as the ordering of its life within the on-going time of history and its succession, which makes time for meeting with the risen and ascended Lord. It is an ordering of the historical and temporal life of the Church that binds it to that one place in history and time in the historical Jesus, but because in Jesus the eternal breaks into our history and time giving us, through the Spirit, freedom to meet with the living God within time and history, it is also an ordering that will not allow the life of the Church to be tied down to the temporal framework of mere succession on the stage of this world. The ordering of the Church's life and ministry in time means giving it such a new orientation within on-going time and all its limitations, that the time-forms of the Church's historical existence become the signs of the new divine order that already breaks in upon the Church in history. Thus for example the historical succession in the ordering of the ministry, far from involving the Church in bondage to the past, attests the binding of the Church to the historical Jesus and so becomes the sign of the new ordering of the Church's life in Jesus Christ. Historical succession does not secure or guarantee the binding of the Church in Christ, for he, the risen and ascended Lord, is not bound by the forms of fallen time; for by his resurrection he has triumphed over them. Historical succession, however, binds the Church to that one time within our fallen history where the risen and ascended Lord keeps tryst with us as the Lord of all time and history, and where alone we may freely meet him. It attests the fact that, through relation to the historical Jesus, Christ binds us to himself on the ground of the historical Incarnation, atonement, and resurrection, and declares that we cannot find any life or salvation in detachment from the historical Jesus.

All this is wonderfully enshrined in the Lord's Supper. "This do in remembrance of me. As often as you do this, you proclaim the Lord's death till he come." In the Supper the Church's life and ministry is so ordered that it is bound to the historical Jesus, to his death on the Cross, but at that very point in time the Church is given to have communion with the risen and ascended Lord and to share in his new humanity, and from the Supper it is sent out to proclaim that until he comes again. Thus the ordering of the Church's life and ministry should follow the pattern enshrined in the Lord's Supper. "For I have received that which I also delivered unto you . . ." It is celebrated in that succession or tradition, and it is ordered within that continuity, but within that continuity it is the risen Christ, the Lord of the Supper, who comes through closed doors, through all the limitations of our fallen time and sinful history, and gives us to eat and drink with him in the new time of the kingdom of God. While the Supper is to be ordered therefore within the historical continuity of the Church, it is such an ordering that room is left within it for the new time of the kingdom, and in the presence of that new time all the historical time-forms of the Church are relativized and given new orientation—they are taken under the command of the risen and ascended Lord, are made obedient to his real presence, so that instead of being mere limitations to the Church's life and ministry they are the signs pointing beyond to the reality of the new time of the new creation. In so doing they are themselves transcended, and made subordinate to communion with Christ in the time of his new humanity.

3. Order in regard to Space and Time

Space and time cannot be separated in the Church. The Church on earth and in history is inescapably involved in space and time and in all the machinery of physical existence, for it is sent out to minister the gospel in space and time. It is in that involvement with space and time that lies the significance of its order. The Church's very bodily and historical existence and mission require spatial and temporal order if it is to perform its divine purpose in space and time, but it can only live its life and fulfil its work in space and time, if its place on earth is ordered in obedience to its share in Christ's heavenly place, and if its time on earth is made obedient to its share in Christ's heavenly time. Church order concerns the ordering of the Church's life and ministry in the meeting of heaven and earth in the place of the Church, and in the intersection of historical continuity and immediate unity with the risen and ascended Christ. The place that the Church has in the space-time form of this world is not abrogated, but in that place the Church is given to share in the real presence of the new man and real time of the new creation. Until Christ comes again to change the space-time form of this fallen world (not to eliminate it but to change and renew it) the Church shares in the real presence of the new man and the real time of the new creation, under the form of space and time as we know it in this on-going world, as under a veil, as in a mystery. The actual space of the Church, its physical place in this world, has to be regarded as the trysting place of Christ on earth; and the time of the Church, its historical actuality, has to be regarded as the time appointed by Christ for meeting with him.

This space and this time have to be used therefore in obedience to his appointment, in subordination to the space and the time of the historical Jesus, that is, the actual founding of the Church upon the rock of the apostles, and to the actual tradition of the historical Jesus which we have received from the apostles, for it is in that obedience within the space-time form of the Church on earth to the historical Jesus that the Church goes into history as his servant, the obedient body of which he is the head. Only as that body is it his Church. Therefore, the ordering of the Church in space and time is concerned with its obedience to Christ, to the risen Lord in the space and time of the historical Jesus alone. Then it is, however, that through the Spirit Christ keeps tryst with his Church in history and bestows upon it his real presence, so that the time and place of the Church become Christ's own time and place among men. Then it is that the Church lives and works as the earthly and historical form of Christ's body (as Karl Barth has called it), obedient to him, its risen head and Lord, and as such it is the instrument he is pleased to use to proclaim his word to all nations and to manifest himself to all who believe.

In all this the Church looks upon itself as covenanted with Christ, and as gathered into union and communion with him as his covenant partner. Just as its historical succession in time and space does not secure or guarantee its unity with Christ, but only serves to attest its binding to him in the time and space of the historical Jesus, so the Church's obedience to the time and space of its foundation in the apostles and to the apostolic tradition does not secure or guarantee that it is the body of Christ. Throughout all its succession in the relativities and contingencies of our sinful history, throughout all its life of faith and obedience, in which the Church cannot but acknowledge its unfaithfulness and disobedience, the Church relies upon the new covenant that Christ has made with it in his body and blood. It is only in that covenant undergirding all its historical relativity and all its unfaithfulness that the Church's security rests. In obedience the Church relies not upon its own obedience but upon the obedience of Christ, and acknowledges that it is given a ground of faith and reliance beyond all the changes and chances of this passing world and all its own unworthiness. The Church can never justify itself, therefore, by claiming historical succession or doctrinal faithfulness, by reference to its own place and time on earth and in history, but must cast itself upon the justification of Christ's grace alone, and rely upon his covenant mercies who promised that the gates of hell would not prevail against his Church, and that he would be in its midst until the end of the world. The ordering of the Church can never be allowed to assume a role of independence and authority as if the duly ordered Church, even in its obedience to Christ, could be anything more than an unprofitable servant. Order must always be maintained in ever renewed amazement at the grace of God, and in ever renewed thankfulness for his undeserved grace and justification.

To sum up. The Church is ordered in its life and ministry on earth:

(a) By being obedient to the historical Jesus Christ in space time in the tradition of the apostolic Church, in which he, the risen and ascended Christ, comes to rule and order the Church by his Word and Spirit, making it his body and servant in history;

(b) By sharing in the obedience of Jesus Christ in space and time through the communion of the Spirit in which he, the new man, gives it to share in his new humanity as he, the Lord, undergirds it in all its frailty and weakness by his new covenant, so that already it is given to abide in the life and time and order of the new creation;

(c) By looking beyond the historical and institutional forms of its ordering in space and time to the fullness of its life in Christ, who comes to meet it in mercy and judgment, and who at his *parousia* will unveil the full reality of the Church in the glory of the Son of man.

In this threefold way the Church looks upon its ordering in the space and time of this on-going world as the required form of its obedience to Christ or the attestation of its reliance upon the new covenant founded for ever in the historical Jesus, as the sign that points to the new divine order of the Church's life communicated to it even now through word and sacrament in the Spirit, and as the provisional form given to it, until the redemption of the body, of the order of the new creation which will be revealed only at the final advent of Christ.

CHAPTER 5

Consecration and Ordination[1]

IN ORDER TO UNDERSTAND the New Testament teaching about consecration and ordination we have to examine the rites and language of the Old Testament tradition. The rites were not carried over as such into the Christian Church, for they were fulfilled in Christ and abrogated; but the New Testament does use the language of the rites to speak both of Christ and his Church, and it does adapt some of the Old Testament rites for its own use, but with entire freedom and with quite new significance. The basic line we have to consider is the consecration of the priest, and king, and prophet in the Old Testament, and see how they are fulfilled in Christ, and then see how in this Christ the New Testament thinks of the ministry as consecrated and ordained.

The Consecration and Ordination of the Priest

The main passages that concern us are Exod 28 and 29; Lev 6, 7, 8, 9; and Num 8. It is worth remembering right away that the Leviticus passages fell in the Jewish Lectionary for the Passover week, and are clearly reflected in the Gospels, especially in John 13–17.

To get the proper perspective we have to remember that Israel was consecrated in the covenant to be a holy people, a kingdom of priests to

---

1. Prepared for the use of the Aids to Devotion Committee of the Church of Scotland, November, 1957, and reprinted from the *Scottish Journal of Theology* 11 (1958) 225ff.

God (Exod 19:6; Lev 20:26; Deut 7:6; 14:21; 26:19; 28:9; cf. Isa 62:12). As such, too, Israel was God's "first-born son"; that is, it occupied among the human family the part of "the head of the house" (the *ben-bayith*, the householder or steward of God's holy purposes, reflected in several of Jesus' parables). Within Israel it would appear that the primitive priests were the first-born sons, the heads of the house, which is preserved in the Passover rite where the ceremony is conducted by the head of the house. But the first-born were "redeemed back" for life among the people and their place was taken by the tribe of Levi (Num 3:12f., etc.). Thus within Israel as a priestly nation, one tribe is set aside for priestly functions instead of the first-born, and within the tribe of Levi the "sons of Aaron" are set apart for special functions as liturgical priests. The Old Testament priesthood has thus an interim institutional character, and its importance lies in its functions and in its obedience to the divine ordinances. It was the business of the Levites and priests to teach the law to Israel, and so they lived scattered through the twelve tribes. The sons of Aaron came to be divided into twenty-four courses, twelve functioning in the temple and twelve in Israel, although all twenty-four came up to Jerusalem for the great festivals.

How then were the priests consecrated and ordained? This is very fully described. The whole congregation (*ekklesia*) assembled at the door of the tabernacle where they were addressed by Moses and told they were about to act in accordance with God's ordinance. Then he "brought forward" or "brought near" or "presented" Aaron and his sons. They were solemnly washed at the laver, and clothed with priestly garments. Aaron was anointed with oil by pouring, but his sons were only sprinkled with his anointing oil. Aaron only was called "the anointed," the *christos*. Then there followed sacrifices, the most significant of which was the "consecration offering" or "fill-offering." Some of this along with unleavened bread was offered for the consecration of Aaron and his sons, some of it was broken up into portions, and portions of flesh and bread were put into the hands of Aaron and his sons, who offered them as peace-offerings. Then Aaron and his sons repaired to the door of the tabernacle and in the presence of the congregation partook of a sacred meal of what remained of the flesh of the fill-offering and bread of the consecration offering—that was called "a sacrifice of praise and thanksgiving." This was repeated for seven days, during which they stayed within the tabernacle.

It is to be noted that in this rite the chief and proper subject is Aaron the High Priest, although his sons are consecrated through association with him, and have their hands filled too and share with him in the sacred meal of consecration. But Aaron alone is the *christos*. (In an extended sense, of course,[2] all Israel is spoken of as *messiah* = anointed, Ps 84:9; Hab 3:13; Ps 89:38, 51.) That act takes place only once and does not need to be repeated. The *Minhah* that Aaron offers avails for himself and the sons of his house. On his death, his eldest son was clothed with his high-priestly garments and was consecrated with his priests in the same way—but the anointing was apparently not repeated, except to recover a break in the priestly line (2 Chr 13:9). It has also to be noted that although the priests were consecrated only once, every time they went in and out of the tabernacle or temple they renewed their consecration through washing their hands and feet, while the High Priest renewed his consecration through solemn and total baptismal ablution once a year in preparation for the renewal of the covenant on the Day of Atonement. It should also be noted that the consecration of Aaron and the sons of his house to the priesthood was called "the covenant of salt."

What about the Levites? In Num 8 we are told that all the Levites were cleansed and "separated" within Israel, cleansed by the sprinkling of the water of expiation (used at circumcision and in cleansing the leper to restore him to membership in the priestly race) and then they were "presented" to God with the same offerings as Aaron and his sons; but in addition all the Levites had hands laid on them by the children of Israel (doubtless acting through their elders) gathered at the door of the tabernacle, who offered them up to their holy use as their representatives. Then Aaron took the Levites and offered them before the Lord as an oblation on behalf of the people that they might do the service of the Lord. Here the laying on of hands indicates the representative part played by the Levites, but as such they are offered unto God. Thus in their case ordination is twofold: laying on of hands and commissioning

---

2. Earlier printed texts have "of cause" which is possible, but "of course" is how TF would have normally spoken, and this was originally a spoken address [editor].

by the whole priestly people, and offering to God as consecration for his service.

What about *Moses* in all this? As Augustine pointed out long ago, Moses stands above all this without any ceremonial consecration. It is he who offers the sacrifices for Aaron and his sons, offers them to the Lord, and consecrates them. He himself had no other consecration than that of his supreme relation to the Word of God alone. Moses did not therefore pass on a consecration he had himself received; he acted only as "the servant of the Lord," and the entire validity of the consecration of the priesthood depended on God's command and grace alone—not on any 'priestly grace.' The priesthood is represented as God's "gift" (Num 18:7) and rests on its 'givenness.' Hence the Hebrew word "to give," *nathan*, is frequently employed for ordaining to the priesthood; it is an appointment of grace.

The Language of Consecration and Ordination in the Old Testament

The general term used for 'consecration' and/or 'ordination' in the Septuagint is *hagiazo*, meaning "sanctify" or "make holy." The emphasis here is always upon the fundamental fact that God will be sanctified or hallowed in the midst of his people (Exod 31:13; Lev 20:8—cf. also the incident of Nadab and Abihu in Lev 10:1-2, etc.). All consecration or hallowing is a sharing in God's hallowing of himself in the midst of his people, and has its significance only within the covenant in which he is holy and requires his people to be holy too.

Three distinctive terms are used, however, to describe this sanctification or consecration of the priest in holy things:

(a) To clothe with priestly garments—"to put on" (including baptismal ablution, etc.);

(b) To anoint with holy oil (the preparation of which was a secret) given along with sprinkling of blood;

(c) To "fill the hands," which was accompanied by a special sacrifice of consecration.

Of these three it is the third that is the distinctive term for consecration or ordination—the priest has his "hands filled": *mille' yadh* (Exod 28:41; 29:29; 35:35; Lev 8:33; 16:32; 21:10; Num 3:3; Judg 17:5, 12; 1 Kgs 13:33; 2 Chr 13:9; cf. 2 Chr 29:31; Isa 43:26). The offering of consecration was called "filling" (*millu'im*).

What "filling the hands" means exactly is not clear. Generally it means that the priest has the priesthood committed to him; he receives it as a gift. Specifically it means that the act of consecration is brought to its fulfilment or completion when his hands are filled with the holy oblations. It can also be applied in an extended sense to the consecration of the altar through having the oblations laid on it. Its meaning is thus twofold, which comes out very well in the Greek of the LXX in its twofold translation of *mille' yadh*:

(a) *Pleroun tas cheiras*. Cf. Lev 7:29; Exod 32:29.

(b) *Teleioun tas cheiras* or simply *teleioun* as applied to the priest as object or in the passive with the priest as subject. It is almost equivalent to *hagiazein*. Cf. Exod 28:41; 29:33.

These words are used, then, to describe the act of the consecration of the High Priest in whose self-consecration the sons of his house are also consecrated; that consecration is brought to its completion in the filling of the hands with the oblations and in the sacrificial meal of flesh and bread, "the sacrifice of praise and thanksgiving."

The Language of Consecration in the New Testament

Although in the Old Testament "to fill the hands" was the more technical term, it does not make very good Greek when translated literally. It is natural therefore that in the Greek the word *teleioun* should be preferred to *pleroun tas cheiras*. The latter expression is, perhaps, to be detected lying behind John 3:35, which has reference to Christ's baptismal consecration in the Jordan and his anointing of the Spirit. If so, the underlying Aramaic has been turned into smooth Greek, and the "filling of the hands" is not very recognizable except to one familiar with the Old Testament rite. Along with this should be compared John

17:2–4; cf. also John 4:34; 5:36. Possibly the Pauline *pleroma* hints of this too sometimes, cf. Eph 1:23ff.; 3:19.

It is, however, the word *teleioun* that is prominent in the New Testament, especially in the Fourth Gospel and in the Epistle to the Hebrews. The verb *teleioun* is, of course, often used in the New Testament with no relation to the conception of priestly consecration, but when it is found in John 17, Christ's high-priestly prayer, which clearly reflects the reading of Lev 7–8, we must see it in a different light. The evangelist also uses the other word *hagiazein*, e.g., 17:17–19: "Sanctify them in the truth. Thy Word is truth. As thou hast sent me into the world, even so have I sent them into the world, and for their sakes I sanctify myself, that they also might be sanctified through the truth." Then in verse 23 Jesus prays that the disciples might be consecrated in one (*teteleiomenoi eis hen*).

When we turn to the Epistle to the Hebrews there are several instances of *teleioun*, which refer to the consecration of the High Priest, while the word *hagiazein* is used in a sense parallel to the usage, both in the Old Testament and in John 17. Thus Heb 2:11: "For both he who sanctifies [or consecrates] and those who are sanctified are all of one, for which cause he is not ashamed to call them brethren." In Heb 7:28 and 9:9 the other word, *teleioun*, is used of the consecration of Christ the High Priest. In the tenth chapter the writer uses both terms, *hagiazein* and *teleioun*, to describe the fact that through Christ's own self-offering once and for all we are consecrated. By consecration the author of this Epistle meant what Paul meant by justification through the blood of Christ and sanctification through his Spirit. It is Christ's own consecration of himself on our behalf which both justifies us and sanctifies us as his holy servants, giving us to share in his consecration in such a way that through Jesus Christ our High Priest we all, with our bodies washed with clean water and with our consciences sprinkled with his blood, draw near to worship God, that is as priests in the house of God. It is interesting also to note that in this Epistle the institutional priesthood of Aaron is set aside because fulfilled and abrogated in Christ, and that he is High Priest as God's first-born Son, and therefore we are all first-born sons in him, while the Church is the Church of the first-born. That is to say, here where the institutional priesthood is done away all

God's children are priests after the fashion of the first-born in Israel. Just as we are given to share in Christ's sonship, so we are given to share in his priesthood. In Christ sonship and priesthood are the same.

The Consecration of the King

The classical passage about this is found in 2 Kgs 11:12, 17 which describes the consecration of the king by Jehoiada, and which reposes upon Deut 17:18–20. It is also based on the rites formed under King David and carried out with regard to Solomon (1 Kgs 1:33ff.; 1 Chr 29:22f.; cf. 2 Chr 6:42). The main elements here are as follows:

(a) Anointing, possibly along with washing in the Gihon. David and Saul were the first to be anointed, and the anointing was accompanied by the gift of the Spirit (1 Sam 10:1; 16:13; cf. 1 Sam 26:11; Ps 2:2 with Acts 4:26). David himself was anointed three times, cf. 2 Sam 2:4; 5:3. This was regarded in the Old Testament as indicative of the Messiah, cf. Ps 45:7 and Hab 3:13.

(b) The kings were enthroned and crowned—the royal insignia of David were apparently used in later times.

(c) The putting of the "Testimony" into the hands of the king. According to Deuteronomy the king had to copy out the book of the Law with his own hand, so as to remember it and rule by it.

(d) A covenant was made between the king, God, and the people. In the case of God's covenant with David it was known as "a covenant of salt," like the covenant made by God with the house of Aaron. In the case of Solomon's consecration we know that there was also prayer and sacrifice—see 1 Chr 29:22f.

Here, then, in the consecration of the king the fundamental pattern of consecration was similar to that of the consecration of the priest, involving: anointing, filling of the hands, and affirmation of the covenant relation. The difference lies chiefly in that to which the king is consecrated, kingship, not sacrifice, and that the king's hands are filled therefore not with oblations but with the law. He is crowned and enthroned, which does not apply to the priests.

The Consecration of the Prophet

We have even less information about this, but a clear instance of the consecration of Elisha by Elijah is given in 1 Kgs 19:16. It was by anointing followed later by investment with the prophet's mantle. In Ps 105:15 "the anointed" and the prophets are synonymous. The anointing of both Saul and David gave them prophetic gifts, and presumably that meant that the anointing of kings was an extension of the anointing of prophets through whose word proclaimed and enunciated God ruled as King.

In Isa 61:1 the Servant of the Lord speaks of himself as anointed to preach the gospel, which Christ claimed to be fulfilled in himself, Luke 4:18; John 10:36.

In addition to this Old Testament tradition, it should be noted that in the Judaean Scrolls the Anointed of the Lord, the Messiah, is regarded apparently as deriving both from the house of David and from the house of Aaron—the anointed priest-king. The members of the community initiated into the new covenant are spoken of as "anointed ones" and as forming a holy and "priestly" messianic community. That may have some influence on the New Testament, e.g., on 1 Peter.

Summary of the New Testament Teaching

Jesus Christ is the fulfilment of the threefold consecration to the office of priest, king, and prophet in the Old Testament. We have seen something of the fulfilment of priestly consecration in Christ, but kingly and prophetic consecration was also fulfilled in him (Luke 4:18; Acts 4:26; 10:38; Heb 1:9). This was all fulfilled in his anointing by the Spirit, which no doubt referred to his birth of the Spirit as well as to his anointing at his Baptism in the Jordan; it was as the anointed Son of the Father that he gathered up and fulfilled the threefold anointing of prophet, priest, and king. The Church, which he has made his own, was anointed with Christ's Spirit at Pentecost by the Baptism of the Spirit, so that through

Baptism all who come to Christ are not only given the right to be sons of God but are anointed with his anointing, receive the chrism of the Spirit (1 John 2:20, 27; 2 Cor 1:21), or are given the seal of the Spirit, as St. Paul puts it.

Here, then, in Christ the first-born Son of God and our High Priest, we are restored to the priestly kingdom, for he has washed us from our sins in his own blood and made us kings and priests unto God. Every one who is a son of God through Christ the Son belongs to this royal priesthood, and shares in Christ's self-consecration on our behalf. Christ alone is the *Christos*, the anointed and consecrated one (John 10:36), but we who follow him in baptism are given to share in it, putting off the old impurity and putting on Christ as our priestly garment, clothed with his righteousness, his consecration, and his holiness. Here there is no institutional priesthood like that of the Aaronic priesthood. That was an imperfect interim-measure only, necessarily done away when the true priesthood of sonship, the priesthood of the firstborn, was restored in Christ. Here priesthood and sonship are the same, but when this is so, it is Baptism, through which we are consecrated as sons of God, which is our consecration to priesthood in Christ.

Consecration and Ordination of the Ministry in the New Testament

When we turn to the consecration and ordination of a special ministry as Christ's gift to his Church we find that this has its place only within the consecration of the whole membership of Christ's body, and therefore within the ministry of the whole body, which it has through sharing in Christ's vicarious self-consecration. But within that there is something else. There are in fact two things: (1) the special consecration of the apostles in Christ's self-consecration; and (2) the apostolic ordination of others through the laying on of hands and prayer.

(1) The Special Consecration of the Apostles in Christ

The accounts of Christ's appointment of the apostles, his 'making' of them, of his drawing them into a very private and close relation to himself and to his teaching and his passion, and above all his special purpose for them in the Last Supper, as reflected in the Fourth Gospel as well as the Synoptics, are of special importance.

Although the Lord's Supper belongs to the whole Church, its first enactment belonged peculiarly to the apostles, who were at that point given a special place in the new covenant and in the Kingdom of Christ, appointed to sit upon twelve thrones judging the twelve tribes of Israel, as the patriarchs of the new Israel, the foundation of the Church. Jesus' solemn washing of their feet and his deliberate actions at the Supper clearly designed for the disciples peculiarly, and his high-priestly prayer of consecration in which he prayed above all for the disciples, make it clear that he regarded himself, in going forth to the cross, as the High Priest in whose self-oblation and self-consecration he was giving the disciples to share in a most intimate way as "the sons of his house." His self-consecration as the *Christos*, his action as the High Priest on the great Day of Atonement, was fulfilled once and for all, and can never be repeated. Just as when Aaron acted all Israel acted in him and through him, for he acted for all Israel, but at the same time the sons of his house had a special place in it, being sprinkled with the blood of sacrifice and with the oil of anointing, so when Christ went forth to the cross all his people were given to share in it, for he acted on their behalf and in their stead; and yet in a special way the Twelve were given to be related to it. They alone went forth to the events of his passion after having shared with him the consecration meal of the bread and wine of the Last Supper, and they alone, as it were, were sprinkled with his blood in Gethsemane where they were taken to watch and pray with him in his awful agony; and they alone when he returned from his sacrifice had breathed upon them his Spirit in the Upper Room and so were anointed with his anointing. As such the apostles belonged to the once-and-for-all events of the founding of the new covenant in the body and blood of Christ; they remain for ever the authoritative witnesses of the new covenant, the pillars of the Church, in whom and through whom Jesus Christ made an everlasting covenant of salt with his Church, making it a royal priesthood in himself.

The apostle-disciples were appointed to their ministry like Moses directly through the Word, and were given to sit, as it were, in Moses' seat, or rather in Christ's seat, inasmuch as they mediated his Word to the Church and in Christ's name were appointed to rule and order his Church; but, like the sons of Aaron, the apostles shared peculiarly in the self-consecration and anointing of their High Priest. All that is something that cannot be repeated, and therefore cannot be extended. The apostleship can have no successors, for the apostles remain under Christ as the permanent authorities over the Church, the foundation upon which all other ministry within the Church depends. And so they were sent out by Christ with his Commission to engage in the mission of reconciliation. It was in the fulfilment of that commission and mission that they came to ordain others to the ministry, giving the sign of the laying on of hands to attest that they were sent to fulfil their ministry within the one commission of Christ given to his apostles, and within the once and for all consecration of his Church upon the foundation of the apostles. But in taking an entirely different method of ordination from that which they had received the apostles showed unmistakably that they were in no sense extending their office to others, but ordaining a ministry in dependence upon their unique ministry in Christ.

(2) The Apostolic Ordination of Others through the Laying on of Hands and Prayer[3]

(Acts 6:6; 13:3; 1 Tim 4:14; 5:22; 2 Tim 1:6; cf. Acts 14:23; 2 Cor 8:19). The laying on of hands is the only ceremony that is taken over from the Old Testament by the New Testament Church for the consecration and ordination of its ministry. The consecration of the Church and of its ministry in the apostles had of course already taken place, and taken place once for all, so that whenever in the history of the Church there is an ordination to the ministry, that ordination is grounded upon the once and for all consecration of the Church and its apostolic ministry in Christ; it shares in it, takes place only within it, and is the means whereby that consecration is through prayer related directly and particularly to those set apart for the ministry within the sphere of the apostolic commission and mission.

3. In this section, TF says he is indebted to the discussion of A. Ehrhardt, *The Apostolic Ministry*, SJT Occasional Paper no. 7, chapter II.

It does not appear that the early Church took over the rite of laying on of hands from Judaism so much as from the Old Testament. The elders in the Sanhedrin were instituted apparently only by enthronement in Moses' seat, but later on ordination by laying on of hands took the place of this. This rite may have had earlier usage in Judaism which influenced the New Testament Church, but the evidence on the whole suggests that the apostles went back directly to the Old Testament itself for their guidance.

In a recent work, Professor Daube has pointed out that three different words are used in the Old Testament for a rite of blessing or ordination with hands:[4]

(a) *Nasa* to describe the priestly blessing when hands are lifted up, e.g., in the Aaronic benediction. This was an act of prayer and blessing in which the name of God was put upon the people—the act used by Jesus in blessing his disciples at his ascension.

(b) *Sim* or *shith* which describes the act of placing hands upon someone for blessing, as in the patriarchal blessing of Joseph's sons by Jacob. It was possibly this act that was used by Jesus in healing, and perhaps by the early Church at Baptism.

(c) *Samakh* which describes the solemn act of laying (literally "leaning") on of hands as applied to sacrifices when sins are symbolically transferred to a victim, or used where the transference of guilt or association in responsibility is indicated, e.g., in stoning a blasphemer or in instituting someone to responsible office. (I cannot agree with Professor Daube's psychological interpretation of *samakh* as "the pouring of personality" from one person to another.) There is no evidence that Jesus ever used this. In Judaism the laying on of hands was not used for the ordaining of "the seven of a city" or local "elders," although their appointment to the local presbytery required the authorization of the Presbytery of the People or the Sanhedrin in Jerusalem. In the second century (and possibly in the first) rabbis were ordained

---

4. David Daube, *The New Testament and Rabbinic Judaism* (London: Athlone, 1956), 224f.

by *samakh*, the solemn laying on of hands, called "the laying on of hands of the elders."

There are two instances of laying on of hands in the Old Testament important for the Christian precedent:

(a) The laying on of hands through which the Levites were ordained to their office. This was an act carried out by the people, presumably through their elders, and was a lay act in which the Levites were inducted into responsible representation of the people, appointed to stand for the first-born of the people in their ministry at the Tabernacle. The act of laying on of hands was completed when they were offered to God by the priests.

(b) The other instance is the, act of Moses in ordaining as his successor in the leadership of the people. In doing so Moses was commanded to "put of his honour upon Joshua" (Num 27:18, 23; Deut 34:9). With this act God bestowed upon Joshua his Spirit to enable him to fulfil his appointed task. Joshua was not of course ordained to take Moses' place either as a priest or as the mediator of the Word of God, but simply in civil and military leadership of the people. He was a lay governor under the kingship of God. This was in a different sense an act of lay ordination.

Laying on of Hands in the New Testament

The first case of laying on of hands was that of the seven elder-deacons in Acts 6. Here, as we have noted, hands were laid on the seven by the congregation, not by the apostles (except according to *Codex Bezae*), but they were set before the apostles, to indicate that the apostles had part in the act. It was, however, an act of lay ordination like that of the Levites in the Old Testament. At the same time the language used in the Old Testament of Joshua's ordination is reflected in Acts, in the choice of seven men in whom there was the Spirit. But again the language also seems to reflect the appointment of the seventy elders in Num 11:16, when, without any laying on of hands, God put his Spirit upon them to enable them to fulfil their office on appointment to the Presbytery of Israel. The laying on of hands upon the seven elder-deacons in Acts was accompanied by prayer, and these ordained were given the Spirit in fulfilment of their ministry. The fact that the apostles did not lay hands on them suggests that they were not being appointed as their deputies, but only as their assistants (i.e., as Levites!).

The instance of the separation of Paul and Barnabas by the command of the Spirit and their ordination at the hands of a group of prophets and teachers to which they belonged at Antioch seems to be (as Professor Daube suggests) a case of ordination for special embassage, in which they were commissioned to carry out a particular task on behalf of the rest. They were not ordained as 'Rabbinic' pupils or disciples, but rather sent out as 'apostles' of the community on a limited mission. The language used here, e.g., "separate me Paul and Barnabas," also suggests that used of the Levites in Num 8:6f. It does not seem to refer to ordination in the proper sense. This sort of thing was a common Rabbinic practice in the second century, but may well have been used earlier.

The most important instance of ordination by laying on of hands in the New Testament is that of Timothy, described in two verses, 1 Tim 4:14 and 2 Tim 1:6, which have to be taken together with the other passages in Timothy and Titus regarding the appointment and ordination of other ministers.

In 1 Tim 4:14 we read: "Neglect not the gift that is in thee which was given thee by prophecy with the laying on of hands of the presbytery." In 2 Tim 1:6, we read: "Stir up the gift of God which is in thee through the laying on of hands." Putting these together, as I think we must, I make the meaning to be as follows: Timothy has been carefully instructed in the faith and trained in the *didaskalia* which he exercises; in that training it was clear that he was called to the ministry, that God had imparted to him a gift for its fulfilment; at the same time that gift is looked on as imparted formally through the act of laying on of hands, authorizing him as an accredited teacher and minister, but used by God as the means of imparting to him a *charisma* for the ministry. The act of laying on of hands has been carried out by Timothy's teacher Paul, and by the presbytery acting together. It is possible, as Professor Daube suggests, that the laying on of hands of the presbytery (*epithesis ton cheiron tou presbyteriou*) is simply a Rabbinic term for "the ordination of elders" (*semikhath zeqenim, Bab. San.* 13 b). But it seems more likely that it means that the presbytery as a whole laid on hands, while Paul acted along with them and doubtless presided over them in the act of ordination. The fact that Timothy, who is put in charge of missionary churches by Paul and commanded to appoint elders in them, is not to lay hands suddenly on people, indicates that he would himself be the chief minister in ordaining presbyters in that area under his supervision, but that he should only do it after due and careful training. According to Rabbinic rules a man was not to be ordained to teach until he had reached the age of forty. It may be with that in mind that Paul exhorts Timothy not to let anyone despise his youth, for, young as he is, he is fully authorized by Paul and the presbytery to undertake his ministry.

This instance is of fundamental importance for a number of reasons:

(a) It provides us with a clear case of what even Professor Daube (who sees it, however, as parallel to Rabbinic ordination) calls "apostolic succession." Timothy is not appointed to be an apostle, but he has the full authorization of Paul the apostle to do the office of a minister, and indeed of a bishop; and as such he is to fulfil the same office in ordaining others as Paul fulfilled in ordaining him.

(b) But this ordination is a corporate act of the presbytery. It was the presbytery that was the repository of authorization at the local level, although the presbytery had also to be acting within the sphere of the apostolic commission and mission, a link that was supplied by St. Paul. It is not suggested that it was the local presbytery that joined with Paul in ordaining Timothy. At any rate it is clear that the presbytery is the medium of ordination although Paul has a special part in it, and Timothy afterwards takes a similar place in the ordination of others. Presumably, however, he would not act apart from the presbytery, except perhaps in founding a new church and appointing and ordaining new presbyters, in which instance he would be the authorized person acting within the apostolic commission to undertake that; but once established the presbytery would act as a body with Timothy. Here both "presbyterian" and "episcopalian" elements are clearly held together.

Now in interpreting what the New Testament has to say about ordination and its adaptation of Old Testament rites, we have to remember that nowhere does the New Testament take over an Old Testament rite and develop it as such. What it always does is to lay several images or rites together, elements of which are then used in the freedom of the apostolic Church for its own purposes in forming a new image or a new rite which derives its significance not from the Old Testament ceremonies or images as such but from Christ and from what the apostolic Church makes of it. How then are we to interpret the New Testament concept of ordination?

(1) The first thing to note is that by selecting this rite of laying on of hands, which was essentially a lay rite both in the Old Testament and in Judaism, the Christian Church made it decisively clear that the Christian ministry was not to be interpreted in the sense of the priesthood of the Old Testament. That had been fulfilled in Christ who alone is Priest. But because all that was fulfilled in Christ, permanent elements of significance in it might well be transferred from Christ to the interpretation of the Christian rite. That is what happened.

(2) The main element in the laying on of hands seems undoubtedly to be the commissioning of ministers of the Word to proclaim the *kerygma* and teach the *didache* in obedience to the apostolic witness to Christ and in following their example and ordinances. Ordination is for those who labour in the Word and carries with it acknowledged authorization to do so, authorization that derives from the apostolic commission as an attestation of the tradition of the apostolic teaching and preaching of the Gospel. Here we recall the old rites of consecrating the king by filling his hands with "the testimony," and the consecrating of the prophet through whose Word it is God who acts and rules.

(3) But this ordination has other elements associated with it; the gift of the Spirit, the bestowal of a special charisma for the ministry; and it is performed with prayer. It is difficult to resist the conclusion

that, while in the Old Testament three different sets of expressions are used to describe three different forms of laying on or lifting up of hands, the New Testament seems to blend elements of all three together. That was certainly done immediately after New Testament times. Thus in addition to the strict concept of *samakh*, commissioning with authority to minister the Word, ordination also draws into its orbit the concept of blessing the one ordained through prayer, and calling upon him the gift of the Spirit, who brings a special charisma to the one ordained for the fulfilment of his ministry. But also the other idea found in the practice of *samakh* in the Old Testament is not absent: that of offering or presenting the one upon whom hands are laid before God, symbolized by the presentation of the seven before the apostles, as Joshua was presented before Eleazar by Moses when he ordained him, or the Levites were presented before the tabernacle and then offered to God. That is a concept that Paul applies to his missionary congregations; he offers them to God as an oblation. According to Calvin this element is a powerful ingredient in ordination, for the ordinand after the analogy of the Old Testament sacrifices is through laying on of hands offered to God for his service and so consecrated. This act of ordination takes place in the name of Christ the King and Head of the Church, so that all the ordinand does when ordained is to be done in the name of Christ. That name is his sole authority; nothing is to be done apart from it. But to ordain in the name of Christ, and to act in the name of Christ, is to act within the self-consecration of Christ on our behalf, as the language of the name of God declared by Christ to the apostles in John 17 indicates.

(4) Ordination thus means ordination in the sphere where we are all consecrated through participation in Christ's self-consecration on our behalf. We recall that the disciples were specially related to the self-consecration of Christ at the Last Supper, for in his solemn prayer of consecration they were associated by Christ with himself as those who would take his Word to others so that others would believe through their word and be drawn into the unity of the one Church of Christ. We cannot dissociate ordination in the name of Christ from that fact. Those ordained are to be regarded as drawn in a special way within the sphere of Christ's self-consecration so that it is only as they share in his self-consecration that they can minister the Word to others in his name. It is

in this connection then that we have to see the relation of ordination to participation in the Lord's Supper, and see the Lord's Supper as the New Testament counterpart to the meal of consecration in which Aaron and his sons participated at their consecration, "a meal of thanksgiving and praise." That expression is reflected in an important passage in Heb 13 which speaks of the ministry in several injunctions and adds: "Through him then let us offer up a sacrifice of praise to God continually, that is the fruit of the lips which make confession to his name continually." It was not unnatural therefore that in very early times, as in the Apostolic Constitutions, the rite of ordination to the ministry was looked upon as being brought to its completion when the one ordained first celebrated the Lord's Supper, for it was when the gifts of bread and wine were put into his hands that the Lord himself fulfilled the act of consecrating his servant to his ministry, as he consecrated the apostle-disciples at the Last Supper. It is significant therefore that all the earliest consecrations and ordinations known to us took place in a Eucharistic context. This is a practice that should still be followed. The act of the presbytery in ordination should be followed by the celebration of Holy Communion in which the newly ordained person should dispense the Sacrament for the first time. The early Church of Scotland practice of "fasting" at ordination seems to have been derived from the old rite of the consecration of the priests with its seven days of separation.

The Doctrine of Ordination

In gathering up our discussion to present a doctrine of ordination we must consider it from three aspects:

(1) The source of ordination: its derivation from Christ through the ministry of the Church.

(2) The end of ordination: that to which a man[5] is ordained determines the nature of ordination.

(3) What the act of ordination means and how it is carried out.

---

5. This paper was given in 1957, before women were allowed to be ministers in the Church of Scotland.

Consecration and Ordination

(1) The Source of Ordination

Who is it who ordains a man to the ministry? In answer to that question we have to give the unambiguous answer: Jesus Christ himself. Ordination is *his* act. It is *his* authority that stands behind it, and therefore it can be done only in his name. But Christ ordains within his Church, which he founded upon the apostles, and it is through that Church that he acts. Here we are confronted with a fundamental duality, but it is also the fundamental duality of Revelation. Revelation is the act of Christ, which is brought to bear upon us directly through his Spirit, but it is Revelation which he communicates to us through the Word historically mediated in the Holy Scriptures. The risen and ascended Lord has bestowed his Spirit upon the Church, but the Spirit utters to us what Christ has already said: he does not speak of himself and does not teach us anything new, but takes what Christ has already revealed and leads us fully into its truth. The Church is thus bound to the New Testament Scriptures, but in and through the New Testament Scriptures the risen and ascended Lord communicates himself directly to his Church in the communion of the Spirit. So it is with ordination. It is the risen and ascended Lord who acts directly through his Spirit ordaining his servant to the ministry, but he does that in and through the Church, which he has once and for all established in the apostles and bound to the Revelation that he has committed to the Church through the apostles.

The Church is bound to act in obedience to the apostolic teaching and commands, and through them it is bound to the historical Jesus Christ. When the Church from age to age ordains men to the ministry in the name of Christ, it does that only within that obedience to the apostolic teaching and ordinances, and only within the sphere of the apostolic commission and mission given by Christ in founding the Church. That duality is apparent already in the New Testament Church. It is the risen and ascended Lord who bestows gifts upon the Church through the Spirit, but these gifts are bestowed for exercise within the one Church founded upon the apostles and within the sphere of their commission by Christ. The apostles appointed the rite of the laying on of hands to mark out and delimit the sphere of their commission, and to attest the propriety of a ministry within that sphere. That laying on of hands cannot be regarded as determining or delimiting the sphere of the operation of the Holy Spirit, for although Christ has bound the Church to its foundation in the apostles, he is himself sovereignly free over the apostles as the risen and ascended Lord. The laying on of hands cannot be understood, therefore, as securing or guaranteeing the presence or the operation of the Holy Spirit, but as the apostolically given sign witnessing to the presence of the Spirit, attesting the obedience of the Church to its apostolic origins and binding its continuance, and the continuance of its ministry, within the sphere of the apostolic commission and authority. It is Christ, not the apostles, not the Church, who bestows upon the ordained minister the Spirit and the gifts of the Spirit for the exercise of his office; nevertheless it is clear that the laying on of hands was given by the apostles with the promise of Christ to impart spiritual gifts for the fulfilment of the ministry.

Ordinarily and normatively we are to understand the laying on of hands as the apostolically appointed sign and instrument used by the Spirit in bestowing the charisma for the ministry. Its necessity is one of obedience to the apostolic ordinance, and it attests that the ordination of the ministry derives from the historical Jesus and his historically communicated authority to the apostles. But the historical Jesus is risen and ascended, and it is he who from generation to generation continues to bestow his Spirit upon the Church and continues to bestow the grace-gifts for the ministry of Word and Sacrament within the Church. Therefore it is Christ the living Lord who is the actual ordainer in ordination, although he makes use of the ministers who have been sent by him already to carry out the ordinance within the Church on earth. It is only in this togetherness of 'the risen Lord' and 'the historical Jesus,' who is one Lord Jesus Christ, the King and Head of the Church, that we must think of ordination. The risen Lord sends us back to the historical Jesus and sends us back always to the commission He gave to the apostles, so that ordination is through the historical communication of the apostolic Word and the apostolic commission. The historical Jesus still commissions his ministers through that external and historical succession, and therefore the historical mediation or communication of ordination is of fundamental importance as attesting the binding of the Church to the historical Jesus and the historical Revelation.

The Church which separates itself from the historical Jesus ceases thereby to be Christ's Church, for it cuts itself off from its historical rooting and grounding in the historical Revelation and Incarnation. But within that historical communication it is the risen Lord himself who ever comes to his Church acting obediently in his name and himself ordains. He himself is really present where we meet in his name to obey his command, and he fulfils what he promises, and his presence in grace and in the power of his Spirit undergirds all our actions. We rely in all ordination therefore not upon the faithfulness of the Church, nor upon the unbroken nature of the historical succession, for these are all involved in the relativities and contingencies of this fallen world; but upon the faithfulness of Christ who remains with his Church that lives and acts in his name. It is his covenant faithfulness undergirding our weakness and faltering faithfulness, and renewing our participation in him, that is the ground of our reliance in every act of ordination.

It is this same fundamental duality in ordination that gives the concept of the so-called "validity of orders" its elusive ambiguity. Validity must refer absolutely to the fact that it is Christ the Lord who ordains, and ordains to ministry in the Church of God. He it is who honours that ministry as his own gift to the Church and makes it efficacious through his Spirit. But validity also refers to the responsible transmission of authorization from generation to generation, attesting the obedience of the Church in all its ordinations to the apostolic teaching and ordinances. Because this involves historical communication and responsible action it involves a duly intended and orderly act of ordination. It cannot be given in abstraction from the ordering of a Church's life, from its discipline and polity. Thus validity has also a juridical aspect, in which the term is relative to the legal structure of a Church in history. It refers to the responsible authorization of a Church in history, which orders its life and discipline in obedience to the apostolic Church and therefore is bound up with the canonical way of administering life and discipline in that Church.

In the Church of Scotland we ordain a man to the ministry of the Word and Sacraments in the Church of God, because we believe it is

Christ himself who ordains, but in ordination the Church (through its authorized ministers) commits to him due authorization to minister the Word and Sacraments within the discipline of the Church of Scotland within which he also promises at ordination to be subject to the Church. But the Church of Scotland does not thereby claim that, in that sense of authorization, it has authorized its ministers to administer the Word and Sacraments in every other Church. It does not necessarily acknowledge the authorization of those ordained in other Churches as giving them authority to administer the Word and Sacraments in the Church of Scotland, but it does not for that reason question the validity of their orders in the sense that their ordination is an act of Christ and is honoured by him in making their ministry efficacious. The Church of Scotland does claim, however, that in obedience to the teaching and ordinance of the apostles "the laying on of hands of the presbytery" is the proper and responsible way of ordaining the ministry and of transmitting in the historical communication of the Church due authorization for the ministry of Word and Sacraments within the sphere of the apostolic commission and mission. While it acknowledges that authorization for the ministry of the Word and Sacraments is inescapably bound up with the discipline of the Church of Scotland and is therefore relative to its own structure and law, it claims that its careful and orderly transmission of ordination from generation to generation is in full conformity to the apostolic ordinance and teaching, and therefore reaches beyond what is merely relative to the particular legal institutions of the Church of Scotland itself to what is valid in the Church of God.

(2) The End of Ordination

Ordination means ordination to the ministry of Word and Sacraments, that is to dispensing Word and Sacraments. Strictly, therefore, 'ordination' should be used only for the order of those who dispense the Word and Sacraments. It is using 'ordination' in a somewhat loose sense to speak of ordaining deacons or deaconesses or ordaining elders, for they are not ordained to dispense the Word and Sacraments but are set apart or consecrated to assist in that ministry, even though a rite of laying on of hands may be used. A rite of laying on of hands is used also in

Consecration and Ordination

some baptismal rites or in confirmations, but it does not therefore mean that those who have hands laid on them are ordained—what determines ordination is the end to which ordination is directed and intended by the Church. This involves two important points.

(a) That which a man is ordained to minister, the Word and Sacraments, is more important than ordination. Ordination is in order to minister the Word and Sacraments, and therefore ordination is subordinate to the Word and Sacraments, which it serves. In other words, the ministering of Word and Sacraments is subservient to the Word and Sacraments themselves. The ministry is but an earthen vessel, as St. Paul put it, but it contains the heavenly treasure, and must never be confounded with the heavenly treasure. Therefore in the ministering of the Word and Sacraments, the mysteries of God, the ministering itself must be dependent upon that which is ministered and can never exalt itself over it. Ordination does not give the minister authority over the Word and Sacrament, but sets him in a servant-relation to them. They are always transcendent to the ministry and their efficacy cannot be tied to the ministry or only be relative to the worth of the ministers. The very authority which a minister has for ministering Word and Sacraments lies in the Word and Sacraments and not in himself—that is another way of saying that the ministry is at every point dependent upon the apostolic Word and Ordinances, for it is through the apostles that we have committed to us the Word and Sacraments and it is only in obedience to the apostolic ordering of the ministry that we administer them.

(b) There can, in the nature of the case, be no higher ministry than that of the ministry of Word and Sacraments, for that would be to suppose that there was a higher authority than that of the Word and a higher sanction than that of the seals of the word directly instituted and given by Jesus Christ. If ordination is defined by its end in the ministry of Word and Sacrament, and Word and Sacrament are more important than the ministering of them, it follows that there is only one order of the ministry in the proper sense; that of the minister dispensing Word and Sacraments. The order of the presbyteral ministry is not only the highest order, but in the strict sense the *only* order of the ministry. Other so-called orders are either for the assistance of this order or for the convenience of maintaining unity and concord and discipline among those so ordained. The fact that there is only one order of the ministry in the strict sense is the meaning of the so-called parity of ministers in a Presbyterian Church, but this does not preclude distinctions in jurisdiction either in the Church Courts to which presbyters are subject or among presbyters themselves. Thus, as Calvin says, "The political distinction of ranks [i.e. distinctions in Church polity, not 'politics'] is not to be repudiated, for natural reason itself dictates this in order to take away confusion; but that which shall leave this object in view, will be so arranged that it may neither obscure Christ's glory nor minister to ambition or tyranny, nor prevent all ministers from cultivating mutual fraternity with each other, with equal rights and liberties."[6]

There can therefore be no doctrinal grounds for any distinction between a presbyter and a bishop or a presbyter-bishop, nor any ground at all for a distinction in order, though there may well be ecclesiastical or historical grounds for making a distinction in function and therefore for adding some measure of jurisdiction to one presbyter to enable him responsibly to fulfil that extra function. But such a distinction in function could not make a bishop more of a minister or give him a higher ministry in relation to Word and Sacrament than that of any other presbyter. The doctrine of parity of ministers must not therefore be confused with differences in function or relative distinctions in jurisdiction; Thus in the Reformed Church we acknowledge that some presbyters are set apart and are acknowledged to have a special charisma for teaching doctrine and for keeping a 'watching brief' over the purity of the Church's proclamation and doctrine in obedience to the teaching of the apostles. These are the 'doctors' of the Church, and they are responsibly commissioned to exercise their functions with appropriate jurisdiction, not in their case in Church or pastoral government, and so they are not given ecclesiastical jurisdiction of any kind but in the teaching and training of the ministry and in doctrine. That does not in any way do away with the 'parity of ministers' in the sense that the doctors have a higher ministry or a superior order to other presbyters. The same would apply to the 'bishop-in-presbytery,'[7] although in that case where his

6. Commentary on Numbers 3:5.

7. Between 1954 and 1957 (and later from 1962–66) conversations were held between the Church of Scotland, the Scottish Episcopal Church, the Church of England, and the Presbyterian Church of England. TF was speaking at a time when such an

special function would be concerned with pastoral discipline he would naturally be set apart for that in the appropriate way by the Presbytery, in "the laying on of hands by the Presbytery," so keeping him under its own authority but commissioning him to act responsibly for it in the ways the Church would lay down. Here the nature of "the laying on of hands" would be determined by the end intended and determined by the Church. In this instance it would not be determined simply by the Word and Sacraments, but by something else: a function to act as spiritual counsellor and guide to his fellow-ministers, and to act in a presidential capacity or even a representative capacity for the presbytery in its solemn acts and deliberations. But because the bishop-in-presbytery could be given no higher relation to the Word and Sacrament—that is in the nature of the case impossible—he could have no higher order than that of his fellow-presbyters.

(3) What Ordination is and How it is Carried Out

Ordination is the solemn setting apart to the ministry of Word and Sacraments of a man who has been called to that ministry. It is an act in which the whole Church concurs, although the act of ordination itself is carried through by those who have already been ordained, for they only are the proper instruments for 'regular' association of others with the commission they have received and which they in obedience to the apostolic ordinance devolve upon others. It is not that they thus transmit 'grace,' or the Holy Spirit, nor that they transmit divine authority; but in so doing they attest that it is Christ alone who acts, and they make evident that they are acting only in obedience to Christ's own commissioned apostles. But, as we have already noted, the act of ordination is also the lawful act in the discipline of the Church where responsibility in office is devolved in an orderly or canonical way upon others in succession to their fathers in the same office. It is an act that takes place in space and time: in the space or place of the Church where Christ has put his name on earth, the visible Church, and in the time or historical continuity of the Church which Christ has sent out into history

---

office was moot as a way of allowing the Church of Scotland to unite with Episcopal Churches.

to proclaim the gospel of his kingdom until he comes again. Thus the physical, visible, and temporal action in ordination attests the binding of the Church to the physical, visible, and temporal incarnation and the Church once and for all founded by the incarnate Son on the apostles and prophets. Just as the Church's life and worship is neither timeless nor spaceless, but in the historical and risen Jesus Christ, so the act of ordination is not a spaceless and timeless act in which the visible and temporal element is of no importance.

On the other hand, the act of ordination is not a Sacrament in the proper sense—although Calvin himself was not averse to calling it a sacrament. It is certainly not a 'Sacrament of the Gospel,' that is, a sign and seal of a saving ordinance through which salvation is bestowed in the unity of Word and appointed sign; but because ordination is the appointed ordinance with its accompanying and appropriate sign for the ordering of the ministry of the Word and Sacraments, it necessarily partakes of the sacramental character of the Word and Sacraments and is rightly performed only within the Church as the body of Christ, within the covenant-signs-and-seals of the Church's incorporation into Christ. No unbaptized person can ordain or be ordained, for no uncovenanted person can be commissioned within the ministry of the new covenant; and no one who is not himself a communicant member of the Church can ordain or be ordained, for no one who has not himself shared in the communion of the new covenant and in the self-consecration of Christ, sealed upon his own at the Holy Supper, can be a consecrated minister of the new covenant. Just because ordination has this setting within the Church's incorporation into Christ in Word and Sacrament, it must take place in the context of Word and Sacrament as well as in the context of the Church's solemn judicial action in a sacral Court.

This dual aspect of the rite of ordination reflects its dual character. It takes place in and through an act of the Presbytery met and constituted as a sacral Court of the Church. Ordination is not properly and validly enacted by any association of presbyters, but by an association of presbyters duly convened within and according to the discipline and constitution of the Church by a resolution of the appropriate court as a whole; for it must be an act in which the whole Church concurs and which therefore has the acknowledged authority of the Church. That is the judicial aspect of ordination, which has its appropriate ceremonies such as the interrogation and response, the taking of vows and the signing of the formula in the Church's roll, and the solemn act of laying on of hands, which in part is an essential legal act attesting the lawful and responsible bestowal of a commission or the canonical conferring of authority to minister the Word and Sacraments within the bounds of the Church and its mission. This judicial part of ordination is not carried out in and by itself apart, but only within the whole spiritual action of ordination, though it is particularly in the laying on of hands that the overlap between the judicial and the spiritual aspects of ordination is most apparent.

Ordination is primarily a spiritual act within the Church in which Christ himself is the principal agent, and in which the ordained ministers (those preaching presbyters to whom it belongs to act thus in Christ's name) act as servants of Christ and only in obedience to his commands. The whole act of ordination is therefore dependent upon the Word of God as mediated through the apostolic tradition. If ordination is by Christ in accordance with his Word, then it is carried out only in 'sacramental' dependence upon his Word—it is the Word which commissions to the ministry, and the Word which is the sole repository of divine authority in the Church and which bestows that authority as the Church acts in obedience to it. The Word is the sceptre through which Christ the risen and ascended Lord continues to govern and rule his Church and continues to call men into his ministry and to command them in his service. Ordination takes place therefore in accordance with the apostolic warrant, in solemn declaration of the Word, and in the context of the Church meeting to wait upon that Word in its proclamation through the heralds sent by Christ to the Church. Only when the royal proclamation of the Word of the King has been made does the Church through its ministers act in obedience to it in the ceremony of ordination.

The other parts of this ceremony are prayer and the laying on of hands. The *Westminster Form of Church Government* puts the laying on of hands first, but the *Second Book of Discipline*, following the order of the *First Book of Discipline* and the teaching of Knox and Calvin, puts prayer first. That indicates that the primary element in ordination is the *epiclesis*, the response of the Church to God's Word made in the prayer calling for the bestowal of the Spirit upon him being set apart to the ministry. It is Christ himself who ordains through the sending of his Spirit, and it is entirely the divine intention and act that determines the nature of the ordinance and its effect. The emphasis upon the act of prayer as an *epiclesis* also makes clear that the formal act of laying on of hands, necessary and important as it is juridically, is not to be regarded mainly as a legal act, but as the apostolically appointed sign attesting that it is Christ who ordains, that it is the Spirit who acts, and that the rite of ordination has its root and ground beyond in the self-consecration of Christ in his own prayerful self-oblation on our behalf. Within that act of prayer the laying on of hands has its essential and indispensable place. But when it is taken within that act of prayer we must say with Augustine: "*Quid aliud est manuum impositio quam oratio super hominem?*"[8] The imposition of hands is primarily the lifting up of hands in prayer, so that actual tactual laying on of hands is really secondary. On the ground of biblical teaching, however, in which it is clear that the act of *samakh* was the main ceremonial act, we lay stress upon tactual imposition as well as the laying on or lifting up of hands in blessing; for in the biblical teaching tactual imposition itself is recognized as an act offering and presenting the one who is the object of laying on of hands to God in dedication and consecration for his service. It is because of this extremely close relation between laying on of hands in prayerful offering and the lifting up of hands in prayer in blessing that many of the earliest books of Church Order omit its actual mention, for the stress was laid upon the act of prayer and was considered to be implied in it. That was the attitude of John Knox in 1560, although in 1572 (if not actually earlier) the imposition of hands was restored in detailed action and has ever since been regarded as indispensable in the Church of Scotland.

Accompanying and preceding the act of ordination there are other rites which have their proper place and are designed to attest the fact that the person ordained is acknowledged as one who has himself received a divine call to the Holy Ministry, that his own private recognition of that call is confirmed by the Church acting through its duly con-

8. *De Bap.* III xvii 21.

stituted Courts, and confirmed by the congregation which has called him to be its minister in the name of Christ. The act of ordination thus requires the *imprimatur* of the Church as a whole and the acclaim and acquiescence of the local congregation, who also take vows in support of the minister and in obedient acknowledgment of the fact that their minister has been sent to them by Christ himself. The minister himself takes vows which bind him to the continuity of the Church's obedience to the apostles in doctrines and ordinances, and in which he solemnly promises to fulfil his ministry with devotion to Christ as his servant, and, without lording it over the flock, to seek their good in the Lord. At the same time he acknowledges that the government of the Church is agreeable to the Word of God, promises to be subject to its discipline, to take his due part in its affairs, and to seek the unity and peace of the Church. But in his undertaking these vows, as in the administration of ordination to him, the Church makes it clear that the minister acts not on his own charges or on his own resources, but only on the command and therefore only in reliance upon the promise of Jesus Christ who remains the same yesterday, to-day, and for ever, and who never fails to keep his Word.

CHAPTER 6

Service in Jesus Christ

I

THE SCOTTISH DIVINES OF the sixteenth century used to distinguish between what all Christians should do "of their charity" and what some have to do "of authority." That was a distinction regarding not so much the *kind* of service as the *mode* of service rendered. All members of the body of Christ are constrained through love to bear witness to him and to pray for others, but some have this ministry laid upon them as a special task, so that they fulfil it not only out of love but in obedience to a specific commission from the Lord and with the definite authority of that commission behind them. It was this authoritative "sending," they held, which distinguished the "solemn" preaching of God's Word, accompanied by the divine "seals," from the service of all the faithful in their proclaiming of Christ and his Gospel. While that is no doubt a valuable distinction, it would be wrong if it were interpreted to mean that, in contrast to the special ministry within the Church, the service of all members of the body of Christ is to be referred back only to the free movement of their love and to be understood as its spontaneous expression. The great characteristic of all Christian service or *diakonia* is that while it is certainly fulfilled under the constraint of the love of Christ it is a service *commanded* by him and laid by him as a *task* upon every baptized member of his body.

We must not forget that even love is commanded by God. As Jesus himself taught us, the love of God and the love of our neighbour are the supreme commandments upon which all the others depend, and in our love to him we are bound in a relation of unconditional obedience to his commandments, among which is the specific commandment to love one another. This is the context in which *diakonia* is to be understood. Christian service is commanded of us. It is to be referred back to the lordship of Christ and is to be understood as the pure service rendered to the Lord by those who are his servants.

In the New Testament two principal terms are used to speak of the servants of Christ, *douloi* and *diakonoi*, slaves and waiters. The former refers to status rather than function and describes the relationship that determines the very structures of existence in Christ. The *doulos* lives under the total claim of God and is completely subordinate to Jesus Christ, to whom he belongs body and soul. The latter refers to function rather than status and describes the service of those who exist in an absolute relationship to Christ as Lord. The *diakonos* is one who has been given a task by his Master, and who does only what is commanded by him, not what he thinks out for himself. The servants of Christ (whether we think of them as *douloi* or *diakonoi*) are not their own masters, for they belong to another. They do not carry out their own wishes or minister to their own glory, but they do only what they are told and serve only the glory of their Lord. The way in which the New Testament uses *doulos* and *diakonos* lets us see that Christian service or *diakonia* is not something that is accidental to the Christian, but essential to him, for it is rooted in his basic structure of existence as a slave of Jesus Christ. It is a form of service in which he is not partially but completely committed in the whole of his being before God, and which he discharges not occasionally but continuously in the whole of his existence as a follower of Jesus Christ.

We would misunderstand this servant-existence of Christ's followers if we did not see that their servitude in the Lord is the mode of their freedom, and their service of the Lord is the movement of their love, the true freedom and true love into which they have been redeemed. It is Christ's to command and theirs to obey, but both commandment and obedience are modes of the divine love in Jesus Christ in which service and freedom are the obverse of each other. But we would also misunderstand Christian service if we construed it simply as the expression of Christian love, intrinsically intelligible in its own requirement and inherently compelling as an end in itself, for then we would detach Christian service from its heteronomous ground in the Lord himself and give it a basis in the autonomous existence of the Christian; we would think of it as arising out of himself and explain it as the Christian's self-imposed way of life in which his existence comes to its truest self-expression. Christian service is not the service of love for love's sake, but, service of love though it is, the duty rendered by *servants* to their *Lord* in obedience to his commandment. Hence while it is fulfilled in the form of service to others in the world, it is not fulfilled as something they have freely chosen for themselves but as a task that Christ has laid upon them in the entirely new situation that has overtaken them in him. Faithful servants do not arrogate to themselves the authority for their actions, nor do they assume responsibility for the results of their service. They act simply as servants who live in subjection to their Lord, but who are free from the necessity, and the anxiety, of having to justify their service. They act responsibly by doing obediently what he commands, and act freely in leaving to their Lord alone the responsibility for the consequences of the service he has laid upon them. Obedience is demanded without any secondary motive, and likewise service is rendered without secondary motive, without any thought of claim upon the Lord and without any thought even of thanks from those to whom service is rendered.

Diakonia is pure service fulfilled in accordance with the requirements of an external Authority, that of the Lord, yet *diakonia* is intrinsically related to that Authority through its content of love. The content of the commandment and the content of the service in obedience to it derive from the self-giving of God himself in Jesus Christ the Lord. He gives what he commands and commands what he gives. He commands a service of love, and he gives the love that empowers that service. It is this inner relation between commandment and love, or between "authority" and "charity," that is so distinctive of service in Jesus Christ.

Diakonia of this unique kind is possible only because the Lord himself has come in the form of a servant, incorporating our servant-existence in himself and incarnating among us the self-giving of God in sheer love and compassion for mankind. He came not to be served but to serve, to live out on earth the life of unconditional obedience to the Father in heaven and the life of pure love poured out to all men in unrestrained mercy. He was himself the complete embodiment of the commandment of love and of the love commanded within our human existence, and as such he constitutes in himself the ultimate source for the inner relation between commandment and love and the creative ground of all true Christian service. This is particularly apparent in the Sermon on the Mount, which is at once the self-portrait of our Lord in his life on earth as Son of man and the promulgation of the will of the Father as unconditionally binding on all men. This is the life of the Servant: "Be therefore perfect as your Father in heaven is perfect." This is the service of the Lord: "Be therefore merciful as your Father also is merciful." It is only in this Jesus that we learn what *diakonia* really is, the loving service in mercy that looks for no reward beyond the knowledge that we do what is commanded of us and looks for no thanks from those to whom mercy is extended, but it is only because this Jesus has made our cause his very own, sharing our existence in servitude and sharing with us his own life of love, that we may and can engage in this kind of *diakonia* in him.

Our particular concern here, however, is not with the structure of the Christian's existence as *doulos* of Jesus Christ and therefore with the general ethos of life in him, but with the form of the Christian's service as *diakonos* of Jesus Christ and therefore with the specific function of life in him. That is to say, we are concerned with *diakonia* in its concrete sense as *deaconing*, both as the charge that Christ lays upon the Christian community and as the office to which some are called within the community. *Diakovia* describes not only the relationship of service to which the whole membership of the Church and specific individuals within it bear to Jesus Christ, but the form which that relationship takes in the mutual service of members to one another and in their service to their fellow men in the world. It is natural that at this point the spotlight, so to speak, should fall upon the *deacon* himself, for it is his specific office, as a humble representative of the people of God, to prompt them in their response to Christ and his gospel and to seek the fruit of that response in their life of deaconing toward their fellow men, and thus in his special vocation as a deacon to fulfil in an exemplary way the kind of *diakonia* we are all called to exercise in Jesus Christ. It was for this reason that the early Church saw delineated in the deacon's office more than anywhere else the likeness of Jesus Christ the Servant of God.

II

Before we consider this diaconal ministry we must examine its source and ground in Jesus Christ, for it was the kind of person he was and the kind of ministry he undertook that determined the form and mode of all Christian service. He was sent by the Father to carry out the redemption of human existence, not by dealing with it from the outside but by operating from within it, not by the sheer fiat of divine power but by humble acts of service in all the weakness and frailty of human creaturehood, i.e., as a man among men, holding messianic office and exercising ministerial function. And so he came qualified by his incarnation to act for the human race within its structures and limitations, and consecrated in his capacity as a humble representative of the people for messianic office within their conditions of alienation and subjection. Hence his mission took both a human and a menial form, the ministry of the Son of Man and of the Servant of the Lord, the *Christos*. Now, we have been accustomed to expound this ministry of Christ in terms of his threefold office as the anointed Prophet, Priest, and King, but this has tended to obscure or to discount two essential aspects of his ministry: *(a)* that he fulfilled his ministry as a human office within the conditions of the community which he served and sustained by direct personal and individual acts on his part; and *(b)* that he gave this ministry content and pattern by deeds of love and compassion in the healing and succouring of sick and suffering and outcast human beings. That is to say, the *diaconal* nature and significance of our Lord's ministry of mercy have tended to fall out of the picture, so that the Church throughout history has had great difficulty in relating to their proper source and ground not only the diaconal office within the Church but the deaconing of the whole community.

It is to this neglected aspect of Christ's ministry that we turn our attention in order to lay bare its permanent significance for Christian *diakonia*. Christ was himself the *diakonos par excellence* whose office it was not only to prompt the people of God in their response to the divine mercy and to be merciful themselves, not only to stand out as the perfect model or example of compassionate service to the needy and distressed, but to provide in himself and in his own deeds of mercy the creative ground and source of all such *diakonia*. He was able to do that because in him God himself condescended to share with men their misery and distress, absorbed the sharpness of their hurt and suffering into himself, and poured himself out in infinite love to relieve their need, and he remains able to do that because he is himself the outgoing of the innermost being of God toward men in active sympathy and compassion, the boundless mercy of God at work in human existence, unlimited in his capacity to deliver them out of all their troubles. Thus through the Incarnation it is revealed to us that God in his own being is not closed to us, for he has come to share with us the deepest movement of his divine heart, and so to participate in our human nature that the heart of God beats within it. We know that in the springs of his own eternal life God is ever open and ready and eager to share the weakness and sorrow and affliction of others and to spend himself in going to their relief and in saving them. It is the very property of God's nature to be merciful, and in mercy it is that nature that he has come to share with men and women in Jesus, that they, too, may be merciful as he is merciful.

This is mercy that is quite limitless in its extent, mercy that will not stop short at any point in being merciful. It is not just mercy to man in his creaturely weakness and abject need, but mercy freely and unstintingly extended to him at his wickedest and worst, in his revolt from the divine love and his opposition to the divine grace; mercy that regards man's resistance to God's mercy and man's inability to be merciful as his most desperate affliction and his greatest need. It is in man's proud contradiction of God's love and in his contempt of mercy, in man's sin and guilt, that the real sting of his misery lies, but it is precisely at that point of ultimate extremity, in the terrible sharpness of his distress, that God's mercy is extended and refuses to be limited even by man's arrogant scorn and refusal of it. But this is mercy that operates by stopping to suffer all the worst that man can do and be, by entering into his revolted and alienated existence and by dealing with sin from within the depths of human life, by attacking and vanquishing guilt from the inside of its own movement, imparting itself where there is no mercy, until it begets mercy even where it has been scorned.

Now, what distresses God so deeply as he looks upon man in his fearful condition is not simply his sickness and pain, nor even the torment of anxiety that gnaws at his inner being, but the fact that in his hostility to God man has become possessed of sin in his very mind and is caught in the toils of a vast evil will that extends far beyond him, and what vexes God also is that man's existence breaks up under the pressure of his guilt in it all and under the threat of the divine judgement upon him. In view of this tragic state the mercy of God takes on a dynamic and creative form in miraculous acts of grace and power in which he allies himself with man against the evil that has entrenched itself within him and against the threat of demolition that has come upon him. That is what we see actually going on in the miracles of Jesus in which he was at work reclaiming lost humanity, not by accusing men in their sickness and sin but by shouldering all their *astheneia* upon himself, i.e., not by throwing the responsibility back upon them but by taking their responsibility on himself. That is surely the most miraculous thing about the healing acts of Jesus, the fact that in him God has come into our enslaved existence in such a *way as* to make himself responsible for men and even to assume their sin and culpability upon himself. That is why there took place in Jesus such a struggle with evil, a struggle that was waged between God and evil power not only in the heart and mind of man but in his bodily and historical existence, and a struggle to reclaim the existence of man as human being from its subjection to futility and negation.

That is the pitiful condition of man that lies at the root of his anxiety, for his deepest being is menaced by chaos and slips away from him into corruption and destruction, since his existence is subjected to vanity in its contradiction of God and in its judgement by God. Here God's mercy takes a real form, for it is of the sheer mercy of God that he enters into this very being and existence of man under the dominion of evil power and under the doom of unavoidable destruction, and takes this human being and existence upon himself. That is to say, God penetrates into the very negation of evil as it is entrenched in man, suffers it in himself, and so, as it were (how can we find words to express what is so unutterable here?), 'hazards' his own existence and being as God for the sake of man. Moreover, he enters into this banned and sentenced state of man to live in it precisely *as man* under all the assaults of evil, within the entire limitation of the creature exposed to evil power and to the judgement of divine holiness, in order to struggle with evil and vanquish it just where it has dug itself in so deeply, in the self-will and resistance of the creature toward God, and in the obdurate and brazen character of its hostility gained under God's rejection.

That is the meaning of the incarnate life and ministry of the Son of God and the whole passion of his existence as Man among men, made under the law, and obedient unto death, where evil pays its fullest wages and delivers its ultimate assault upon God's creatures and where that assault gains its fateful force from the very judgements directed against it. No wonder St. Paul insisted that our sin gains its strength from the very law of God! That is why the 'hazard' to which God submits as he stakes his own being on our behalf and for our salvation comes not from the attack of evil itself but from the judgement and negation of evil—it is that fact that makes the cross and its *Eli, Eli, lema sabachthani* so indescribably terrible, the sheer anguish of God bowed under his own judgement on sin, a judgement not mitigated in the slightest but utterly fulfilled. Thus the existence of man into which God enters, and within which he lives as Son of Man, is a lost existence that is already breaking up and crumbling away not only under the negation of evil but under the negation of the divine judgement, where the rejection of evil serves to harden and make final the threat to demolish human being. It is into that dark and doomed existence under the divine judgement and into its corruption and destruction under negation that God enters in unutterable mercy in order to save mankind.

Now we can grasp something of the extreme gravity of man's plight, and the nature and extent of his need in the inseparability of his spiritual and physical existence and in the disintegration of his whole creaturely being as man before God. Now we can understand also something of what lay behind the cross and the descent of the Saviour into our bottomless pit of evil and guilt and death, and so of what was involved in every act of healing and mercy in which Jesus through sharing our human existence sought to release distressed humanity from its subjection to evil and vanity, from its imprisonment in chaos and disorder and disintegration, and sought to restore it to the truth of God's creation, in which God affirms as good that which he has made, and so makes good his own Word in the creation of man.

The miracles of Jesus were concerned, then, with the saving of creation. In them God asserted his claim over the human beings he had made and proclaimed his will to maintain them in integrity of being in face of everything that threatened their existence and to restore them to natural life in the freedom and joy of his creation. The miracles reveal not only that the salvation of man involves a total negation of all that is opposed to God's creative purpose but that it can take place only within the healing and remaking of a human being in his actual physical and spiritual existence. Only through the Creator's full participation with us in our human life on earth can atonement for sin and redemption from evil power issue in the actual restoration of what God has made. The miraculous acts of Jesus are thus the luminous points in his ministry, proleptic to his resurrection from the dead, where it is disclosed that the whole life and sojourn of Jesus Christ among us is the absolute miracle within which and through which the new creation takes place.

Without the Incarnation of the Creator Word the fallen world would crumble away finally and irretrievably into nothingness, for then God would simply let go of what he has made and it would suffer from sheer privation of being. But the incarnation has taken place—once and for all the Creator Word has entered into the existence of what he has made and bound it up for ever with his own eternal being and life, yet the incarnation had to mean, in this union of the Creator and the creature, the final negation by God of all that resists his creative will. That is the stupendous and bewildering miracle of Jesus that just because in him divine nature and human nature are united in the unity of his one person, the judgement and & expiation of sin had to take place as an inner determination of the life he lived among us from birth to death (and how he was straitened until that inexpressible agony was accomplished!); and the new creation took place in the healing and sanctifying and regenerating of the human nature he assumed from our fallen and corrupt existence (and how joyful and radiant was the fulfilment in his resurrection from the grave!). It was through the sovereign *parousia* of the Creator Word within our flesh at the points of enslavement and disintegration that the integrity and wholeness of man in his spiritual and physical being were restored and that human nature was reclaimed for the heavenly Father. That is what Jesus was in his healing and helping acts. He was the Redeemer at work serving the creature from below and from within his broken and divided existence delivering him from inner bondage, redeeming him from deeply-rooted tension and anxiety; the Creator himself at work recreating what he had made by sharing in its humble creaturely existence in all its distress and trouble and futility, and sharing with it the healed and sanctified humanity in the perfect life of the Son of Man.

III

This work Jesus Christ fulfilled from two sides: from the side of God toward man, and from the side of man toward God. He came as God himself, drawing near to man in all his sovereign freedom and grace, bringing his Kingdom to bear directly upon human life and history. He came as the mighty Son breaking into the realm of darkness to deliver men from their thraldom and shame, and to redeem them from the whole power of evil in triumph over sin and guilt and death and hell itself. Yet, Son of God though he was, he came among us as an infant of days in great humility within the darkness and helplessness and poverty of man, in order to work out through his own human life and deeds among us the faithful answer of man to the saving grace and power of God. Hence he came issuing out of human history as a son of Adam, of the seed of David, in order to wrestle with our perverse human nature from within our disobedient life until he had converted it back in obedience to the Father and offered it to him in the perfection of filial trust and love.

Within this twofold work Christ came identifying himself with man in his hopeless misery and abject need, and making man's cause his very own. By Incarnation and Atonement, he who had been the ground of man's existence from beyond his existence now forged such a bond of union between man and himself that he became the ground of man's existence in his existence, undergirding and sustaining it from within and from below, overcoming its vanity and privation of being and giving it meaning and reality in himself. Hence Christ is to be found wherever there is sickness or hunger or thirst or nakedness or imprisonment, for he has stationed himself in the concrete actualities of human life where the bounds and structures of existence break down under the onslaught of disease and want, sin and guilt, death and judgement, in order that he may serve man in re-creating his relation to God and realizing his response to the divine mercy. It is thus that Jesus Christ mediates in himself the healing reconciliation of God with man and man with God in the form, as it were, of a meeting of himself with himself in the depths of human need. And it is thus that the Father looks upon every man in his need only by looking at him in and through the atoning presence and suppliance of his incarnate Son that meets him there, for the incarnate Son is the outgoing of his own divine being toward every man and the pouring out of his own eternal love upon him in unrestrained mercy and grace.

As we have already seen, Jesus ministered this divine mercy as a humble representative of the people into which he had incorporated himself and within which he had been consecrated to the vocation of the Messiah, the elect one, the Servant. This office of *Christos* he fulfilled as *man,* not therefore by a compelling display of mighty power, but by meek and personal service as he went about doing good, helping and healing others, and so through fellowship with men in a shared existence. That was his diaconal ministry to men in their enslavement and disintegration which gave meaning again to human life and sustained it in such a relation to the Father that within it atonement could issue in communion and redemption in new creation. It was indeed only in continuous fulfilment of this diaconal ministry that he went forth at last to offer himself in sacrificial expiation for the sin of mankind, so that when his atoning work was accomplished in death and resurrection and ascension and the message of reconciliation with God through Christ was freely proclaimed, it could be heard and received by men whose very existence was sustained in its relation to God by the hidden presence of the incarnate and crucified and risen Christ within it. That is the permanent and immense significance of his humble *diakonia* in the flesh, which has been given continuing effect through the pouring out of Christ's Spirit at Pentecost, for it is that *diakonia* in the flesh that gives material content to his presence through the Spirit.

Now, in the fulfilment of his earthly ministry, Jesus drew to himself a company of disciples whom he formed and instituted into one body with himself as the inner nucleus of the Church, incorporating them into his messianic mission and sending them out to exercise his own *diakonia* in helping and healing, in preaching and forgiving. He set himself in their midst as their Lord and their example in the service of mercy. Through their union and communion with him in his mission he gave structure to the Church he founded upon them and shaped its ministry of the divine mercy in his name. That is to say, in constituting them as his body, baptized with his baptism and partaking of his cup, he so assimilated them into his own diaconal life and service on earth that he made *diakonia* an essential mark of the Church redeemed by him and built up round his own person as the Christ. They were in him a messianic community anointed for service, through sharing in his own anointing and his own self-consecration for mankind. It cannot be doubted that this diaconal character of life and service in Christ is a basic and permanent sign of the Church sanctified in him, for it is here that Christ's own image and likeness most clearly appear: in the *diakonia* of the divine mercy within the spiritual and physical existence of man. The Church cannot be in Christ without being in him as he is proclaimed to men in their need and without being in him as he encounters us in and behind the existence of every man in his need. Nor can the Church be recognized as his except in that meeting of Christ with himself in the depth of human misery, where Christ clothed with his gospel meets with Christ clothed with the desperate need and plight of men. It is never the *diakonia* of the Church to be itself the *Christ,* but through its humble service to Christ clothed with his Gospel and its service to Christ clothed with the misery of men to seek and to pray for their meeting and so to be in history the bodily instrument which Christ uses in the proclamation of the divine mercy to mankind and in prompting their responses to that mercy.

Diakonia in this sense is not only the charge which Christ has laid upon the whole membership of his body but an office to which some within it are specially called and for which he bestows through his Spirit the appropriate charisma. Here Jesus stands among us both as the *Kurios* who gives the charge and as the supreme *Diakonos* whose example is to be followed in all *diakonia* of the divine mercy. He would have us minister to one another and to others as he ministered to his fellows in the form of a servant.

What were the distinctive features he exhibited in this ministry?

(a) He served God in his mercy and man in his need with the secret of the cross in his heart. As he went about doing good, he healed not as a doctor but as a Saviour, and he helped not as a wonder-worker but as the holy one who absorbed into himself the affliction of men. Though it was by the finger or Spirit of God that he brought divine power to bear upon the realm of evil and broke through the thraldom of sin and sickness in miraculous deeds of mercy, he fulfilled his ministry in meekness and lowliness in order to bear the onslaught of evil upon himself and so to get at the heart of it. It was by living a life of holiness among us in perfect obedience to the Father that he engaged with the inhuman forces of darkness that had encroached upon the bodies and souls of men. Therefore, when Jesus healed a man even of a physical affliction he did so only through a struggle with evil will. Nowhere did he heal simply as a kindly physician, but as one who wrestled personally with evil and overcame it through the conflict of his own holy will with the powers of evil spirit. That is why again and again Jesus groaned in agony and grief of spirit as he cured men's bodies and minds and had to renew his strength constantly through prayer, while prayer itself was a battle with the rebellious will of an alienated creation. This was not simply the service of kindness for kindness' sake, but a far profounder service of mercy that dealt with the real sting of evil by penetrating into its sinful motion and undoing its guilt in atonement. It was the kind of service that could not be rendered apart from vicarious divine sorrow for the sin of the world.

(b) He ministered the mercy of God to man at the sharpest point of his need and misery, where he is not only unmerciful but resents mercy, and is therefore bitterly hostile to this ministry. Although it was the mercy of God freely ministered by Jesus that provoked the resistance of man to its sharpest point of hostility toward God, yet in this ministry of mercy Jesus met the hostility of man by making it the supreme object of his compassion, by accepting it and bearing it in himself and then by making an end of it in his own death. It is easy enough, as Jesus pointed out, to be merciful to others when it meets with some return, but to be merciful without any hope of return and without ever looking for any return, to go on being merciful in the face of unremitting unthankfulness, and always to make every act of ingratitude, no matter how bitter and obdurate, the very occasion for mercy, is to minister a mercy that is quite limitless. That is real mercy, and that is what it means to be merciful as God is merciful. Such was the mercy ministered by Jesus, triumphant mercy which drew out human unthankfulness and resentment to their ultimate point where he limited it by absorbing it in himself and put a final end to it in the very death which it inflicted on him—mercy that cannot be defeated.

(c) Jesus carried out his ministry as a humble servant on earth in utter reliance upon his Father in heaven, refusing to do anything except what he had been sent to do and refusing to discharge his mission except in the weakness and selflessness of pure service. At no point did he seek to change the nature of his ministry as service, and therefore he rendered it only through constant recourse to prayer in order to let it take effect solely through the good pleasure of the Father. The true and faithful servant does not arrogate authority to himself or build up round him instruments of power or even an aura of prestige through which he may exert pressure to attain his ends; otherwise he would betray the essential nature of his service as *service*. Hence Jesus warned his disciples, as he washed their feet in menial service at the Last Supper, to beware of allowing their service in his name to gather a worldly prestige in which its nature as service would be lost or to take the form of a munificent patronage that could lord it over mankind. *Diakonia* in the name of Christ has only one source of power: in prayer and intercession, for Jesus Christ himself, the supreme *Diakonos,* will rule over the ages and the nations only through the weakness of the man on the cross.

Such, then, is the pattern of service which Christ has instituted in himself for the Church and for all who within it are called to be deacons. It is a charge to be merciful as the Father is merciful and a call to follow Christ in the form of a servant, that all members of the body of Christ may be fellow labourers in his work and that deacons, reflecting in themselves the pattern of Christ's service, may prompt the whole people of God in the ministry of divine mercy.

IV

Without doubt this is a very difficult charge that Christ has laid upon his Church, and one that is desperately hard for the Church to fulfil in its corporate capacity as Church and therefore in the form of a service rendered by the community as such. How can it render this service as *service* and render it *effectively* within the power-structures of humanity?

Here the Church is up against a twofold temptation. On the one hand, it is tempted to use worldly power in order to secure the success of its service. As an organized community within the national, social, and economic structures of human life the Church cannot isolate its ministry of the divine mercy from the organized services of the State for the welfare of its people. The Church knows only too well that the need of men is bound up with the injustices inherent in the national, social, and economic structures within which people live, and is often directly traceable to them, and therefore in order to meet human need adequately and rationally attention must be given to the factors that create it and aggravate it. Certainly as far as hunger and poverty and want are concerned, what is required is the application of scientific methods in the production and distribution of goods from the vast wealth with which God has endowed the earth. But how can this be done without economic and political power? And so the Church is constantly tempted not only to institutionalize its service of the divine mercy but to build up power structures of its own, both through ecclesiastical success and prestige among the people and through social and political instruments, by means of which it can exert pressure to attain its ends and impart power to its service in order to ensure its effectiveness. What church is there that feels deeply the burden of human need, and takes seriously its service of mercy, that does not fall into this temptation?

On the other hand, the Church is tempted to leave the corporate responsibility for the need of men wholly to the State and to restrict itself to the ministry of forgiveness. How can the Church participate in the planned and controlled welfare of mankind without actually compromising its freedom and secularizing its life in the worldly forms of society? And so the Church is tempted to retreat into an area where it could not come into conflict with the power-structures of organized social welfare and where it thinks to avoid the subtle snare of using its success in the relief of human suffering as a means of enhancing its own image or of pressing its own claim upon the people. This could take a quietist and other-worldly form through the restriction of Christian service to inward 'religious' concerns, but it could also take the form of a flight into the anonymity of 'religionless' behaviour or the so-called 'metachristianity' of the 'new man.' But in either case the Church would decline the burden of human need at its sharpest point and deflect the real force of Christian witness, and so run away from the agony of being merciful as God is merciful.

Whichever alternative the Church chooses, on the one hand or the other, it contracts out of the actual charge Christ has laid upon it and betrays the essential nature of Christian service as *service*. Can the Church engage in the pressure groups of organized society in order to ensure the success of its own enterprise, and so suffer assimilation to the forms of this world, without compromising its real nature as the body of Jesus Christ? Can it hide its light under the natural forms of man's cultural and scientific development without losing its soul? Can it follow Christ, the Servant of the Lord who steadfastly resisted every temptation to use compelling demonstrations of glory and power to fulfil his ministry, without like him suffering the hostility and ridicule and ignominy that are heaped by the world on powerless and selfless service of God's mercy? Can the Church really fulfil the charge Christ has laid upon it and therefore take up his cross without renouncing itself for him, without, as it were, hazarding its life or losing its identity in recognized historical existence for Christ's sake and the gospel's? Can the Church go forth from Christ clad with his image in the form of a servant without laying aside the pride and glory and power of the nations, and without taking into its own mouth in triumphant agony his cry before the judgement seat of Pilate: "My Kingdom is not of this world?" And how can the Church go forth from Christ to engage in authentic service in his name without immersing itself in the need and misery and desperate plight of men in complete solidarity with the world under the judgement and grace of God, without participating deeply in the divine mercy that has put an end in the crucified body of Christ to our restless striving for power and vain snatching at glory, and to our resentment of meek and humble reliance upon the heavenly Father?

Difficult though it is for the Church as such to carry this burden and fulfil the role of a servant, God in his mercy has instituted within it special ministries to dispense to it the Word of life and to seek the fruit of it in the lives of its members, to guide the Church and to prompt it in its service. This is the two-fold ministry that we may speak of as "the service of the Word," and "the service of response to the Word." *The service of the Word* is the ministry of Word and Sacrament through which Christ is pleased to be present, offering himself as Saviour and implementing his salvation by the power of his Spirit. But it is a *service*, a *diakonia*, in which ministers only *serve* the proclamation of Christ and cannot make that proclamation effective by imparting to it their own strength, and in which they only dispense the Sacraments as *stewards* of the mysteries in utter reliance upon Christ to fulfil his own ministry of himself in Word and Spirit, in grace and power. *The service of response to the Word* is the ministry of the divine mercy to the people in which Christ himself is pleased to be present, acting as their representative in lifting them up to the face of the Father in thanksgiving and worship and in making them his fellow labourers in the pouring out of the divine mercy to all mankind. But it is a *service*, a *diakonia*, in which deacons only *prompt* the people in their responses of prayer and praise and do not act on their behalf, and in which they guide them in their service to mankind and do not undertake it for them, but in which they remind the people of Christ's own promise to meet them in all their deeds of mercy to the hungry and thirsty and naked and sick and imprisoned, and so to give effect to their service in the depths of human need.

These two ministries are essentially complementary and are mutually dependent, since each requires the other for its proper fulfilment and one is obstructed by the lack of the other. It is through that double ministry that Christ communicates himself to man by bringing God's presence to bear upon man and by bringing him in his need to receive that presence, by ministering the mercy of God toward man in his guilty estrangement and by freeing him in his desperate need for the response of faith and trust in God, and he does that by incarnating God's love in himself for man and by sustaining through his own presence the existence of man for fellowship with God. It is thus that Jesus Christ mediates in himself the healing reconciliation of God with man and man with God in the form of a union of his own presence in the gospel with his own presence in the depths of human need. The service of the Word serves Christ clothed with his gospel, so that through it he draws near to man with forgiveness in unconditional grace; and the service of response to the Word serves Christ clothed with the misery of man, so that through it he sustains and upholds man in unutterable compassion until he finds the sheep that is lost and counts that he has found it when it hears his voice and follows him.

Now, while the New Testament uses the term *diakonia* both for the service of the Word and for the service of response to the Word, it is especially used and indeed technically used for the service of response to the Word, that is, for the ministry of the *deacon*. We may thus distinguish between the two forms of ministry as the *presbyteral* ministry through which the Word and Sacraments are dispensed and the *diaconal* ministry through which the responses of God's people in worship and witness or intercession and mercy are guided and prompted. The term *diakonia* is peculiarly appropriate to the latter ministry, for while the presbyteral ministry is one in which the ministers act not as representatives of the people but only as those sent by Christ and commissioned by him with authority to dispense his word of forgiveness, in the proclamation of the gospel and the administration of the Sacraments, the diaconal ministry is one in which the deacons act as representatives of the people and as examples of the way in which Christ identified himself with their need, and therefore as sent by him to engage in a ministry of pure, unassuming service without any commission to exercise authority or pastoral control. They are as necessary and as indispensable to one another as husband and wife, and father and mother, in the same family.

It is an immense tragedy that throughout its history the Church has so often lacked a proper *diaconate* to guide it and prompt it in the ministry of the divine mercy, and to seek the full fruit of that mercy in the activities of the community and in the lives of its members. This has had disastrous consequences for the ministry of Word and Sacrament, for left on its own, without its other half, it has succumbed to the temptation to arrogate to itself a false glory and to fulfil its authoritative commission not by obedient *service* but by usurping control and mastery over the Lord's inheritance. But it has had disastrous consequences also for the service of the Church in its corporate capacity, for without the example of pure service, which it is the office of the deacon to set forth, the Church has fallen into the temptation to give itself out as the patron of goodness and welfare and to assume worldly powers in order to achieve success in its works of relief, and thus has betrayed the very nature of its ministry as service of divine mercy to mankind. This has also meant that the ministry of Christ clothed with his gospel has been kept apart from the ministry of Christ clothed with the need and plight of men, with the result that the ministry of the gospel has so often lost its relevance to men in the concrete actualities of their existence, and the ministry of the divine mercy has lacked its penetrating power to strike into the deepest root of human need in man's guilty estrangement from God—thus grave disorder has appeared in the life of the Church and its mission is often fraught with a deep sense of futility.

The Church needs today a massive recovery of authentic *diakonia* if it is to hold forth the image of Christ before mankind and is to minister the mercy of God to the needs of men in the deep root of their evil and in the real sting of their misery. Such a recovery would go far to heal the breaches in the life of the Church and to supply what is lacking in its mission. Three areas in particular call for drastic amendment and far-reaching reform.

(a) *Intercession.* There is no more basic form of the Church's ministry than prayer, for it is in prayer that it renders its supreme service of worship and thanksgiving to God, and it is only through prayer that the Church can engage in the pure service of divine mercy in utter reliance upon God and in the renunciation of every attempt to put the Word of God into effect through its own cunning or strength. The Church does not minister through the power of its own action but only through the power of its Lord, and therefore it cannot fulfil its *diakonia* on earth without continuous engagement in intercession through its great high Priest at the right hand of God almighty. The frantic attempts of the Church in modern times to find ways and means of making its message relevant to men, of clothing its ministries with worldly power, or of evolving methods and instruments which will ensure the popularity and success of its enterprise, are open admission that the Church has ceased to believe that the gospel is really able to effect what it proclaims and of tragic disbelief in the power of intercession, i.e., in the active intervention of the Church's heavenly Mediator which is echoed through the Spirit in the Church's stammering prayers on earth. The intercessory prayer of the Church is direct engagement in the mighty apocalyptic battle between the Kingdom of Christ and the kingdoms of this world and in the triumphant reign of the enthroned Lamb over all the forces of evil and darkness in history. The Church's greatest need is to *believe again* in the intercession of Christ and to find through prayer the sole source of power in its mission. Nothing can ever take the place of this basic service, the *diakonia* of intercession.

(b) *Witness.* Witness is the form which service takes as it moves from worship and intercession in Christ toward men in their estrangement and separation from God. It is open and transparent witness to Jesus Christ as the incarnate love of God, the Lord and Saviour of men, and witness directed above all to the deepest point of man's misery in his guilty alienation from God and to the sharpest point of his need in his hostility to God's grace. It is thus witness in the face of resistance and even persecution. The Christian Church is under constant pressure by the world to conform to its ways and thoughts, to adapt its message to its desires and ambitions, and thus the Church can only bear witness by entering into affliction. It is because the Church is a servant of Christ and is assimilated to his mission in its essential life that it suffers the same hostility as he suffered and shares with him the weakness and helplessness of his passion. It is because Christ crucified and risen again dwells in the Church and makes it the earthly and historical form of his body that he leads it into the unavoidable conflict between the mercy of God and the inhumanity of man and between the holiness of God and the sin of mankind. The Church cannot withdraw from the affliction and suffering which this conflict brings without contracting out of its witness and betraying its Lord. Yet this is the very point where the

Church today in its faint-heartedness and scepticism seems to have lost its nerve, and where under pressure from the world it makes its message easy and acceptable to human hearing, adapting the gospel to modern man instead of bringing modern man face to face with the gospel. But the actual point of relevance and communication lies at the point of offence where the real hurt of man is exposed and divine healing takes place. It is a betrayal of *diakonia* to heal the hurt of God's people lightly, saying peace, peace, where there is no peace. The Church cannot discharge the task that Christ has laid upon it without offering unadulterated witness and engaging in pure evangelism, cost what it may in scorn and ridicule or oppression. If at this point the Church seeks to save its life it will lose it, but here if it is ready to lose it for Christ's sake and the gospel's it will find it. It still remains true that the blood of the martyrs is the seed of the Church, and that it is through bold and suffering witness that men and women serve Christ most faithfully.

(c) *Reconciliation.* The Church that is committed to the *diakonia* of the divine mercy must live the reconciled life. It cannot proclaim reconciliation to the world without standing in solidarity with the world under the total grace and judgement of God and without carrying within itself a solidarity of communion in the redemption through the blood of Christ. It cannot offer healing to mankind without being healed in its own body. It cannot minister reconciliation to humanity in its bitter divisions and hostilities without being reconciled in its own membership and purged of its internal bitterness and strife. What can obstruct or damn the service of the Church more than to act a lie against what it proclaims and by perpetuating division within itself to blaspheme the blood of Christ shed to make men at one with God and at one with each other? What is demanded of the Church by Christ is that it should serve the divine mercy in the actualities of physical and spiritual existence where the bounds of human life break up under the divisive forces of evil, and that instead of allowing the divisions of the world to penetrate back into the life of the Church, to make it equivocal and futile, it should live out in the midst of a broken and divided humanity the reconciled life of the one unbroken Body of Jesus Christ—that is *diakonia*.

Until the Christian Church heals within itself the division between the service of Christ clothed with his gospel and the service of Christ clothed with the need and affliction of men, and until it translates its communion in the body and blood of Christ into the unity of its own historical existence in the flesh, it can hardly expect the world to believe, for its *diakonia* would lack elemental integrity. But *diakonia* in which believing active intercession, bold unashamed witness, and the reconciled life are all restored in the mission of the Church will surely be the service with which Jesus Christ is well pleased, for that is the *diakonia* which he has commanded of us and which he has appointed as the mirror through which he reflects before the world his own image in the form of a Servant.

CHAPTER 7

The Church in the Last Quarter of the Twentieth Century[1]

WHAT WILL THE LAST quarter of the twentieth century be like? How will the Church of Christ fare in it? How is the Church of Scotland to fulfil its mission within it?

Many people today seem to take for granted that the future will be dominated by Marxism, or even by some form of Communism. They see ahead a state of affairs in which, under pressure from economic forces from below, there will increasingly take place organized control of our social life through State legislation. Certainly not a few seem to have capitulated to what they consider the inevitability of that kind of take-over, and have been trying to adjust their expectations to fit in with it. I do not say that this is always deliberate, for often they are just caught up half-thinkingly in the stream of prevailing trends, and yet, on the whole, the Churches seem bent on adapting themselves to the ceaseless onrush of socio-political change, under the naive impression that this is the 'progressive' or 'enlightened' thing to do, and that neither preaching nor theology can be relevant unless it is 'politically involved.' Infecting this outlook seems to be a milder and more subtle form of the Marxist fallacy that religion is the opium of the people, namely, the idea that the less people think of the other-world, the more they will love their

---

1. Address by TF as Moderator, at the close of the Church of Scotland General Assembly, 1976.

neighbours—which, of course, is the exact opposite of the teaching of Jesus. But there have also taken the field today militant 'theologies of liberation' which have assimilated the prophetic passion of Jewish messianism and the revolutionary nature and impetus of the Christian message to Marxist ideology. They presuppose a Marxist interpretation of history as the outcome of class conflicts leading through an inner necessity to a future in which all human miseries will be eliminated, for they believe that Karl Marx has uncovered the fundamental 'laws of motion' governing society, and thereby turned the understanding of our social problems the right way up. But all this does involve, admittedly, a causal interpretation of human affairs and a materialist framework for all human ideals, while the kind of utopia which it holds out ultimately relies for its fulfilment on violence.

I believe that such an alliance of Christianity with Marxism is a grave mistake, for any socialization or materialization of the Church's message along these lines can only empty it of its biblical and evangelical content, as well as undermine the freedoms to which traditional Christianity has given rise. There is no possibility along that road of transmuting human society into a community of love, for Marxism has no gospel of salvation from man's self-centredness and greed, but can only clamp down upon human life the enslaving structures of group egoism. But even apart from that, I believe that Marxism has no real future. Let me offer two broad reasons for this conviction.

(1) The great advances we have been making in fundamental science have steadily been destroying the foundations of Marxism in the obsolete ideas of a closed mechanistic universe and the hard instrumentalism that goes with it. The Marxist conception of the technological society is a product of the old positivist view of science, operating with causal mechanisms that it imposes upon every aspect of natural and human existence. But all this is now collapsing: an enormous revolution is taking place in the foundations of knowledge in which there is emerging a very different outlook upon the universe characterized by open structures, in which mechanistic concepts are found to have only a limited and low-level validity. The correlate of this new science is a freer and open society in which personal and social relations will be emancipated from the tyranny of impersonal forces. However, even apart

from the scientific destruction of Marxist premises, we find everywhere today a vast instinctive revolt against the imperialism of socio-political institutions, evident not least in the reaction of the young against social mechanization and establishment structures. But this kind of reaction has nothing constructive to offer, unlike what is now developing out of the new science.

Before I pass on to my second reason, let me say this: I do not believe that the Christian Church has anything to fear from the advance of science. Indeed the more truly scientific inquiry discloses the structures of the created world, the more at home we Christians ought to be in it, for this is the creation which came into being through the Word of God and in which that Word has been made flesh in Jesus Christ our Lord. The more I engage in dialogue with scientists and understand the implications of their startling discoveries, the more I find that, far from contradicting our fundamental beliefs, they open up the whole field for a deeper grasp of the Christian doctrines of creation, Incarnation, reconciliation, resurrection and not least the doctrine of the Holy Trinity. You will not be surprised, therefore, at my reaction to those theologians and churchmen who claim that in the space age we can no longer believe in the Incarnation of the Son of God or the bodily resurrection of Jesus; I can only regard them with sorrow and shame, since they do not seem to know what they are talking about and are only misleading the flock of Christ through their scepticism. On the contrary, this is an age in which we are being emancipated from the tyranny of a narrow-minded scientism, and in which true science and theology are thrown closely together in the service of God the Father Almighty, Maker of heaven and earth, and of all things visible and invisible.

(2) Now I come to my second reason why Marxism has no real future: the rise of an immense hunger for *spiritual realities* which will not be satisfied with merely technological or social reorganization of human affairs. Even science itself, as Michael Polanyi has shown us for many years, cannot do without transcendent grounds, for it perverts and destroys itself when it cuts itself off from spiritual reality and ultimate beliefs. Science has reached the boundary point where it realizes its own limits; hence it is positively dangerous, as Sir Bernard Lovell has shown in his recent Presidential Lecture to the British Association, to delude

ourselves with the idea that through natural science we have the only avenue to a true understanding of the universe. Scientists themselves are everywhere acknowledging the need to probe into a deeper dimension of the spirit, without which everything in the technological society is futile and meaningless.

Wherever we seem to look we find that human civilization is sick with its diet of materialism and secularism, and surging up from below is an unquenchable longing for otherworldly and divine resources. This is widely evident, as we have been hearing again in recent months, even in Russia. The very fact that the Soviet government has to use secret police and brute force to suppress the distribution of the Bible and the dissemination of the gospel is itself a mighty, unwilling tribute both to the power of Christianity and to a desire for spiritual life that will not be denied. In the Western world, this longing for spirituality sometimes takes bizarre, antinomian forms in what we call the counter-culture, but behind it all there is surely a desperate hunger for God, a craving for the bread of life. The human spirit has been made for communion with God and will not be stifled with social or institutional substitutes.

But, of course, the most startling fact of our times is the tide of pentecostalism which breaks through the confines of religious and ecclesiastical formalism and opens up a strange new world of experience with a transcendent reference. The most significant thing about it is its refusal to have anything to do with a distant, inactive deity, and its insistence that God is alive and dynamically at work through his Spirit in the personal and social life of believers, moving them towards Jesus Christ. But whether or not the charismatic movement as such breaks out among the Churches, undoubtedly a steady spiritual eruption is taking place, in which common people, bored and depressed by the incessant moral denunciations they hear all round them and frustrated by sermons lacking evangelical joy, clamour for the sheer, stark simplicity of Jesus, and the good news of the gospel of salvation he proclaimed.

I do not find the situation very different in Scotland. In the last few months many people have written or spoken to me of a deep hunger in people's hearts, a cry for spiritual help, a yearning for deeper faith in Christ, and a new desire for prayer. I believe a spiritual awakening is on the way and it is rising from the grassroots of the Church.

If we look into the last quarter of the twentieth century in the way I have been trying to do, we can see that the Church is faced with an unparalleled opportunity. The deep changes going on in our way of life which (in spite of outward appearances at the moment) lead to a free and open society, together with the recognition that human thought must be lifted on to a higher level of spiritual reality, even for the progress of science, give us a magnificent chance to hold up Jesus Christ before men and women in such a way that the gospel is allowed to exert its own transforming power in the depths of human culture, and thus shape the fundamental pattern of our social order. But this does mean that we must reach a profounder understanding of the essential mission of the Church, moving away from our ecclesiastical pragmatism and legalism, and bringing the great truths of Christ clothed with his gospel to bear directly upon the heart and soul of our people day by day, for it is there that the real battle for the future will be won. Tinkering about with the institutional structures of the Kirk will only affect superficial patterns of religious behaviour. We are in the midst of a serious spiritual crisis, and only a movement of a profoundly spiritual and evangelical nature can carry us forward to our great goal.

Now let me indicate something of the way in which I envisage this mission of the Church in our own land, by referring to the Early Church and to the Reformation.

(1) Surely the most impressive fact about the Early Church was the irrepressible, spontaneous outburst of Good News with which it exploded upon the ancient world in land after land. Its daily life throbbed with mission and expansion in such a way that every believer seemed to be a missionary. At least everyone was a witness, for to be a Christian and a witness to Christ were one and the same thing, so that it was the hallmark of a Christian that he was ready to pay the cost of witness and discipleship in martyrdom. There were no missionary societies in those days, there was no organized mission such as we know it, but everyone worthy of the name of Christ sealed upon him in baptism testified to Christ, and the gospel spread like a forest fire, until within three hundred years the civilized world was claimed for Christianity. There was no programme to commit all members of the Church to political involvement, and no attempt was made to carry through a programme

of social change, and yet society was profoundly transformed—the Christian Church proved to be most effective in changing the world by being faithful to its evangelical mandate.

What was the secret of it all? The Early Church had a divine message, and they really believed in it. I am not thinking here of the great doctrines of the Faith to which they gave such classical expression in the Creeds, so much as belief in the active intervention of God himself in our human life and structured existence in space and time. They could not get over the utterly staggering significance of the Incarnation, God manifest in the flesh, nor of the resurrection of Jesus Christ from the dead, leaving an empty tomb behind him, which knocked a gaping hole clean through all mundane religion and philosophy. This is the Creator himself at work in our human life and death, the Saviour of the world. And it was because they really believed in that kind of direct divine interaction with this world that meditation, worship, prayer, intercession occupied such an enormous place in the life of the Church—it was real interaction on their part with the living God himself. In addition to all this, the Early Church had a positive and theologically structured existence, which affected all its life and pervaded daily existence in home and school, in market and hippodrome, wherever the gospel took root in common life.

Such a Church with such a message was able to penetrate into the fabric of culture and society, and reshape them from within, and thus put a profound Christian stamp upon the very foundations of our western civilization. It was because the Church's message was free from ideological mixture, that it could create new situations in society and in the world in which the transforming power of the gospel left such an impact that all subsequent history has been affected.

Why not today? I believe that we are now confronted with such an opportunity as we have not had for many centuries, to carry out the same kind of mission. But if so, we must learn from the fact that the Early Church had a crystal clear message and really believed in its divine power. We have been so habituated to trying to fit in with the current patterns of society, obsessed with the idea that the message of the Church be *made* relevant, that what we actually do is to belittle the Christian message and imprison it in what is merely transient. I believe that whole procedure is now utterly bankrupt, and is to a large extent responsible for the fearful slump in our Church membership, over the last twenty years especially. What we need, and need desperately, is a profound renewal in the very springs of our faith in the *living God*: not some God so far removed from us that he does not answer prayer, not a God so inert that he does not interact with the world he has made, not some vague Deity behind the back of Jesus Christ, but the God who has come himself among us in his own mighty eternal being, and personally has to do with us in Christ crucified and risen as the Redeemer of the world. God has been using the chaotic forces of the modern world to plough up our culture and civilization, so that they are now ready in a new way to receive the message of the gospel and allow it to shape and direct our way of life. Of course, this is going to take a great deal of hard thought and work, but what is supremely required from all of us is really to believe again in Jesus Christ as the Incarnation of God, and in the transforming power of his passion and resurrection. We must rehabilitate the essential mission of the gospel in which through preaching and witness we hold up Jesus Christ as the Saviour of mankind. No Church that goes forth in the name of Christ like that, and is prepared to pay the cost of the implications of the gospel for our physical and social existence, can fail to achieve today what the Early Church achieved in its own centuries. And that is what I am sure the Church of Scotland can do and will do in the days and years ahead.

(2) With the *Reformation* we have another great period in the history of the Church in which there was an irrepressible, spontaneous outburst of the gospel, the good news of God's unconditional grace and forgiveness, which proved to be evangelical and social dynamite in country after country, including our own. Arising out of research into the original sources of the Church, its apostolic foundation in Christ, there took place a massive rediscovery of the centrality of Christ, and that evoked a movement to bring the Church back into conformity to him, and thus restore the face of the ancient Catholic Church, as John Calvin put it. Somehow the institutional Church through its alliance with worldly power had come to usurp the place of Christ, and the voice of the Church seemed louder than the voice of God. In contrast, the great emphasis of the Reformers was upon the mighty living Word of

God, which is no mere word, but the Word-Act of God, still operating through his Spirit in saving, transforming power. That is the aspect of the Reformation to which I wish to refer now.

I had a vivid experience of what this meant when I was a young student in Greece. I had set out to climb Mount Olympus, and at the end of the first stage lodged at a small Monastery on the lower slopes. That evening as I sat by the stream outside the Monastery reading my Greek New Testament, an aged monk, bent with the years, came to sit beside me. When he saw what I was reading, he became very excited. Apparently he had never held a New Testament in his hands before—all they had in the chapel was a lectionary. And so I gave him my copy and he tucked it away in the folds of his cassock like a treasure. On my return from the top I stayed at the Monastery again, and down by the stream I found my friend the monk absorbed in the Gospels. A light shone out of his eyes, which I shall never forget. He was so utterly changed that he seemed even physically transfigured.

It was a spiritual renewal of that kind on a vast scale that happened in the sixteenth century when the living Word and Spirit of God transformed the face of Europe. It is a recovery of that Reformation experience of God's Word, which we need if we are to meet the challenge presented by the opening structures of our way of life, and are to direct the tide of spiritual regeneration now going on. It was through the Word of God that the worlds came into being; it was through that Word incarnate in Jesus Christ that the powers of darkness were vanquished, and the barriers of the grave were torn away; and it will be through that same Word, read and heard in the Holy Scriptures and ministered faithfully, that Jesus Christ, clothed with the same Spirit by whose power he rose again from the dead, will surely transform our own life and society. But it does mean in the first instance a recovery of Bible reading throughout the Kirk and a renewal of the ministry as a proper instrument of the gospel. And by that I mean two things: we must recover both genuine preaching of the Word and genuine pastoral visitation.

May I be allowed to say that far too much of our preaching today seems to do little more than reflect prevailing trends in society, for often we preachers seem no more than servants of public opinion? We do not spend sufficient time in the study wrestling with the Word of God so that the content of our sermons tends to be boring and trivial, made up of scrappy ideas suggested by the public media, which leaves the human heart still hungry for the bread of life and the basic pattern of our social existence unchanged. I do not believe there is any other way to inject the creative truth and dynamism of the gospel into the stuff and fabric of our life than through faithful ministry of God's holy Word. If we fail here, we will not match up to the challenge that beckons us so excitingly. But it is no less important to minister that Word, as Calvin used to say, *privatim et domatim,* privately and from house to house, for it is there that we really minister the gospel to people as *persons,* and not as just functions of industry, or cogs in the machinery of trade union power, or pawns of the politicians. Humanity is made up of real people interlocked in deep personal connections, and it is there where birth, marriage and family, life and death are of the very substance of our existence that the gospel must be planted and allowed to grow, for it is deep in the human heart that we need to be redeemed and changed. How can we do that except by complementing proclamation of the Word from the pulpit by personal, pastoral ministry of the same Word in the home? I wish to stress this for two reasons: because genuine pastoral visitation has seen a disastrous decline in our midst, and because we seem to be allowing a secular psychology to replace spiritual counselling. I do not want to detract from the valuable help the ministry can derive from good psychologists, psychiatrists and sociologists, but I do object when all this is allowed to relegate into secondary importance, and even to replace, a distinctively Christian understanding of man; and some doctrine of self-fulfilment, or what a friend of mine calls 'auto-salvation,' replaces justification by the grace of God. I do not believe anything can be a substitute for the evangelical insight into human nature which a minister gains as he prays with people in their homes and directs them to Jesus Christ as they open their hearts to him; nor do I believe a minister can preach the gospel from the pulpit relevantly to his congregation unless he converses with them about spiritual realities in their homes. This is not a ministry that can be adequately fulfilled by one man on his own. Pastoral care of this sort must be shared with the eldership revitalized as a spiritual office. Even so, I believe, it is very difficult for a minister to be a shepherd to more than six hundred souls if he is to engage in pastoral care as he is commissioned to do by the great Shepherd of the Sheep.

Here I find myself rather disquieted by our recent policy in the Kirk regarding union and readjustment of Churches, and recuitment for the ministry. I realize that a considerable, tactical redeployment of our resources is needed, but how far, I ask myself, is this programme merely the rearguard action of a weary institution, and how far is it really the operation of the Church militant? Where is our vision when we are content with tailoring our mission to suit a depleted manpower, treating the ministry as a sort of ecclesiastical civil service to keep the institution going, when we ought to be sounding a trumpet call throughout the Kirk for a host of younger people to come forward for a ministry which will seriously undertake the mission of Christ to *all* the people of Scotland? Former students of mine in the ministry tell me there is a host of young people in our midst who are largely outside the Church, or often only half within it; they really believe in God and are desperate for spiritual guidance and clear convictions, but they recoil from the institutional Kirk because somehow its formalism and legalism get between them and Christ. This is a situation where direct personal and pastoral contact of the kind I have been speaking of has a considerable contribution to make. These are fine young people in whose hands the future of Christianity in the last quarter of the twentieth century may lie—and it would be fearful if we lost them. I believe that from generation to generation the Kirk relies more than anything else on the parish ministry. No doubt the concept of the parish needs modification through assimilation to that of the community, while the ministry also needs restructuring to give greater place to a shared or corporate ministry, and no doubt other forms of ministry have their proper role today, but even so nothing can replace the parish ministry as the staple ministry of the Church. If we can develop this once again as a vigorous ministry of the Word matching a revitalized proclamation of the gospel, I believe the Church of Scotland will be more than able to cope with the challenge of the times, for in that way it can turn the life of our people in a radically Christian direction,

I am full of hope for the future. Charged with a great heritage from the past, the Church of Scotland has a religious balance and a theological stability that are the envy of many. It has ample resources of mind and man-power waiting to be tapped for mission far beyond the bounds of its immediate membership, at home and abroad. My prayer is that God will pour out upon it such a measure of his Spirit that it may effectively fulfil its mission in our beloved land and at the same time serve the reconciliation and unification of all mankind in Christ the head of the new creation.

CHAPTER 8

God, Destiny, and Suffering[1]

I AM PARTICULARLY DELIGHTED to be here this evening to say a word of profound appreciation from the Church of Scotland for all the work that the E.M.M.S. has done through the years, both in helping to train doctors and in the actual work in the field. I would also take the opportunity to express my own personal gratitude to the E.M.M.S. I recall the first time I enjoyed the hospitality of the hospital in Nazareth in 1936 and again that same year when the now defunct hospital in Damascus looked after me when I had a bout of sandfly fever. So in many ways throughout the years I have a great debt to the E.M.M.S.

This evening I thought I would head my address "God, destiny, and suffering" and offer you some thoughts arising from my recent visit to the Middle East.

My reflections have centred largely on the enormous contrast between religious Jews and Muslim Arabs: two peoples with a profound sense of God and an equally profound sense of destiny in the will of God. For both of them, belief in God and their way of life are inextricably intertwined—and for Arabs, certainly, religion and politics are inseparably related as well. That also applies to Zionist Jews. What of the Christian Church, and the Christian Mission in that kind of context?

Everywhere I went from Turkey to Egypt I found a rising Islamic militancy. Here we see reborn the impulse to conquest that dates right

1. Address by TF to the annual meeting of the Edinburgh Medical Missionary Society in 1977, during his year as Moderator of the General Assembly.

back to Mohammed and has certainly had an enormous impact in the Middle East throughout the centuries, bringing in turn, of course, opposition from Christian countries in the Crusades, who sought to retard the Muslim advances upon the Holy Land and upon Europe.

Today we have, surprisingly, a new religious crusade: a very sharp missionary activity on the part of the Muslims that carries with it the old ruthless exclusiveness towards Christians in particular. In Turkey, I was very interested in the remnants of the Greek Orthodox Church, for in the last century and a half, hundreds of Greeks have been rubbed out and their churches destroyed. All we have left is a handful of Christians in that corner of Europe and yet they remain, bearing a Christian witness. Turkey is supposed to be a secular state but in spite of that, one senses very deeply a rising Islamic consciousness determined to assert itself in the old way. In Egypt I was told that non-Coptic Christians were unable to buy property or to build churches and a group of reformed Christian Arabs came asking me to help them find a church. This I was able to do through my contact with the Greek Orthodox Church and I hope it will result in a Greek Orthodox building being put at the disposal of the Presbyterian Arabs. Now the reason for this is simply that there is a strong sense of Islamic dominance in Egypt. No Moslem, for example, is by law allowed to become a Christian, unless he becomes a Copt. There is little doubt that the eight million Copts in Egypt preserve Egypt from becoming ruthlessly Islamic. The Muslim rulers have to rely upon the eight million Copts in order to maintain themselves and, therefore, their considerable deference to the Copts is not because they are Christians. The Copts are the original ancient inhabitants of Egypt and the Arabs were, after all, the invaders who took over the country. The respect for the Copts has increased as modern Egypt has become more and more aware of its ancient heritage as archaeologists unearth its hidden treasures.

The Arabs today have a sense of destiny that I do not find easy to understand, but it is rather 'predestinarian'; they feel that they are involved somehow in the 'will of Allah' and ultimately that it is this which will prevail. So their religion, their faith, and their activity have behind them a profound sense of destiny. Now it is that sense of destiny bound up with their way of life and their belief in God which inevitably conflicts very sharply with that of the Jews. They, too, have a deepening sense of destiny and of God, a sense that is considerably intensified with the return of the Jews to the Holy Land. The interrelation between the people and the land is a profoundly religious concept. For the Jews, in contrast to the traditional Islamic role, there is no room for empire beyond the bounds of historic Israel. Beyond what they consider as the historic boundaries of Israel the Jews do not want to expand or conquer other lands. They do want to secure the frontiers of Israel, yet they have actually been seeking to do that beyond some of the old boundaries of Israel from Dan to Beersheba. By and large, however, the relationship of the Jews to other faiths and other people does not involve the imperialism that one finds arising in Muslim countries. And here, one must contrast what goes on in Israel with what goes on, in let's say the Turkish area of Cyprus, where Christian places have been desecrated. In Cairo, the Anglican Cathedral is to be pulled down to make way for a motor road and a site has been designated for re-building, that will not be in the public eye. Another long established church, St. Andrews, is apparently also to be pulled down and turned into a bus garage, but we do not know whether an opportunity will be given to build a reformed church in Cairo in its place. That could hardly happen in Israel, as even in regard to mosques, the Israeli record is better than the record of the Muslim treatment of synagogues.

In Israel today, however, there is a new openness and an objectivity towards holy places and historic sites which are not present in places where Muslim consciousness is deepening and sharpening as in Libya. Jews and Arabs—I'm speaking here of Muslim, not Christian Arabs—both have a profound sense of the one God, a profound sense of destiny. The tensions between the two are somewhat impossible to resolve, yet they rest on grounds so fundamentally similar that again and again one thinks of this tension between Jews and Arabs as between brothers—brothers who are engaged in some sort of internecine conflict and struggle. It is in that context that Christian churches have to bear witness and fulfil their mission. How are they to do that? The fundamental question we have to raise with both of them is "Who is God? Is he the living God who exercises active control over peoples and destinies of nations?" We say to the Jews, "Who is this God that you seem to have found again in the Six-Day War when you said 'The Lord of Hosts is among us; this is not our doing but the Lord's doing.' Who is that God of active providence, and how does he relate to the problems of suffering and pain and destiny? Or is God immutable and impassible?" These are the questions that Muslims also have to raise and so do we Christians. It is with that kind of dialogue, whether we engage in medical missions or any other kind of mission, that we must bear witness to Christ and his Cross. But within the Christian Church we too must try to reach an understanding of and come to grips with the sense of destiny which in a different way Muslims and Jews have. This is the field of eschatology, the bearing of the Incarnation, passion, and resurrection and the advent of Christ on the destiny of humankind. It is in that context that we bear witness to Muslims and Jews alike and relate the Christian gospel to their sense of destiny and of God in their own history.

Let me now share with you three profound impressions arising from my visit to Israel.

1. The example set us by the Greek Orthodox Church in its witness and its tenacious adherence to Christianity throughout the centuries of Islamic oppression and persecution. Many Protestant Churches—the sects which move into the Holy Land—seem to think that the Orthodox are fair game for their evangelism, but this is a profound mistake. I believe that if it were not for the Orthodox Church the whole of the Middle East would long ago have been completely swamped by Islam and lost to the Christian faith. It is because the Orthodox have held on to their holy places and churches, held on to their witness in spite of the overwhelming odds of the Islamic world around them, that they have maintained a position whereby all Christendom has a continued concern and a continuing place in the Middle East. Today in Israel the holy places are opened up in an unparalleled way. Access is given to peoples of all races and faiths, even if they are agnostics and atheists or merely interested tourists, to visit the holy places. This provides an unparalleled opportunity to bear witness in the holy places to the historic faith of our Lord and Saviour, Jesus Christ. The Orthodox Church have suffered a good deal throughout the years when they have been forced to hold together, and, as it were, to shelter behind the walls of their monasteries and their churches because of the tide of Islam. They suffered a loss of

missionary impulse—but that is now changing. In Egypt, for example, the Greek Orthodox Church has been busy turning monks into theologians or missionaries, with the result that the Alexandrian Church has had considerable missionary success in different countries in Africa. And so we find the Orthodox emerging again as a powerful Christian force. I believe it is up to us in the Western Church to support them, to encourage them in their missionary enterprise and to stand by them in helping them to bear witness to all who visit the holy places by pointing them to the passion and resurrection of Jesus Christ.

The Orthodox have another lesson to teach us; they never sell any property; they hold on to it because they believe in looking far ahead to the day coming when property held in trust from God will be used again in the service of the gospel and the Church. We, alas, in the Protestant Churches, have retreated in the Middle East, giving up property. In Egypt, in Israel, in Syria and elsewhere, if we had held on to the property we once had, we would be able today to match the opportunities that are now upon us. The Orthodox, who have a long-term policy in Christian witness, have a great deal to teach us and I would to God that those of us who are concerned with work in the Middle East, would take a leaf out of their book, and at any rate co-operate with them.

2. The second thing I want to share with you is the experience I had of being taken around what is called *Yad Vashem*. Now that is a staggering place in Jerusalem; it is a documentary museum which provides pictorial and written evidence of the experiences of the Jews in Europe as they were sent into the concentration camps where six millions of them were ruthlessly and fearfully slaughtered and butchered. It is an immensely moving and overpowering experience; in fact, I could not linger too long on it. All the time there kept coming to me the question, "What is the relation of God to Dachau, Belsen, Auschwitz and all that abomination? What is the relation of the living God, the God in whom we believe, the God of history, of destiny, of providence to that terrible holocaust? If God remains utterly and completely detached from that, can we believe at all in such a God?" I noticed on a monument that they had erected outside the words, "In thy bloods, Live" . . . words taken from the liturgy of circumcision and taken from the 16th chapter of Ezekiel. Afterwards as I talked to the two Jewish guides that the Mayor

of Jerusalem had provided to take me around, I said "How do you relate God to all that?" and they said "What do you mean?" I said to them, "You believe in the living God," (and I was referring to their experience in the Six-day War) "that God is alive, that he is still with you, in the midst of you, in this Holy Land, watching over you; but if that is the living God, how do you relate him to the holocaust of six million Jews? How do you relate God to that abominable suffering, to that terrible wickedness, for unless you can relate God to that, what does he mean to you?" They were silent and then they said, "We have no answer." And so I pointed them to those words of the monument, "In thy bloods, Live," and said, "That's the blood of the Covenant cut into your flesh from generation to generation and the blood of the Covenant remembered annually in the Passover. That's the blood that speaks of the faithfulness of God who will not abandon you." But there is the blood of the New Covenant to which we must bear witness for there is only one answer to the unappeasable agony of human violence and suffering, God in the Cross of Christ.

I remember an unspeakable experience during the war in Italy. We had been driven into the ground for over a week, hammered day and night by shelling; when it ceased we emerged from cover and I went round to see the devastation. I found the most awful sight you could ever imagine; bits of bodies all over the place. As I scooped up the brains of a friend of mine and tried to gather the arms and flesh and bits of soldiers together to bury them, I kept saying to myself "I could not believe in God, were it not for Calvary," for Calvary tells me that God has not kept himself aloof from our pain, slaughter and hurt, but he has come into the midst of our guilt and agony to take it upon himself. Somehow in and through it all, he meets us and saves us. I believe that is what we have to say to our brethren the Jews. Unless you can relate God to pain and suffering and believe that *God suffers* with you, then there is no answer to the horror of *Yad Vashem*. Unless they can relate God to their suffering, there will be no way for Jews to find reconciliation with the Arabs or other peoples. Some Jews in a kibbutz said to me, "We have given up God because God abandoned us in the concentration camps of Europe." That haunted me all through Good Friday as the words "*Eloi, Eloi, lama sabachthani*" echoed in my ears: "My God, my God, why

God, Destiny, and Suffering

hast thou forsaken me?" It is that cry upon the Cross that can penetrate through the darkness to those Jews who have abandoned God, because they think God abandoned them. It is our duty to bear witness to them of the God of the Cross, in the face of their suffering. There is only one answer to their cry of dereliction; the incarnate God who suffered and rose again in Jesus Christ.

3. The third thing I would bring to you is the utter obscenity of division at the Cross of Christ. This was brought home to me acutely by another Israeli, the Mayor's best guide who took us round Jerusalem. We ended our tour at the Church of the Holy Sepulchre. I was staggered at what I found. I had not seen it before without the scaffolding; but here under Israeli protection, more has been done for the Church of the Holy Sepulchre than I had known previously. As we came away, the guide said to me, "Why are you Christians divided here at this holy place?" What a thing for a Jew to say to a Christian! At the site of Calvary Greeks and Latins and Copts and Ethiopians and Armenians all struggle for a due share in the Church of the Holy Sepulchre. They are so sharply divided that a Muslim family has to hold the key to the building! Christians fighting at the very place where Jesus Christ was crucified! How can we preach the gospel of Christ when we tolerate that kind of division in the heart of the Christian Church? My experience there at that holy place brought home to me, as I think nothing else, the obscenity of the division among Christians and Christian churches. If we are to bear witness to Christ to Muslims or Jews, we may do that only if we ourselves live out the gospel of reconciliation we preach. So long as we are divided, so long as we practice 'apartheid' between different churches, we are acting a lie against the very blood of Christ shed to make us one.

What of our Christian mission in this context? Two things: First, much deeper dialogue is needed than ever before between Jew and Muslim about God and suffering, about God and destiny, about God and the unappeasable agony and guilt of mankind. I believe that is the way we are being called to take. Twice over this year I have given a lecture to Christians and Jews in which I have discussed these questions. On each occasion it was the relation of God to suffering which opened up dialogue in question after question from our Jewish brethren. I believe that it is at this level that we must bear witness. Mushy

Christianity, even mushy evangelical Christianity of which there is far too much in certain parts of the Holy Land, doesn't cut much ice. True evangelical Christianity is concerned to bring the gospel into the depths of Israeli thought and Muslim thought and to confront them in the depths of their thought with the God who penetrates into, takes charge of, their destiny by the passion and resurrection of Christ. That alone will count in the end. But words are not enough. Christians have to act their concern for the pain and suffering of man, and this is where hospitals count so much. Let me say that everywhere I went in Israel, as years before in Transjordan and in Arab countries, I found immense respect for the work of the Church of Scotland and of the Edinburgh Medical Missionary Society through their hospitals. When I visited an Orthodox Kibbutz between Nazareth and Tiberias one of the leaders said to me, "My eldest son was delivered in the hospital in Tiberias by Dr. Walker." It was something which he had never forgotten. The new Mayor of Tiberias told me that he had been twice operated upon by Dr. Herbert Torrance and he could not speak highly enough of him. It is goodwill of that kind which has opened not only hearts but minds to Christian reflection and to Christian witness. Let us do that in the right way without trying to change Jews into Gentile Christians which they cannot become without betraying the God of Abraham, Isaac and Jacob. Rather let us show them how to become Jewish Christians, as we try to show Arabs how to become Arab Christians. We must beware of imposing our Western culture upon these people. That is what many Protestant churches do not understand; they seek to impose their ways of worship upon other people instead of allowing them to worship God in and through their own language and culture, and so really to worship God in the name of Jesus Christ as *their* Saviour and Lord. If we Christians act in this way toward Arabs and Jews, and at the same time act out in our own life and work what we believe to be the relation of God to suffering, and thus actualize the message of reconciliation, then I believe the door will be open for us in the Middle East in a way that has not been for centuries and centuries.

My overwhelming conviction coming away from the Middle East is that this is a time of unparalleled opportunity. But in face of that challenge what we need is Christian co-operation in which we make the best use of our material resources and our manpower. If we can co-operate in reconciliation with one another in word and act, if we can proclaim the gospel of healing and combine that with medical care, I believe we can do something which can go far to create a bridge between Israel and Jordan and thus lay the basis for peace throughout the whole of the area. We thank God for all the magnificent work that has been done in the past, for the doctors and nurses who have given their lives to medical missions in the Holy Land, but it is some time since we have matched that with an adequate theological dialogue such as used to be carried out by the Revd. S. Semple of the Scots College at Safed or the Revd. G. Sloan of Tiberias. We need ministers of that calibre today who can talk with Arabs and Jews at that level. If we can match that kind of witness in deep dialogue with medical work I believe that we will find the door opening even wider to the Christian Church, far beyond our expectation.

CHAPTER 9

Eldership in the Reformed Church[1]

THE INSTITUTION OF THE office of elder in the Reformed Church in the sixteenth century was an innovation in the traditional structure of the Western Catholic Church and the canonical pattern of its ministry. There were precedents for something like this in the Waldensian and Bohemian (later Moravian) Communities in the twelfth and fifteenth centuries, and there still are features corresponding to it in the leadership of congregational life in Greek Orthodox Churches arising out of the overlap between the worshipping congregation and the cultural community. In the Reformed Church itself the eldership came to be more closely associated with the ministry of Word and Sacrament which has had the effect of linking together 'clerical' and 'lay' service within the corporate priesthood of the Church and in the operation of its 'sacral courts' at synodal, presbyteral, and consistorial levels. The eldership has certainly been a source of inner cohesion and stability in the life of Reformed Churches, leaving upon them characteristics of particular significance in the ecumenical fellowship of Churches.

From the first, however, there have been semantic difficulties with the terms used to designate this office, especially with the English word 'elder,' and there have been persistent ambiguities and problems about the nature and function of the elder's office, not least over the question of explicit justification for it on grounds of biblical teaching and apostolic ordinance. These ambiguities and problems have not unnatu-

1. This was originally a booklet published by Handsel Press in 1984.

Eldership in the Reformed Church

rally come to the surface whenever Reformed Churches have entered into close contact with other Churches in the evangelical and catholic traditions alike. Without any definite or certain biblical evidence for it, and without any canonical precedent for it in the ancient Church, the eldership in Reformed Churches has regularly tended to develop features of its own within the different countries and cultures in which the Reformed Church has spread. In the ecumenical context of today, however, the Reformed Church is bound to take a fresh hard look at the nature and function of the eldership, if only on its own basic principle that it is not only an *ecclesia reformata* but an *ecclesia reformanda*, not just a reformed church but one always open to reformation in the light of what may still be learned from the Holy Scriptures and a deeper understanding of the Christian Faith. This is an obligation that the Reformed Church ought to feel more deeply than most Churches because of its claim that even matters of church order are *de fide*.

This essay is written from within the perspective of the Church of Scotland, and in the light of its historical roots and developments since the Reformation, as well as questions which debate about the eldership has been forcing into the open.

1. How Elders Came to be Introduced into the Reformed Church

During the Reformation and its extensive research into the history and life of the Early Church, evidence was found for the existence of *seniores plebis* or *seniores laici*, lay councillors or assessors, associated with the regular ministry. Questions about their function had been raised by Zwingli in Zurich and Bucer in Strasbourg, while careful investigation was initiated by Oecolampadius in Basel and pursued further by Peter Martyr in Oxford and by John Calvin in Geneva.[2] Attention was drawn to the note of Pseudo-Ambrose allegedly about two kinds of 'presbyter' in the Early Church, to the writings of Origen, Cyprian, Optatus, and Augustine, and later of Isidore of Seville, about *seniores/gerontes*

---

2. For Peter Martyr see *Loci Communes*, 4.1.11; and for John Calvin see the 1559 *Institute*, 4.3.8; 4.11.1, 6, 43; *Commentaries* on Rom 12:8; 1 Cor 12:28; and 1 Tim 5:17.

or 'elders' in the North African Church.³ *Seniores* were the men who were chosen or appointed to form the local councils of North African Communities, the *gerousiai* (as they were called in Greek), civil functionaries presiding over the affairs of the local community and helping to maintain public and moral order.⁴ With the spread of Christianity, however, these 'elders' were sometimes associated with the bishops, presbyters, and deacons and sometimes, as Optatus indicates, subdeacons, of the Christian Churches in superintending the *mores* of the people. There is no record in documents or the many extant inscriptions for their being called 'presbyters' (*presbyteri*).⁵

In their conviction that laymen, that is, people not ordained to the ministry of Word and Sacrament, should have part in the government of the Church, so far as moral and judicial questions were concerned, the Reformers of Geneva introduced the *seniores laici* of North Africa into local Church jurisdiction. In Geneva these 'seniors' or 'elders' were representatives of the City Councils who were associated with the ministers in keeping discipline. Together they constituted the 'Consistory' which comprised twelve members from the City Councils, elected annually, and six pastors, and was presided over by one of the syndics or magistrates.⁶ Their prime function was to act as judges in matters involving spiritual and moral discipline with authority to pronounce censure in the community, but without prejudice to civil jurisdiction. Calvin insisted, however, that councillors joined with ministers in this

---

3. For this appeal to patristic evidence, see Peter Cohn Campbell, *The Theory of Ruling Eldership* (Edinburgh: Blackwood, 1866), 6–12.

4. See especially, *Gesta apud Zenophilum* and *Acta purgationis Felicis*, in the Appendix to S. Optati Milevitani LIBRI VI, CSEL vol. XXI (Vienna: Tempsky, 1893), 187–204.

5. See Vitringa, *De Synagoga Vetere* (Franeker, the Netherlands: Gyzelaar, 1696), ii.3: "care was taken that they should not be called presbyters, lest any one should ignorantly confound them with the elders or presbyters mentioned in Scripture, but *seniores* and *gerontes*." And John Forbes, *Instructiones Historico-Theologicae de Doctrina Christiana, et vario rerum statu, ortisque erroribus et controversiis, jam inde a temporibus Apostolicis ad tempora usque seculi decimi-septimi priora*, (Amsterdam: Elzevirium, 1645), 16.1.17.

6. *Les Ordonnances Ecclesiastiques, Johannis Calvini Opera Selecta*, edited by P. Barth & W. Niesel, vol. II (Munich: Kaiser, 1952), 369f; and J. K. S. Reid, *Calvin: Theological Treatises* (Philadelphia: Westminster, 1954), 63f.

way must leave their batons outside the door where the Consistory met, for they could not exercise their civil authority in the public affairs of the Church. While they had to take an oath similar to that prescribed for ministers, they were not ordained or set apart in any way, and were never regarded as members of the *Presbyterium* which was comprised solely of ordained presbyters, the *Venerable Compagnie des Pasteurs*.

It should be pointed out that 'elders' appear elsewhere during the Reformation period, for example, among English exiles at Frankfurt who were evidently influenced by the teaching of Bucer and Martyr as well as Calvin. Moreover in France, where the Reformed Church did not have the kind of relation to the State found in Geneva, 'anciens' were not just civil functionaries associated with ministers in moral and judicial matters, but came to be more closely related to the worshipping and sacramental life of the Church.

During the Reformation in Scotland, 'elders,' initially taken from the Lords of the Congregation and the Burgh Councillors, were associated with ministers in the Church Courts, in Assembly, and in Synods, and in the General Session or Eldership which, at that time, was something between what we call a Kirk Session and a Presbytery. These elders were not ordained, but were called and admitted on an annual basis. Gradually, however, they came into closer connection with the work of the ordained ministry, and took over some of the functions which in Geneva were carried out by deacons: catechetical instruction of the young, visitation of the sick, and even the reading of prayers in the absence of the minister. It should be noted, however, that these Scottish elders did not take over the function of the deacons in Geneva in giving the chalice at the celebration of the Lord's Supper.[7]

In 1578 under the influence of Andrew Melville (and of Theodore Beza), the General Assembly gave its approval to a revision of the Polity of the Kirk, *The Second Book of Discipline*. It instructed, in contrast to what Calvin had taught, that elders were to be appointed, admitted and commissioned for life, which meant that their office was to be recognized as a fully 'spiritual' one for which they were set apart, though not by the laying on of hands. This was reinforced by the Act of the General

---

7. Steuart of Pardovan, *Collections*, I (Edinburgh: Edinburgh Printing Co., 1837) viii.3.

Assembly in 1582, which in session 12 laid down the order for the election and admission of elders, taking over for the whole Church the particular form used in the Presbytery of Edinburgh. Professor Gordon Donaldson has pointed out that it took some time for the impact of these acts of the Assembly to take effect, as there is evidence of annual elections of elders continuing to take place, while in 1656 it was still believed that the practice of the Church was regular elections.[8] However, together with the account given of the form and practice in 1641 by Alexander Henderson in *The Government and Order of the Church of Scotland*, written at the instruction of the General Assembly to guide the Scots divines at the Westminster Assembly, the Act of 1582 remains the most authoritative statement of the elder's office in the Church of Scotland. It may be pointed out here that in his account of the celebration of the Lord's Supper, Alexander Henderson provides us with early Assembly authority for the practice of the celebrating minister eating the bread and drinking the wine "first himself" before passing them on to the people to share among themselves, and also for the rule that the Elders are to "attend about the Table," not evidently to dispense the bread and wine, but to see that "all who are admitted to the Table, may have the bread and the wine in their own place and order of sitting."

Now when the Reformers in Strasbourg, Basel and Geneva found *seniores* in the North African Church they looked for *biblical* evidence for this, and claimed to find it in a number of passages: Rom 12:8; 1 Cor.12:28, and some of them, on occasion at least, e.g., Calvin with reference to Pseudo-Ambrose, in 1 Tim 5:17. John Knox's *Book of Common Order* referred to Rom 12, 1 Cor 12, and Eph 4, but not to 1 Tim 5:17; the *Second Book of Discipline*, however, did make use of 1 Tim 5:17. The position taken up by Calvin was clearly ambiguous, for while his interpretation of 1 Tim 5:17 appeared to sanction the theory that elders were presbyters, he did not embody it in the constitution of the Genevan Church, for he refused to entertain the idea that elders might be admitted to the Presbytery or that they should join with ministers in

---

8. G. Donaldson, *Scottish Reformation* (Cambridge: Cambridge University Press, 1960; cited from 1972 ed.), 222; cf. W. R. Foster *The Church Before the Covenants* (Edinburgh: Scottish Academic Press, 1975), 69, and W. Makey, *The Church of the Covenant 1637-1651* (Edinburgh: Donald, 1979), 125-27.

acts of ordination by the laying on of hands. However, once the views of Beza and Melville about the ministry were taken up in the *Second Book of Discipline* regarding "Presbyter or Eldar" and "Presbyters or Seniors,"[9] they had the effect of continuing to fuel the theory that 'elder' and 'presbyter' meant the same thing.

All this came up for careful and detailed examination at *The Westminster Assembly* as the Scots, among others, wanted to have elders adopted in all the Churches in the British Isles.[10] Eventually the Westminster Assembly rejected 1 Tim. 5:17 as having any reference to 'elders', and thereby also rejected the specious theory (as Campbell called it) that there were two kinds of 'presbyter' in the Early Church. They did so on the authority of the great Hebrew and Judaic scholars of the Reformed Church, Buxdorf Blondel and Vitringa, as well as of the equally great scholars in the Assembly, Lightfoot and Selden. The Assembly referred instead to 2 Chr 19:8f., Rom 12:7f., and 1 Cor 12:28. Two significant points emerged in the Westminster discussion that should be noted. (a) 'Elders' could be read into these New Testament passages only on the assumption that the early Church had instituted something analogous to the 'elders of the people' (*seniores plebis*) found in the Old Testament; and (b) the Church officials that they called 'other Church governors,' as even George Gillespie admitted, probably corresponded to 'deacons' in the Early Church.

It must be affirmed that the Westminster Assembly decidedly rejected the use of the term 'presbyter' for the elder, and always spoke of elders as "other Church governors," "elders of the people," or "commonly called elders." Against that one must take account of the fact that in the 1611 Authorised Version of the Bible *presbyteroi* was frequently translated "elders." This may help to explain why in the Church of Scotland the reference in Acts 15:23 to "the Apostles and Elders (*presbyteroi*)" could be cited in justification for 'ruling elders,' although the Westminster Divines, like the Reformers, rightly understood the term *presbyteroi* there very differently. Thus the tendency to speak of the elder as 'presbyter' persisted, and along with it the theory that there were two kinds

---

9. *Second Book of Discipline*, 11.6 & IV.

10. See the account of the debate given by Campbell, *Theory of Ruling Eldership*, 32ff.

of presbyter or elder in the Early Church, a teaching presbyter or elder and a ruling presbyter or elder, but both evidently of the same order. This implied that elders should take part in the ordaining of ministers and in the ordaining of elders, which ran sharply against the Reformed (and Westminster) doctrine of the Ministry of Word and Sacrament, as held in the Church of Scotland.

It was inevitable that in Scotland, as in the U.S.A., the theory of 'the ruling elder' would prove troublesome and indeed that the whole concept of the eldership should be reopened. That is what happened in the nineteenth century after the publication in 1831 of the book by Samuel Miller of Princeton on *The Ruling Elder*. The case for the theory that ministers and elders were both 'presbyters,' differing only in respect of their particular functions, was now subjected to a thorough examination, if only because it was held to have associations with 'Brownist' or 'Congregationalist' notions of the Church and Ministry. In the USA this theory of the eldership was demolished by Smyth of Charleston and Hodge of Princeton with immense learning, but the same thing was done much more lucidly and succinctly by Peter John Campbell of Aberdeen, to name only one of those who entered the debate.

Clearly the *biblical grounds* for the conception of elders in the Reformed Church had to be examined more thoroughly than before. As a result Reformed scholars found themselves forced more and more to the conclusion that there is no clear evidence in the New Testament for what we call 'elders,' let alone the theory that there are two kinds of presbyter. The biblical passages to which appeal is made, when objectively considered, cannot be taken to bear the interpretation Presbyterians put upon them. Moreover, they were never understood in this sense by any of the Church Fathers, not even by Pseudo-Ambrose who did not make use of 1 Tim 5:17 in the way that was sometimes alleged. It is also the case that outside Presbyterian Churches, there is no Church that interprets the New Testament passages adduced by them in this way. Hence Presbyterians are isolated from the rest of Christendom past and present in claiming that these biblical texts provide evidence for 'elders' in their sense. The conclusion seems inescapable: Presbyterians adduced this 'biblical evidence' in order to have some authoritative justification for an eldership they found, not within the New Testament itself, but within certain sections of the fourth-/fifth-century North African Church. And yet even there, as we have noted, there is no evidence that these 'elders' were ever called 'presbyters.'

Even if the Church were to follow Calvin and the Westminster Divines (different as they were) in their approach to the eldership, it would still not be possible for it to do more than get biblical evidence for some office similar to that of the Old Testament 'elders of the people' who served in communities of Israel in a civil capacity and thereby shared with the religious leaders responsibility for governing the public life of the people of God. Calvin himself, however, never advanced biblical evidence for what we call 'elders,' but only, and then very tentatively, for what he called 'elders.' He was definitely not a *Presbyterian*! In Scotland, with the Melvillean revolution, the Church embarked upon a course in which it was to substitute *elders*, set apart for life, in place of Calvin's *deacons*, transferring to them the functions ascribed to deacons in the New Testament, and detailed by Calvin in his description of their office in the Early Church, while restricting the functions of deacons in the Church of Scotland mainly to the gathering and distributing of the alms of the congregation in its social care of the needy. Perhaps we may put a better gloss on this departure from Calvin's model by claiming that actually our 'elders' are the nearest thing in any Church today to what the Pastoral Epistles speak of as 'deacons.'[11] However, the fact that our elders are called 'elders' and not 'deacons' means that they cannot draw support from what the New Testament has to say about deacons, and are thus unable to find in the New Testament any description of their specific office as elders. Consequently they can only turn to *Presbyterian tradition* rather than to Holy Scripture for any guidance in the fulfilment of their duties.

2. The Relation of Elders to the Diaconate

It seems to be clear that in the New Testament there is no evidence that can stand up to objective criticism for the title 'elder' used in our

---

11. Cf. *A Manual of Church Doctrine according to the Church of Scotland*, by H. J. Wotherspoon and J. M. Kirkpatrick, revised and enlarged by T. F. Torrance and Ronald Selby Wright (London: Oxford University Press, 1960), 99ff.

way. This does not mean that there are no biblical grounds at all for the kind of office that we refer to under the eldership. It would seem to be entirely consistent with biblical teaching that there should be associated with those specifically ordained to the ministry of the Word and Sacrament others who are 'ordained' to a complementary ministry within the congregational life and activity of God's people. This second use of the term 'ordained' (now in common vogue) has been put in citation marks in order to avoid ambiguity, for ordination in the proper sense, normally and traditionally, carries with it the notion of "the power of order" or *potestas ordinis*, as the *Second Book of Discipline*, I.3f. speaks of it. In the Church of Scotland elders have never been regarded as invested with "the power of order," even for the 'ordination' of other elders, for their distinctive ministry is not the service of the Word but the service of response to the Word.[12] Its distinctive *mode* is not one of 'authority' but one 'of charity', as the sixteenth century Scottish divines expressed it.[13] While ministers are ordained to dispense the Word and Sacraments to the people, elders are set apart to help the people in their reception of the Word and in their participation in the Sacraments, and to seek the fruit of the gospel in the faith and life of the community. Elders are meant to *represent* the people, and to fulfil their ministry from the people toward God. Thus their specific calling is to help the faithful *from* within their midst, prompting them in their responses to the gospel proclaimed to them, leading them in their worship, assisting them in their understanding of the faith, and guiding them in the way of obedience to Christ's commandment of love. To take elders out of that relationship and assimilate them to the order of ministers of Word and Sacrament would have the effect of damaging the two-way movement of service in Christ's Church, from God to man and from man to God, and thus doing away with the complementary functions within the

---

12. *Second Book of Discipline*, 1.6.5: "As the Pastors and Doctors should be diligent in Teiching and sawing the Seid of the Word, so the Elders should be cairful in seiking the Fruit of the same in the People."

13. See, for example, George Gillespie, *An Assertion of the Government of the Church of Scotland in the Points of Ruling-Elders, and of the Authority of Presbyteries and Synods*, (Edinburgh,1641), 14ff.

Eldership in the Reformed Church

corporate pattern of ministry which the introduction of elders in the Reformed Church promoted.[14]

In accordance with the nature of their office elders are set apart or 'ordained' for service in the Church, that is, "solemnly received with lifted up hands."[15] Stress is laid upon the rule that elders are commissioned or 'ordained' only by those who are themselves ordained and commissioned, that is, not by the people, but by those who are called and sent by Christ with authority to act in his name and, in a significant sense, in his stead, as St. Paul expressed it.[16] Although elders may be elected by the people and are their representatives within the corporate ministry of the Church, they are not to be regarded as their delegates, carrying the power of the people and answerable to them. It is by Christ through ministers in his Church that they are commissioned and it is to him that they are answerable. In the view of Reformed or of Presbyterian Churches 'the power of order' is not lodged with the people, and devolved by them upon ministers and other office-bearers in the Church. Power is lodged only in Christ and is devolved by him through those he calls and authorizes to act in his name, yet only in "the form of a servant" in accordance with the example which he gave to his disciples. A clear distinction was drawn in ordination between the 'immediate' act of Christ through his Spirit and his 'mediate' act through the Pastors of the Church. That is to say, the Lord Jesus Christ was regarded as the real Ordinary in the Church: all power and authority

---

14. For the theology that lies behind this diaconal/complementary form of ministry, see 'Service in Jesus Christ', my contribution to *Service in Christ: Essays Presented to Karl Barth on his 80th Birthday*, edited by James I. McCord and T. H. L. Parker (1966. Reprint. Wipf & Stock, 2009), 1–16.

15. Thus A. Henderson, *The Government and Order of the Church of Scotland* (Edinburugh: Bryson, 1641), 1.111. 'Ordain' was the term intruded by G. Gillespie, *An Assertion of the Government of the Church of Scotland*, 15, and is found in Steuart of Pardovan's *Collections*, (edition of 1773), I.VII.4.

16. For ordination of ministers, see *Sec. Bk. of Disc.*, 11.6; T. Smeaton, *Orth. Resp.*, 107; Henderson, *The Government and Order of the Church of Scotland*, 1.1; *Form of Presbyterian Church Government. and Ordination*; cf. Samuel Rutherford, *The Due Right of Presbyteries* (London: Griffin, 1644), 1, 86f; George Gillespie, A *Miscellany of Questions* (Edinburgh: Lithgovv, 1649), 63f.

derive immediately and mediately from Christ himself acting through his Spirit in the Church.[17]

It cannot be claimed that this conception of the eldership prevails in all Reformed or Presbyterian Churches, or that it is held consistently in any one of them. Even in Scotland actual practice through several centuries is found by historians (e.g., Gordon Donaldson) not infrequently to diverge from the formal positions laid down in the Kirk's authoritative standards. Moreover, in the nineteenth century there was a growing reaction against the hard line Melvillean and Westminster authoritarian conception of the ministry, reinforced by Acts of the General Assembly against 'Brownism' or 'Independency.' This was partly due to the demand for a Christ-centred rather than a Church-centred form of Christianity, but due also in no small measure to the general pressure for democratization within the Church. There was so much uncertainty in regard to these matters in the latter part of the nineteenth century that *The Presbyterian Alliance* instituted an investigation of the practice and procedure of Presbyterian Churches adhering to it. It was found that Samuel Miller's notion of the eldership had gained ground in some Churches to such an extent that elders sometimes engaged in acts of ordination, not only of elders but even of ministers. Nevertheless this practice was not found to have been sanctioned by any Church law in any of the Presbyterian Churches adhering to the Alliance at the time of the investigation. Undoubtedly since then there has been some symbiosis between many Presbyterian and Congregational Churches which has allowed some of them to be united, mainly, it must be admitted, on the ground of Reformed principles, although in some instances with a significant recovery of the biblical and early Christian conception of the diaconate. This is a symbiosis that will undoubtedly continue with the formation of *The World Alliance of Reformed Churches*, which includes Churches of the Congregationalist as well as of the Presbyterian type.

The kind of ministry exercised by elders in the Reformed Church does not seem to be inconsistent with the outlook we find in the New Testament, but there is no *explicit* evidence for the eldership as such.

---

17. Cf. Samuel Rutherford, *A Peaceable and Temperate Plea for Paul's Presbyterie in Scotland*, (London: Bartlet, 1642), 2ff; Rutherford, *The Due right of Presbyteries*, 206f; and Gillespie, *A Miscellany of Questions*, 40f.

On the other hand, the nature of the office elders hold and the kind of functions they perform bear a close resemblance to the office and functions of the *deacon* described in the Pastoral Epistles and early Church documents.[18] There we learn that deacons fulfilled an important assistant ministry in the Church in association with bishops and presbyters, and had particularly to do with ministry of the divine mercy and with seeking the fruit of it in the life and mission of the community, and that they assisted presbyters or bishops in serving communicants at the Lord's Supper. Thus it would seem to be the case that our elders now fulfil a ministry that in the New Testament itself is ascribed to deacons. In other words, the best, and indeed the only, biblical evidence for the ministry fulfilled by our elders is found in New Testament teaching about deacons, supplemented by what we learn from Early Church documents. Consider, for example, the Epistle to the Philippians 1:1, in which St. Paul mentions only "bishops and deacons." Are we to include 'elders' here under 'bishops' or under 'deacons'? That is the issue, and when faced with it, Reformed commentators have regularly 'included them under 'deacons.' It might be said, then, that what we call 'elders' are really 'elder-deacons'.[19] This falls closely in line with what a great scholar like J. N. D. Kelly has to say about deacons in his commentary, *The Pastoral Epistles*. Of course, the actual name of the office, 'elder,' or 'deacon,' does not finally matter very much, so long as the nature and integrity of the office itself is maintained. But it would seem right for a Church which claims to be reformed according to the Word of God, and to be continuously open to further reformation in the light of what is learned from that Word, that it should subordinate its own ecclesiological tradition to the holy Scriptures, and in name and office put into practice the New Testament teaching about the diaconate.

---

18. For Calvin's view of the diaconate see J. K. S. Reid, "*Diakonia* in the Thought of Calvin," *Service in Christ*, edited by J. I. McCord and T. H. L. Parker, 101–9, (London: Epworth, 1960).

19. It is not surprising that Steuart of Pardovan could claim that "the office of Deacon is included in the office of a Ruling Elder," *Collections*, VI.2. cf. *A Manual of Church Doctrine according to the Church of Scotland* (London: Oxford University Press, 1960), 80ff, 99ff.

Given this substantial relation between the Reformed elder and the biblical and early Christian deacon, there are two significant implications that should be noted.

(a) The eldership in the Reformed Church, like the diaconate in the Early Church, is essentially a sacramental office closely associated with the celebration and administration of the Lord's Supper or Eucharist. Thus it has long been a primary function of Scottish elders, meeting as a Kirk Session, to join corporately with the presiding minister at the celebration of Holy Communion, rather after the pattern set by Jesus and his disciples at their last celebration of the Passover together, when he solemnly inaugurated the new covenant in his body and blood, thereby instituting the Holy Supper in the Church. In the early centuries deacons acted as *ministerial assistants* to presbyters and/or bishops.[20] They were given an important part in the regular liturgy of the Church, such as in reading the Scripture, prompting the responses and leading the praise, while also assisting in a subsidiary way at the celebration of the Eucharist, but also exercised a stewardship over the gifts that were brought to it for the *Agape* or 'Love-feast.' Hence deacons were charged with the distribution of goods and alms to the poor, as well as with assisting the presiding presbyter or bishop in taking Communion from the central celebration to house-churches within the *paroichia* or "diocese." This association of elders and deacons with the celebration of the Lord's Supper would seem to argue for an integration of their duties in the Church of Scotland. Moreover, it would have the effect of recovering something of the wholeness of their office and of reinforcing the fact that it is essentially *spiritual*. In their own distinctive way elder-deacons are "stewards of the mysteries of God" in the life and mission of Christ's Church.

(b) The fact that the ministry in the Church is essentially corporate with a two-fold activity as 'service of the Word' and as 'service of response to the Word,' argues that our elder-deacons, like deacons in the Early Church, should be regarded as members of the *cleros*, no less than presbyters. It might be claimed, as it was by Clement of Rome (1 Clem. 40), that they have a status within the Church of Christ similar to that of the Levites in the Church of Old Testament who had the Lord himself

---

20. See Forbes, *Instr. Hist.-Theol.*, I.XVI. 1, 21–22.

as their peculiar "allotment" or "inheritance" (Deut 18:2; cf. Acts 1:17), even though they did not belong to the priesthood as such.[21] That is to say, while elder-deacons are not to be regarded as included within the order of those ordained to the ministry of Word and Sacrament, nevertheless they are to be regarded among those who have been solemnly set apart and sanctified for holy office within the corporate priesthood of the Church.[22]

3. The *Diakonia* of The Acts of the Apostles, Chapter 6

How are we to understand the office of "the seven men" appointed and ordained by the apostles to a *diakonia* in the infant Church, as recorded by St. Luke in the 6th chapter of the Acts of the Apostles? This was a matter debated in several Councils of the Early Church, when it was eventually concluded that the incident referred to the institution, not of deacons, but of presbyters in the local community of Hellenistic Jews who had come to believe in Christ, whose function it was in the ministry (*diakonia*) to proclaim the Word, minister the Sacraments, and have the pastoral care of the needy.

When the Church in Jerusalem became too large for the twelve disciples themselves to look after as pastors of the flock, they decided to appoint others to carry out the duties of local ministry, and to devote themselves as apostles to *the Word*, for which they had been specially trained and commissioned by the Lord. They felt themselves uniquely called to provide the Church with the authoritative understanding of Christ and his gospel which the Lord meant the Church to have and which he mediated to it through the apostles—that is what we now have in the Scriptures of the New Testament in which we receive from the apostolic foundation of the Church and through the apostolic tradition the 'deposit' of the faith once delivered to the Saints.

---

21. The Westminster Assembly employed a similar analogy with reference to 2 Chr 19:8–10, in support of those "commonly called Elders": *The Form of Church Government*, "Other Church-Governors."

22. Evidently *seniores plebis* in North Africa, while not *cleri*, could yet be included with them under *ecclesiastici viri*: Gesta apud Zenophilum, Appendix to the works of Optatus, (see note 4 above), 189.

John Lightfoot, the learned Westminster Divine, once drew attention to a very significant reference in Acts 1:15, where we are told that the company of persons in the first assembly of disciples numbered about *a hundred and twenty*.[23] It would appear that the Primitive Church took care to act within the provisions of Jewish law later recorded in the *Mishnah* tractate *Sanhedrin*,[24] a Rabbinic codification of earlier material (*mishnayot*) not infrequently reflected in the New Testament. There we find it laid down that if a community is one hundred and twenty strong it is entitled to have its own little "sanhedrin of seven," appointed through "the laying on of the elders' hands," to exercise oversight over its affairs.[25] That was the legal ruling which the apostles seem to have followed when they laid their hands on seven chosen men, giving them authority to have charge of the local congregation of converted Hellenistic Jews (traditionally separated from Palestinian Jews even in their synagogues). Thus Acts 6 gives us a record of the first community within the rapidly growing Church to have its own ministers. They were those who elsewhere in the New Testament were called "presbyters," not "deacons," although they also seem to have performed functions that were later assigned specifically to deacons.

By way of support for this interpretation of "the seven men" in Acts 6, we may point to the fact that in Rome Jewish synagogues were organized on the *Sanhedrin* model of small communities of worshippers of a hundred and twenty, each with its own "seven,"[26] and that in formal assembly these elders or presbyters, including the *archisynagogos* or "ruler of the Synagogue," were "arranged like the half of a round threshing-floor so that they might all see one another," as we find it

---

23. *The Works of the Reverend and Learned John Lightfoot*, D.D., vol. 1, revised edition (London, 1684), 276 and 279.

24. *Sanhedrin* 1.6; cf. also Babylonian *Talmud, Megillah*, IV.l; Josephus, *Antiquities*, IV.viii.14, 38, and *Jewish War*, II.xx.5.

25. See T. M. Lindsay, *The Church and the Ministry in the Early Centuries* (London: Hodder, 1902), 115ff; W. Lockton, *Divers Orders of Ministers* (London: Longmans, 1930), 22ff; and D. Daube, *The New Testament and Rabbinic Judaism* (London: Athlone, 1956), 237f.

26. Cf. E. Schürer, *A History of the Jewish People in the Time of Christ*. 5 vols. (1885–86. Reprint. Peabody, MA: Hendrickson, 1994) 11.11, 247f.

Eldership in the Reformed Church

laid down in the Mishnah.[27] It is particularly interesting that Christian congregations in first century Rome also followed the same pattern, as we can see so vividly in the Catacomb paintings of the celebration of the Eucharist. The most well known of these, of course, is the Catacomb of Aquila and Priscilla where the seven presbyters (including Priscilla as a *presbytera*!) are depicted in a semi-circle behind the Holy Table with Aquila in the centre as their *proestos* or presiding presbyter-bishop, and the deacons in front with the baskets of offerings. Optatus tells us that even in the fourth century there were more than forty little congregations or churches in Rome, although they were united through the *una cathedra* of Peter the *apostolorum caput*.[28] In Alexandria, on the other hand, where in the first century there was by far the largest concentration of Jews outside Judaea, more than a million of them, the model followed was that laid down for large communities outside Jerusalem who might have twenty-three "elders" or *zekenim* plus their presiding officer, presumably the *Sagan*.[29] It is hardly surprising, then, that in Alexandria the Christian church should have been organized on much the same pattern, with a large presbytery of twenty-four presbyters (twelve from the urban and twelve from the surrounding areas) including their presiding (*proistamenos*) presbyter or bishop.

It might be instructive also to refer to the contrast drawn in the Mishnah *Sanhedrin* between lesser Sanhedrin and the great Sanhedrin in Jerusalem, which numbered seventy *zekenim* (or *presbyteroi*) plus the presiding High Priest and/or the *Sagan*. A similar contrast would seem to be implied in the New Testament between local communities within the Christian Church and the mother community in Jerusalem which, as we know more fully from outside the New Testament, came to have a Christian *Sanhedrin* of seventy presbyters presided over by St. James, our Lord's brother (cf. Acts 15:13; 21:18, etc.).[30] As T. M. Lindsay

---

27. The *Mishnah*, English ed. by Herbert Danby (Oxford: Oxford University Press, 1933), 4.3.

28. LIBRI VII, 2.4, CSEL edition, p. 39; cf. 1.10, p. 12f.

29. See Schuerer, *History of the Jewish People*, 11.11, pp. 55ff, 70ff, 227ff.

30. See R. H. Connolly, *Didascalia Apostolorum* (Oxford: Clarendon, 1929); and F. F. Bruce, *Men and Movements in the Primitive Church* (1980. Reprint. Milton Keynes: Paternoster, 2006), ch. 3 on "James and the Church of Jerusalem," 86ff.

pointed out,[31] James and his presbytery, who had charge over the mother Church in Jerusalem and Judaea, formed a body quite distinct from that of the twelve apostles who were 'ministers at large' having authority over the whole universal Church in accordance with our Lord's solemn appointment recorded by the Evangelists, in Matt 19:28 and Luke 22:29f. It should also be noted that there is an implied contrast between the ordination of the seven presbyters in Acts 6 through the laying on of hands, and the commissioning of the twelve disciples as apostles by Christ, not by the laying on of his hands but by his direct appointment in which he solemnly entrusted them with judicial authority in his Kingdom, as the passages already cited from St. Matthew and St. Luke make clear. This contrast between the commissioning of the apostles immediately by our Lord and the ordination of presbyters through the laying of hands, distinguished presbyters and all other ministers in the Church sharply from the apostles to whom there could be no successors.

It should be emphasized that the use of the word *diakonia* here by St. Luke does not lend any justification to the view that "the seven" in Acts 6 (as even Calvin mistakenly thought) were "deacons." The term refers not to any particular office, but rather to the unique nature and mode of ministry in Christ's Church as a *humble form of service*.[32] *Diakonia* applies to all forms of ministry, of Word and Sacrament as exercised by presbyters or bishops, as well as to the complementary ministry fulfilled by deacons. Even the ministry of the apostles was regarded as a *diakonia* (see, for example, Acts 1:17; 6:1, 4), after the pattern of Christ himself who came "not to be served but to serve" (Mark 10:45; Matt. 20:28; cf. Luke 22:26). It was thus that St. Ignatius of Antioch could point to the ministry of deacons (*diakonoi*) as exhibiting in the most vivid Christ-like way the unique mode of humble ministry which Christ himself, the *Diakonos par excellence*, had exercised on earth and instituted in his Church.

It would appear that whenever in the history of the Church Acts 6 has been adduced to support the institution of deacons, confusion has resulted: problems have arisen which have proved difficult to disentangle. This has certainly been the case whenever Reformed Churchmen

---

31. Lindsay, *Church and the Ministry in the Early Centuries*, 118ff.
32. Cf. again McCord and Parker, eds. *Service in Christ*, 1–9, and 13f.

have wanted to limit the diaconate to the ministry of alms and at the same time find in Acts 6 authority for the diaconate, in spite of the fact that the seven spoken of there were not called "deacons." The ministry of "tables" mentioned there cannot be interpreted as a ministry of 'banks,' that is, a ministry in monetary matters, but rather as a *diakonia* in the distribution of goods from the Lord's Table which presupposes a complex practice in which the Lord's Supper and the Love-feast, the Eucharist and the Agape, and the evangelical mission of the Church, were closely bound together. In the Early Church this *leitourgia* was continued for several centuries in the regular worship and mission of the people of God: while the bishop and his presbyters presided at the Table of the Lord, the deacons, after fulfilling their part in the Eucharistic celebration, distributed to the poor gifts that had been offered at the Lord's Table.

So far as deacons themselves are concerned, there was never any suggestion in the New Testament or in the Early Church that their office was restricted to the ministry of alms and social care. Yet that is what the Church of Scotland unfortunately came to hold, when it transferred many of the functions of deacons to elders. Those functions became distorted in the process. The eldership as such was left without biblical support as an evangelical office, while room was made for deacons only in a very attenuated form. This is largely, I believe, why the diaconate thus conceived has constantly given ground for so much confusion and why it has been so difficult to resurrect and maintain in its wholeness within the Church of Scotland. Much of that confusion might be done away if we frankly acknowledge that we have misread the Holy Scriptures through the distorting lenses of a Presbyterian tradition. It is imperative that we set about once again to reform our church polity in accordance with the revealed Word of God. That should not entail a rejection of the rich tradition of service fulfilled by the Reformed eldership which has often been admired in other Communions, but rather that the eldership, assimilated to the biblical and early Christian diaconate, would recover something of its wholeness as an essentially spiritual and evangelical *diakonia*, taking its distinctive character from the gospel of the Lord Jesus Christ which it is meant to serve. So far as the Church of Scotland is concerned, this would have the much-needed effect of deepening mutuality and complementarity between the *presbyteral* ministry of the Word and Sacrament and the diaconal ministry of shared obedience to Christ. It would also mean that elder-deacons would exercise a more central ministry in the responses of God's worshipping people, in leading their praise and thanksgiving, in guiding their intercession and witness, and in the translation of their love to God into a living liturgy of service in the depths of human need. Such a reformation in the office of the elder-deacon within the Reformed Church might then even play a modest ecumenical role in prompting fuller recovery of the biblical and early Christian pattern of *diakonia* in other Churches as well.

CHAPTER 10

The Ministry of Women[1]

I

IN ONE OF THE earliest of the Catacomb paintings in Rome in the *Capella Greca*, within a century after the death and resurrection of Christ, there is a remarkable mural depicting the breaking of bread at the celebration of the Eucharist. Seven presbyters are seated in a semi-circle behind the Holy Table, assisted by several deacons. This is known as the "Catacomb of Priscilla," for Priscilla is seated to the right of the presiding presbyter (presumably her husband Aquila), the *proestos* or bishop, and is actively engaged with him in the Eucharistic rite. There are two points about this painting on which I would like to comment.

The first has to do with the number seven. In the great Temple Synagogue in Jerusalem there was a Sanhedrin of seventy-one elders (*zekenim*) or presbyters together with its president or *sagan*. What of the smaller synagogues in the communities outside Jerusalem or in the *diaspora*? According to the *Mishnah* tractate *Sanhedrin* it was laid down that a large Jewish community might have twenty-three elders, presumably plus its president, making twenty-four in all, but if a community were 120 strong it was allowed to have its 'seven' elders, which would normally be presided over by an *Archisynagogos*, such as Jairus or Crispus of whom we read in the New Testament. *Sanhedrin* tells us that these presbyters were to be arranged "like the half of a round

1. A booklet published by the Handsel Press in 1992.

threshing floor so that they all might see one another." It was thus in accordance with the regulations of Jewish law that at Alexandria, where there were well over a million Jews in the first century, the local sanhedrin numbered twenty-three or twenty-four, while at Rome the Jewish community, which was differently distributed, was served by a number of smaller synagogues each with its sanhedrin of seven elders.

Regarded in this light, the fact that the number of disciples, who with Peter formed the original Christian community in Jerusalem, was numbered about 120 (Acts 1:15), is rather significant. It helps us to understand why shortly afterwards the Twelve Apostles appointed specifically seven disciples (presumably as 'presbyters' not 'deacons' as is usually held) to serve the needs of the primitive Church in Jerusalem, while they gave themselves over "to prayer and the ministry of the Word" in fulfilment of their universal apostolic ministry. We also learn, however, that in due course with the growth of its membership the Jerusalem Church came to have a Christian sanhedrin of seventy presbyters, probably in line with the seventy disciples sent out by Jesus on the mission of the Kingdom mentioned by St Luke (10:1, 17), but again in accordance with Jewish regulations, presided over by James, not the Apostle but the brother of our Lord.

It is not surprising, then, that in Alexandria the Church had twenty four presbyters, twelve for the city and twelve for rural districts around the city, presided over by one of their number whom they elected and consecrated as bishop. Nor is it surprising that in Rome, on the other hand, as we learn from Optatus,[2] there were at least forty small churches, which evidently had their due number of presbyters after the pattern of the Jewish communities in Rome, but with bishops rather than rulers of the synagogue as their presidents. Incidentally this helps to explain why 'monepiscopacy'—having a single bishop—was comparatively late in developing in Rome and why Clement acted as the chosen spokesman for all the churches in Rome to those beyond. It is in the *Capella Greca* that we are given a vivid glimpse into the assembly of one of these small congregations of believers meeting in the catacombs with their seven presbyters, Aquila and Priscilla and five others, arranged in a semi-circle "like the half of a round threshing-floor." Moreover, the Jewish as

---

2. *Libri VI, CSEL, XXI*, pp. 187–204

The Ministry of Women

well as the Christian character of this Eucharistic celebration, together with its very early date, is accentuated by a rough Hebrew inscription in the foreground.

The second point about this wall-painting to which I wish to draw attention is that a woman is presented as concelebrating with men at the breaking of bread. Priscilla (or Prisca) is a *presbytera* officiating along with *presbyteroi* in the central act of the worship of the Church. At first sight this is rather startling in view of the statements of St. Paul: "As in all the churches of the saints the women should keep silence in the churches. For they are not permitted to speak, but should be subordinate, as even the law says. If there is anything they desire to know, let them ask their husbands at home. For it is shameful for a woman to speak in church" (1 Cor 14:33–35). If our Jewish friends are right, what St. Paul has in view here relates to the customary arrangement of synagogues in which women, who usually occupied seats apart from, or overlooking the main area, were forbidden to chatter or otherwise interrupt the conduct of worship. That may well be how we are to regard St. Paul's injunctions here. Otherwise the passage is rather difficult to understand, since in an earlier chapter in the same Epistle it is assumed that women do pray and prophesy aloud in church—although it is made clear that when they do so they must have their heads covered, if only out of respect for their husbands' authority over them (1 Cor 11:31). Thus it would appear that the Apostle has no objection to women praying or prophesying in church provided that they wear a fitting cover over their heads. In the same Epistle (1 Cor 16:19) he refers to the church in the house of Aquila and Prisca in which it is hardly likely that Prisca kept silent!

Another passage from St. Paul's First Letter to Timothy must also be considered: "Let a woman learn in silence with all submissiveness. I permit no woman to teach or to have authority over men; she is to keep silent" (1 Tim 2:11–12). Here women are explicitly enjoined not to talk (*lalein*), but also not to teach (*didaskein*) in public, and perhaps also not even to teach their husbands in private! This hardly accords with the way some Jews interpret the passage just cited from First Corinthians, but whatever it means it must surely be understood in accordance with the activity of Prisca in Ephesus, as recorded by St. Luke, when along with Aquila, she expounded the way of God more accurately to Apollos (Acts 18:26). It is hardly surprising, then, that St. Paul applies to her along with Aquila the term "fellow-worker" (*synergos*) which he used to refer to people associated with him in the ministry of the gospel like Timothy (Rom 16:3, 21—cf. also 1 Tim 3:2; 1 Cor 3:9), or Clement (Phil 4:3), or Mark and Luke (Phlm 24).

One must also recall how St. Paul mentioned in a similar way women such as Nympha—like Priscilla she had a church in her house (Col 4:15)—or Junia, his female relative, to whom he referred as a noted apostle (Rom 16:7). Reference should be made as well to the four virgin daughters of Philip the Evangelist who were spoken of as endowed with the gift of prophecy, that is, with the gift of proclaiming the gospel as well as foretelling events. In his own list of those endowed by the ascended Lord with gifts for the ministry St. Paul put apostles first, prophets second, evangelists third, followed by pastors and teachers (Eph 4:11). That order gives some indication of the way in which the great apostle to the Gentiles regarded the ministry of women like his kinswoman Junia and the daughters of Philip. St. Paul also speaks of women as holding the office of deaconess (1 Tim 3:11), with explicit mention of Phoebe in the church at Cenchrea (Rom 16:1), with which should be associated the order of 'widows' who were not ordained but held a place of honour in the apostolic Church in fulfilling a ministry of prayer and intercession (1 Tim 5:3–16).

All this must be taken fully into account in reaching any balanced understanding of what St. Paul meant in the two passages commonly adduced by those who oppose the ordination of women in the ministry of the gospel. When we consider all that is recorded in the New Testament in this regard, it is rather difficult, to say the least, to accept the idea that there is no biblical evidence for the ministry of women in the Church. It also helps us to understand why the early Christians, who were hounded to death in the Catacombs of Rome for their fidelity to the gospel and the normative tradition of the apostles, should have left the Church with such a definite depiction of the place of a woman presbyter at the celebration of the Lord's Supper.

The office of deaconess was developed in the early centuries of the Catholic Church, appointed through the laying on of hands by the bish-

The Ministry of Women

op (*Apostolic Constitutions,* 3:15), but there is no canonical record of any office of woman presbyters. There were evidently no women serving with men in councils of "elders of the people" (*seniores plebis*) in the North African Church who, although not reckoned among the clergy (*cleri*), assisted bishops, presbyters, and deacons in the public life of the local community. Mention is sometimes made of elderly women who exercised a prominent role in the worship of a congregation, known as *presbytides*, but, as Epiphanius insisted, they were not to be regarded as female presbyters or priestesses (*Haereses*, 79:4). Attempts were obviously made by authorities in the Early Church to play down the New Testament evidence for women in the ministry, apparent in alterations introduced into the Greek text of St. Paul's references to Junia and Nympha, which were changed to Junias and Nymphas, thereby making them out to be men! However, in spite of this depreciation of the female sex widely found in the Mediterranean Church, there were strange exceptions to the canonical restriction of clerical office to women. For instance, in a mosaic still extant in the Church of *Santa Praseda* in Rome, built by Pascal I toward the end of the ninth century in honour of four holy women, one of whom was his mother Theodora, we can still read around her head in bold letters THEODORA EPISCOPA! And so we have papal authority for a woman bishop and an acknowledgement by the Pope that he himself was the son of a woman bishop! The word *episcopa* was evidently used at times to refer to the wife of a bishop, as *presbytera* was sometimes used (and still is in Greece) to refer to the wife of a presbyter, but that does not seem to have been the case in this instance.

It is, of course, the case throughout the general history of the Church in East and West, and until recently in Protestant Churches as well, that tradition regularly restricted the priesthood or ordained ministry to men, but that was done on grounds of ecclesiastical convention and canonical authority. Appeal has also been made to dominical authority for, as we learn in the Gospels, our Lord appointed only men to be his disciples and apostles, which was in line with traditional Jewish convention. These men, of course, were all Jews, so that it must be asked whether the Church departed from the example and authority of Christ when it appointed Gentiles to be presbyters and bishops. The point is, as

St. Paul himself wrote to the Galatians, a radical change had come about with Christ, for in him there is neither Jew nor Greek, there is neither slave nor free, there is neither male nor female, for you all are one in Christ Jesus (Gal 3:28). This means that in Christ there is no intrinsic reason or *theological* ground for the exclusion of women, any more than of Greeks or Gentiles, from the holy ministry, for the old divisions in the fallen world have been overcome in Christ and in his body the Church. That applies to the division between male and female just as much as it does to the division between Jew and Gentile, or between slave and free.

II

In modern times it has been argued that only a man can represent Christ in the celebration of the Eucharist, for it is only a man who can be an *ikon* of Christ at the altar. To back up this claim reference is often made to the Pauline statement that man ought not to cover his head, since he is the image and glory of God, but woman is the glory of man, for man was not made from woman but woman from man (1 Cor 11:7-8). Appeal is also made to St. Augustine's interpretation of these words offered by way of a comment upon what is written in Genesis: God created man in his own image, in the image of God created he them; male and female created he them (Gen 1:27).

This means, St. Augustine once claimed, that while man and woman together are in the image of God, woman on her own, considered apart from her character as a helpmeet for man, is not in the image of God. Man may be in the image of God apart from woman, but not woman apart from man (*De Trin.* 12.7.10—contrast St Basil, *De con. hom., Or.,* l.22f., and Didymus, *De Trin.* 2:7)! If that were the case, the mother of Jesus considered in herself as a virgin could not have been said to be in the image of God!

This is a quite offensive notion of womankind that conflicts directly with the truth that in Christ Jesus there is neither male nor female; it even contradicts Augustine's own statement in the same passage that "human nature is complete only in both sexes!" And it conflicts directly with our Lord's teaching that in the beginning God made man male and female in such a way that what he has joined together may not be put asunder (Matt 19:4f.; Mark 10:6f.). It thus conflicts with the biblical and orthodox teaching that woman as well as man was made in the image of God, and may therefore be said to an *ikon* of God as well as man. And, of course, it also conflicts with the orthodox understanding of the Incarnation as the saving assumption of the whole human being, male and female, and as the healing of our complete human nature. This must surely be understood as involving the healing of any divisive relation between male and female due to the curse imposed upon them at the fall (Gen 3:16), while sanctifying the distinction between them. It thus rejects any manichaeistic denigration of the female sex (and St. Augustine, it should be remembered, was a Manichee for nine years before his conversion).

Moreover, the fact that the Son of God became man through being conceived by the Holy Spirit and being born of the Virgin Mary, that is, not of the will of the flesh nor of the will of a human father, but of God (John 1:13), means that at this decisive point in the Incarnation the distinctive place and function of man as male human being was set aside.

Thus, as Karl Barth pointed out, in the virgin birth of Jesus by grace alone, without any previous sexual union between man and woman, there is contained a judgment upon man.[3] This certainly implies a judgment upon the sinful, not the natural, element in sexual life, but it is also to be understood as a judgment upon any claim that human nature has an innate capacity for God; human nature has no property in virtue of which man may act in the place of God. Moreover, the sovereign act of God in the virgin birth of Jesus carries with it not only a rejection of the sovereignty of man over his own life, but a rescinding of the domination of man over woman that resulted from the fall (Gen 3:16). Thus any preeminence of the male sex or any vaunted superiority of man over woman was decisively set aside at the very inauguration of the new creation brought about by the Incarnation. In Jesus Christ the order of redemption has intersected the order of creation and set it upon a new basis altogether. Henceforth the full equality of man and woman is a divine ordinance that applies to all the behaviour and activity of the

---

3. Karl Barth, *Church Dogmatics. Vol. 1. Part 2. The Doctrine of the Word of God*. Translated by G. W. Bromiley. Edited by G. W. Bromiley and T. F. Torrance (Edinburgh: T. & T. Clark, 1957), 188ff.

"new man" in Christ, and so to the entire life and mission of the Church as the Body of Christ in the world.

In thinking and speaking of the Incarnation it is important for us to keep close to the biblical witness that in becoming man (i.e., *anthropos*, not *aner*—*homo*, not *vir*) the Word was made flesh, not just male flesh. All human flesh was assumed in Christ, the Son of God, the Creator Word become man, so that now all men and women alike live and move and have their being in him. We must not forget that our Lord regularly identified himself as "Son of Man" (*ho huios tou anthropou*), which clearly had divine and final import, as Jesus acknowledged before the high priest (Mark 14:62). The being of Jesus, the Son of the Virgin Mary, was not just male being but divine-human being with universal import as the Saviour of all humankind. This is not, of course, to deny that he was physically a male, but to hold that the human nature of Jesus as Son of Mary was taken up into and united with his divine nature in one indivisible personal reality—it is as such that he was and is the incarnate Son of God.

Hence it would be a grave biblical and theological mistake to bracket the Incarnation with the gender or sex of Jesus in such a way that everything in his incarnate life and work depended on his maleness, for that would seriously call in question the salvation of female human being and detract from the Incarnation as the assumption of complete human being and the redemptive recapitulation (*anakephalaiosis*) in Christ of the whole human race of men and women. After all, the Greek term for Incarnation adopted by orthodox Christian theology from the beginning, in line with the biblical witness, was *enanthropesis*, i.e., inhomination.

It should be noted that the Pauline argument about the first Adam and the last Adam in the redemption of mankind does not have to do specifically with Adam as a male but with *Adam* as the one made from the ground, *adamah* in Hebrew, and so in Hebrew *Adam* means "earthling," just as our word "human" derives from the Latin *humus* meaning "soil." This is reflected in St. Paul's statement: The first man is from earth (*choikos*, of the dust), the second man is the Lord from heaven (1 Cor 15:47). That is to say, the argument of St. Paul about the saving recapitulation and renewing of the whole human race in Christ the last Adam has to do with the first Adam as "human being," and not just with the maleness of Adam in contrast to the femaleness of Eve (as elaborated rather fancifully in patristic typology), and with the second Adam, while certainly a human being and historically a male, as man "from heaven." The first Adam was not generated (*gennomenos*) like other human beings but brought into existence (*genomenos*) by a creative act of God from the earth as a human being to be the beginning of the human race, and the second Adam so far as his flesh was concerned was brought into existence (*genomenos*) by a creative act of God to be the beginning of the renewed human race—but in contrast to the first Adam he was man from heaven. The new humanity is not begotten through Christ as a male, but brought into existence by the downright act of God from heaven, and it is in him that the whole human race is gathered up and redeemed by him as Lord and Saviour. The maleness of Jesus just does not enter into the argument.

In view of this soteriological nature of the Incarnation, it is understandable and highly significant that the Augustinian conception of man apart from woman was never employed, to my knowledge, in any official council of the universal Church, as a theological reason for the claim that only a male human being may image or represent Christ at the altar (but cf. statements in *Didascalia Apostolorum* 15, or *Apostolic Constitutions* 3.6.1f. to which appeal is sometimes made). This strange pseudo-theological idea is a modem innovation evidently put forward by some rather reactionary churchmen in the nineteenth century, but has recently been revived as a convenient (although specious) argument for the exclusion of women from ordination to the holy ministry, and has been made to look ancient by being cast in the terms that only a man can be an *ikon* of Christ at the altar (a misuse of 1 Cor 11:7 which applies only to relations in the order of creation).

What happens here is that an old ecclesiastical convention is being put forward quite wrongly as a *theological truth* or a *dogma* of the Apostolic and Catholic Church. Hence I believe that Dr. George Carey, the new Archbishop of Canterbury, was quite right in his assertion that the idea that only a male can represent the Lord Jesus Christ at the Eucharist is a serious *theological error*. He was not declaring that those churches and churchmen who reject the ordination of women, because it conflicts with a convention long sanctioned by catholic tradition or canonical authority, are to be judged heretics, but asserting that it is a very grave mistake for anyone to convert such a convention, no matter how strongly enforced by catholic tradition, into a dogma or an intrinsic truth of the Christian faith.

I would also add that it is a serious epistemological error (often denounced by the great theologians of the early Church) to confuse what may be held on conventional grounds (*thesei*) to be the case with what must be held on true on real grounds (*physei*).

Basic to this whole discussion is the theological use of creaturely terms and images taken from God's self-revelation to humankind in the Holy Scriptures. 'Image' is surely to be understood in a strictly *relational* sense in accordance with the Old Testament teaching that God has created human beings (i.e., man and woman) for fellowship with himself in such a way that, in spite of the utter difference between them as Creator and creatures, human beings are made after the image and likeness of God. The Latin translation "*ad imaginem Dei*" is quite right, for it does not mean that the image of God inheres in man's nature, far less in male or female nature, as such, but that it is a *donum superadditum*, a gift wholly contingent upon the free grace of God—that is why St. Athanasius used to refer to the "the image of God" as "the grace of the image" (*he kat'eikona charis*, e.g., *De Inc.* 12). Hence we are not to think that men and women through creaturely human nature, by virtue of some intrinsic analogy of being, reflect God's uncreated nature, but that they are specifically destined by grace to live in faithful response to the purpose and movement of God's love toward them as his creaturely partners, and thereby to live and act in personal conformity to what God reveals of himself to humankind through his Word.

In making himself known to human beings God certainly communicates with them in human forms of thought and speech, so that there is necessarily an anthropomorphic ingredient or coefficient in his revelation which is very evident in the Holy Scriptures. Nevertheless God makes his self-revelation shine through all anthropomorphic forms of thought and speech in such a way that under the transforming impact of his Word they are not opaque distorting media, but become transparent forms through which his divine Word and Truth are conveyed to us.

That is why in the mediation of his self-revelation through the Hebrew Scriptures of the Old Testament which are replete with dramatic imagery, there is a persistent denunciation of all images of God conceived by the human heart, whether conceptual or physical, as forms of idolatry. And that is why there is built into the self-revelation of God an absolute rejection of all naturalizing of religion, typified by the worship of *Baalim* and *Astaroth* with its heathen projection of creaturely sex, male and female, into God.

The proper understanding of 'image' was a crucial issue that cropped up in the fourth-century Church in the debates between Nicene theologians and heretical Arians about the way in which they were to think of Christ as the image of God and of themselves as conformed to his image. Stress was laid by the Church Fathers upon the fact that since God is Spirit (John 4:24), all the language used of God in biblical revelation and in Christian theology must be interpreted in a wholly spiritual, personal, and genderless manner, in accordance with God's intrinsic nature which infinitely transcends all human imaging or imagining. Thus any images taken from creaturely being such as 'father' and 'son' have to be understood in a diaphanous or 'see-through' way; they are to be used like lenses through which vision of truth make take place, and so in such a way that the creaturely relations they express in ordinary mundane usage are not projected into Deity. When used theologically they are forms of thought and speech that refer to truth independent of themselves, and are themselves to be understood in the light of that truth to which under the thrust of divine revelation they refer. In short, when used theologically, creaturely images in language about God have a referential, not a mimetic relation to the divine realities.

It is surely in this way that we are to think of 'father' and 'son,' as terms expressing creaturely images which divine revelation uses and adapts in using about God, and so as transformed terms which Christian theology is bound to use about God. It is only in and through 'father' and 'son' as they are appropriated and adapted by God for his self-revealing in accordance with who he really is, that we are to know him and think of him and worship him in spiritual ways that are true of him and worthy of him, without reading the creaturely relations and images in them back into his divine Nature.

It should be emphasized, then, that the understanding of the words 'father', 'son', 'spirit', 'deity', 'trinity', 'being', 'nature', etc. when used theologically of God may not be governed by the gender which by linguistic or cultural convention they have in this or that language, for sex belongs only to creatures and may not be read back into the being of God as Father. Moreover, since the Son and the Spirit are consubstantial with God the Father (that is, of one and the same being with him), they are likewise beyond sex in their being. This remains true of God the Son, even though as incarnate he is also the Son of Mary, for we cannot speak of his being begotten of the Father before all ages as true God of true God in sexual terms. Moreover, as we have noted, in becoming man it was complete human being and nature that he assumed for our salvation, not just male nature. In all these statements about God, 'father' and 'son', as theological terms and images harnessed to God's self-revelation in Christ, are transformed under the impact of his Word and Spirit and are to be understood *spiritually*, in accordance with the transcendent Nature of God who is Spirit (John 4:24) Just as the self-revelation of God as three persons, the Father, the Son and the Holy Spirit, transcends the category of number, so it transcends the category of sex or gender. Hence, as St. Paul has taught us, human fatherhood may not be used as a standard by which to judge divine Fatherhood, for it is only in the light of the divine Fatherhood that all other fatherhood is to be understood (Eph 3:14–15).

III

We turn back to our consideration of the place of men and women in the ministry. It should now be clear to us that when we are told that the Lord Jesus Christ is the image of the invisible God and that we are renewed in Christ after the image of the Creator (Col 1:15; 3:10), 'image' must be understood in a wholly spiritual and transparent way without the intrusion of material relations and properties such as sex. What are we to say, then, in view of this theological understanding of image, about the assertion that it is only a man or male human being who can image or represent Christ at the Eucharist? Fundamentally, that depends wholly on how we are to think of Christ himself as present at the Eucharist, and correspondingly of the way in which he is represented at the Eucharist by the celebrant. At the institution of the blessed sacrament of the Lord's Supper during the Passover celebration in the Upper Room on the night in which he was handed over, Jesus ministered himself to his disciples, giving them Communion in his own body and blood, which he did in his unique identity as the incarnate Son of God. Thus it is utterly unthinkable that the body and blood given to us by the Lord Jesus in our Communion with him is to be regarded as restricted to male body and blood, for it was the body and blood of *the Son of Man*, the bread which came down from heaven:

> Truly, truly, I say unto you, unless you eat the flesh of the Son of Man and drink his blood you have no life in you; he who eats my flesh and drinks my blood has eternal life, and I will raise him up at the last day. For my flesh is food indeed, and my blood is drink indeed. He who eats my flesh and drinks my blood, abides in me and I in him. As the living Father sent me, and I live because of the Father, so he who eats me will live because of me. (John 6:53–56)

That explanation of Eucharistic Communion was given by Jesus in the synagogue at Capernaum in anticipation of the Last Supper. And so when it actually took place in Jerusalem, as St. John tells us, Jesus ministered to the disciples as he who had come from God and went to God, and spoke to them at length of his oneness in being with God in terms of a mutual indwelling of the Father and the Son in one another.

The union of the disciples with Jesus through their communion with him was grounded in his own union with the Father. There the image of Jesus as male just did not come into the picture, for in the Supper Jesus was present in the midst of his disciples as the Son of Man clothed with the glory of the Father: in receiving him they received the Father who sent him. That is the real presence of the Christ, God incarnate, crucified, risen, and ascended, at every Eucharist: when the appointed celebrant on earth acts not in any representative capacity of his or her own, as male or female, but solely in the name of the Lord Jesus Christ who sent him or her, and only in virtue of his real presence as the unseen Celebrant who in his atoning love communicates himself to us as often as we eat the bread and drink the wine commanded us thus to do in remembrance of him: This is my body, this is my blood given for you. It is as High Priest and atoning sacrifice united indissolubly in his one person, that Jesus Christ comes among us and ministers himself to us in the celebration of the Eucharist, the Lamb of God who takes away the sins of the world and gives us his peace, the Saviour who presents us to the Father in union with himself as those whom he has redeemed and consecrated through his one eternal self-offering.

The general line of our response to the strange idea that it is only a man, or male human being, who can image Christ or represent Christ at the altar, which he himself is, should now be clear. However, three considerations in particular ought to be stressed.

(1) If the notion of image is retained, it must be a diaphanous image through which the reality to which the image is directed can show itself unhindered and unobscured. Since the ministerial celebrant acts in Christ's name, he does not and dare not obtrude himself or his sex into the celebration; he does not image Christ in the form of a transparent medium, which would obscure Christ by coming in between Christ and the communicants. At the Eucharist the minister or priest does not act in his own name or in respect of his own status as a male human being, but only in the name of Jesus Christ and in virtue of his incarnate significance as the one Mediator between God and human being.

It may help us here to recall what happened at the transfiguration of Jesus on the mount when a cloud overshadowed the disciples and a voice came out of the cloud, saying, "This is my beloved Son: hear him." When the disciples looked round they saw no man any more, save Jesus only with themselves. It is surely something similar, *mutatis mutandis*, that takes place at the Eucharist, when the celebrant is robed with the garments of office symbolically blotting his own human self and sex out of the picture so that Christ in his own self-presentation may be the sole focus of worship, unobscured by the opaque image of the celebrant, male or female. If the notion of image is used of the celebrant at all here at the Eucharist, it must be image, not in its picturing or mimetic sense, but in its referential sense in which the image points beyond itself altogether and in so doing retreats entirely out of the picture.

(2) The celebrant officiates at the Eucharist, not as a male or female human being, but as a *person* set apart and sanctified in Christ for this ministry. Christ himself presides at the Eucharist as he in whom human nature and divine nature are indissolubly united in his one *Person*. As we have seen, it was as man, not just as male, that the only-begotten Son of God became incarnate, and it was human nature in its completeness and not just male nature that he assumed and united to himself in his divine Person. Hence to claim that it is only a male who can represent Christ at the altar savours of a heretical Nestorian separation between human and divine nature in the one Person of Christ. Even St. Augustine, in spite of what he had written earlier in the *De Trinitate* about the image of God, finally insisted that while the Trinity himself is three persons, "*the image of the Trinity is one person*" (*De Trin.* 15.23.43). That is to say, if reference is to be made to the notion of image, it is strictly not as man or woman (or man and woman together) that is to be thought of, but man or woman as *person*. It should be remembered, however, that the concept of person, quite unknown in antiquity in Hebrew or Greek tradition, arose under the creative impact of the doctrines of Christ and the Trinity and takes its creaturely pattern from the uncreated relations between the three divine Persons who are the Triune God. This is a concept of person in which the relations between persons belong to what persons are, and is not the same as the modern psychological notion of personality in which the person is turned in upon himself or herself. Christ himself is Person in a unique sense, as personalizing Person, whereas we are persons in a dependent and creaturely way as personalized persons, who exist in inter-personal relations, which transcends the distinction between male and female.

It is person in that contingent relational sense that is the image of God, not male or female human being as such, which fits in very well with the biblical notion of the creation of man for fellowship with God, which we noted above. Hence, it should be argued here, that if Jesus Christ is present to us in the Eucharist as God and man in one indivisible *Person*, we should think of the celebrant acting in his name or representing him as a human *person*, not as a male or female human being, yet even so not in virtue of his or her own personal being but solely in virtue of his or her sacred commission to act in the name of the Lord Jesus Christ alone.

(3) Above all, however, we must take into account what the celebration of the Eucharist means, as the sacrament of the atoning self-sacrifice of Christ made in our place, on our behalf and in our stead, for that governs absolutely the way in which we must think of the celebrant as representing Christ at the altar. We must also remember, as Athanasius expressed it, that the Lord Jesus is both the dispenser and the receiver of God's gifts, who ministers the things of God to us and of us to God (*Con. Ar.* 3.39f.; 4.6J). In becoming man for us and our salvation, he became one of us and united us to himself, really becoming what we are in order to be ourselves in our place in his identity as very God and very man, in such a way that he acts for us and on our behalf in all our responses to God, even in our acts of belief and worship.

Thus we believe in God through sharing in Christ's vicarious faith or faithfulness toward him, and we worship God through sharing in Christ's vicarious prayer, worship, and adoration of the Father. In fact, in a very basic sense Christ Jesus is himself our worship and it is as such that he is actively present with us and in us at the Eucharist, as through him, with him and in him we are brought into such a communion with the Father through the Son and in the Spirit, that we are made to participate in the real presence of God to himself. It is strictly in accordance with this vicarious presence of Christ in the Eucharist that we must think of our part in its celebration whether as participants or celebrants. "Nothing in my hands I bring, simply to thy cross I cling." As participants we hold out empty hands at the altar or the holy table to receive the bread and wine, and by faith to partake of Christ's body and blood, for we bring to it no sacrifice or worship of our own, or if we do we let our worship and sacrifice be displaced and replaced by the sole sufficient sacrifice of Christ, and it is through him, with him, and in him alone that we worship the Father in the unity of the Holy Spirit.

It is not otherwise with the celebrant. At the Eucharist the celebrant ministers not in his own name, but in the name of Christ, acting through him, with him, and in him, and thus in such a way that he yields place to Christ, lets Christ take his place, never in such a way that he takes Christ's place or acts in his stead. That is how his representation of Christ is to be understood, through a personal and liturgical inversion of his/her own role with the role of Christ who is the real Celebrant. The rule of John the Baptist must apply supremely here: "He must increase, but I must decrease" (John 3:30).

If we speak of this celebration in terms of Eucharistic sacrifice, as I believe we should, answering sacramentally to the one atoning vicarious sacrifice of Christ himself on the Cross, it must be asked how we offer a sacrifice, even sacramentally, which by its essential nature is one offered on our behalf, in our place and in our stead. The substitutionary as well as the representative nature of the atoning sacrifice must be kept fully in view throughout when, pleading Christ's eternal sacrifice, we set forth the *anamnesis* (remembrance) of it, which we are commanded to make. That is a Eucharistic sacrifice in which we may not combine any sacrifice of our own with the atoning sacrifice of Christ, and into which we may not obtrude anything of ourselves or seek to harness it with what we are and do; that would be to sin against the unique unrepeatable and completely sufficient nature of the sacrifice of Christ on the Cross. However, in view of this representative and substitutionary nature of the sacrifice of Christ, to insist that only a man, or a male, can rightly celebrate the Eucharist on the ground that only a male can represent Christ, would be to sin against the blood of Christ, for it would discount the substitutionary aspect of the atonement. At the altar the minister or priest acts faithfully in the name of Christ, the incarnate Saviour, only as he lets himself be displaced by Christ, and so fulfils his proper ministerial representation of Christ at the Eucharist in the form of a relation "not I but Christ," in which his own self, let alone his male nature, does not come into the reckoning at all. In the very act of celebration his own self is, as it were, withdrawn from the scene.

It is surely, partly at least, for that reason, that the celebrant wears vestments (which have no reference to his sex), for he does not act in his own significance, or in his own name but only in the name of God, the Father, the Son and the Holy Spirit. It is rather in the office or 'persona' with which he is clothed to act in Christ's name that the representation of Christ is to be recognized, not in the self of the celebrant, and certainly not in his male nature. It is actually the unseen Christ who in the real presence of his divine-human Person ministers at the Eucharist, not the person of the presbyter or bishop as such except in the name of Christ, and then only in a humble, self-effacing way. Hence the celebrant is not to be regarded as a sacrificing priest who repeats the atoning sacrifice of Christ, even though in an 'unbloody' form, but is only one who serves the Eucharistic proclamation of Christ's full, perfect and sufficient, all-prevailing sacrifice, offered once for all. It is upon Christ our ascended high priest that the Father looks and only on the celebrating on earth as found in him. Thus, however we look at it, to insist that man, precisely as man or as male, alone is able to represent Christ, would amount to a serious intrusion of male self-consciousness and assumed preeminence into our understanding of the priestly office of Christ, and would be tantamount to some form of psychological sacerdotalism and Eucharistic Pelagianism.

We conclude that in spite of long-held ecclesiastical convention, there are no intrinsic theological reasons why women should not be ordained to the holy ministry of Word and Sacrament; rather, there are genuine theological reasons why they may be ordained and consecrated in the service of the gospel. The idea that only a man, or a male, can represent Christ or be an *ikon* of Christ at the Eucharist, conflicts with basic elements in the doctrines of:

- the Incarnation and the new order of creation,
- the virgin birth, which sets aside male sovereignty and judges it as sinful,
- the hypostatic union of divine and human nature in the one Person of Jesus Christ who is of the same uncreated genderless being as God the Father and God the Holy Spirit,
- the redemptive and healing assumption of complete human nature in Christ, and
- the atoning sacrifice of Christ which he has offered once for all on our behalf, in our place, in our stead.

And therefore it conflicts also with the essential nature of the Holy Eucharist and the communion in the body and blood of Christ given to us by him.

As in Christ there is neither Jew nor Greek, neither slave nor free, so there is neither male nor female, for all sinful separation and gradation between them resulting from the fall of mankind have been done away, while God-given distinctions have been preserved, renewed and sanctified. Through the Incarnation, death, and resurrection of the Lord Jesus Christ humanity has thus been set upon an entirely new basis of divine grace, in which there is no respect of persons, and women share equally with men in all the grace-gifts or *charismata* of the Holy Spirit, including gifts for ministry in the church (cf. Justin Martyr, *Dialogue with Trypho*, 88).

CHAPTER 11

Preaching Christ Today[1]

PREACHING CHRIST IS BOTH an evangelical and a theological activity, for it is the proclamation and teaching of Christ as he is actually presented to us in the Holy Scriptures. In the language of the New Testament, preaching Christ involves *kerygma* and *didache*—it is both a *kerygmatic* and a *didactic* activity. It is both *evangelical* and *theological*. This is a feature in the Gospels to which my former colleague in New College, James S. Stewart, more than any other New Testament scholar known to me, sought to be faithful in his lectures, which he delivered in a kerygmatic and a didactic mode. He interpreted the text of the Gospels and expounded the gospel in the Gospels in such a way that his students heard the living and dynamic Word of God for themselves. Not surprisingly many of them were converted in his classroom. No wonder that Jim Stewart was such a beloved preacher and teacher of gospel truth. It was James Denney who used to say that our theologians should be evangelists and our evangelists theologians. This is something, I believe, we must learn again in our calling to preach Christ today.

---

1. An address to the Scottish Church Theology Society, founded for the renewal of theology, published in 1994, reprinted by Eerdmans who have graciously returned the copyright.

Preaching Christ Today

I. The Inter-Relationship between Kerygma and Didache

The first thing I want to talk about in preaching Christ is *the inter-relation between kerygma and didache*. The Church's calling is to proclaim Christ kerygmatically and didactically—we need didactic preaching, and kerygmatic theology. The only Christ there was and is, as John Calvin used to say, is not a naked Christ but "Christ clothed with his gospel." By that he meant that Jesus Christ and his Word, Jesus Christ and the truth of his message belong inseparably together and may not be torn apart. With us human beings person, word and act are separate, but this is not the case with Jesus, the Word made flesh, full of grace and truth, for in him Person, Word, and Act are one. That is why when we read and interpret the Gospels and Epistles and let them talk to us out of themselves we find ourselves having to do directly with God in Christ "speaking to us in Person," as Athanasius and Calvin both used to say.

Unfortunately this is the very thing that some New Testament scholarship today does not seem to promote in its so-called quest for the historical Jesus. I think here of one of the most radical New Testament scholars of our times, Rudolf Bultmann of Marburg. He did his best to 'demythologise' Jesus, or strip away from the New Testament 'Jesus' the theological frame in which he is presented to us by the Evangelists and Apostles, on the ground that the didactic or theological material derives not from the historical Jesus but from the early Christian community. But you cannot stop there in peeling away layers of so-called theological interpretation put upon Christ. I recall how one of the Professors in my old University in Basel, Fritz Buri, attempted to do just that, and set himself to strip away from Jesus not only the didactic material in the Gospels but the *kerygma* as well, and so to detach the historical event of Jesus completely from his evangelical message. He decided to give three public lectures on *Entkerugmatisierung*, or the *dekerygmatising* of the Gospel, thereby going beyond Bultmann's demythologising programme in seeking to strip Jesus naked of his gospel. Karl Barth decided to go along and listen to these lectures. Later when he met Fritz Buri in the street he said to him with his customary humour: "Now at last, brother Buri, I know the difference between you and Bultmann. When Bultmann goes in for a swim he at least has a pair of bathing trunks on!"

When you begin to tear these elements in the Holy Scriptures apart, the kerygmatic from the didactic, the historical from the theological, everything goes wrong. Is this not what New Testament Scholarship so often does today in its adherence to what it calls "the historical scientific method," and thereby undermines evangelical and theological preaching?

I was particularly intrigued once in a coming across a similar problem in the researches of the social anthropologists, Evans-Pritchard on the Azande culture in Africa, and Clyde Kluckholn on the culture of the Navaho Indians in the south-western States of America. Let me refer only to the latter. He spent a long time with in direct carefully and meticulously controlled observations of their way of life, but after many years he realized that he had not really understood them. He had made a point of being as scientifically accurate and objective as possible in establishing the empirical data, but the Navahos would not accept his results. The trouble was that he had been interpreting and integrating what he observed with a conceptual frame of thought alien to the Navahos. Then when he set himself to study the institutions and behaviour of the Navahos again through living with them and absorbing their way of thinking in describing and integrating their own way of life, he found that what he wrote up about them not only made sense to the Navahos but made scientific sense as well, for this way of conceptualizing what he observed from the inside, as it were, made his observations and judgments accurate and objective in a way that they had not been before.

Learning from Inverting Spectacles

Let me show you what has been happening in the analysis of the New Testament texts by reference to the results of a famous experiment with inverting spectacles that has been carried out in different parts of the world, for example at Wichita in Kansas. These are spectacles that make you see things upside down and the wrong way round, so that everything becomes disorderly and chaotic. Your orientation to the world around you is completely upset, so that you stagger about. You can't act in a natural and balanced way in relation to the objective realities around you, chairs, tables, doors, and so on, for you bump into them and stumble around. But after eight painful days you become oriented to the world round you in a orderly way again, and can start moving about without tumbling over the furniture or running into things.

What is happening? When you put on these inverting spectacles you tear the visual image away from the mental image—the perceptual image from the conceptual image—and everything becomes topsy-turvy. That is the sort of thing that happens in the kind of New Testament scholarship I have been speaking about when the kerygmatic and didactic elements in the biblical narrative, the empirical and theological factors, are split apart, and their original cohesion is lost.

There is something fundamentally wrong going on here with the so-called historical scientific method, which needs to be carefully understood, for it is terribly important—it has to do with the interrelation of *kerygma* and *didache* and the wholeness of the New Testament witness to Christ. James Stewart was rather hurt when a thesis was published about him, arguing that he didn't appreciate historical scientific method. Actually he knew much better than his critics about the real issues at stake in attempts to interpret the New Testament Scriptures in a way that is both faithful and academic, for he sought to interpret the texts of the New Testament strictly in accordance with what they actually are as they have been handed on to us in the inseparable interrelation of *kerygma* and *didache*, and not in accordance with some analysis and reconstruction imposed upon them *ab extra*. He sought to interpret the apostolic witness to Christ in light of its implicit wholeness in order to let it speak to us as far as possible out of itself.

We must now ask, what is meant by "historical scientific method"?

'Historical' Method

What kind of *history* is being envisaged? Well let's think again of Bultmann, held to be one of the great New Testament scholars of our times. He drew a sharp line of distinction between two kinds of history called *Historie* and *Geschichte*, the kind of history that is interpreted in terms of strict causal connections, and the kind of history that is interpreted in terms of how things appear to us. That distinction goes back through Herrmann and Kant, to Lessing's "ugly big ditch" between necessary truths of reason and accidental truths of history, but ultimately it derives from the radical dualism between "absolute mathematical time" and "relative apparent time" posited by Newton in his system of the world. That is the dualism that lay at the heart of the determinist conception of the universe which has played so much havoc with our understanding of nature and its relation to God, and ruled out of rational consideration any thing that could not be explained in terms of physical laws, so that not a little of our human experience and culture which we cherish and value could be understood and explained only on a subjective basis.

The Newtonian distinction between two kinds of time along with the mathematical formalization of the laws of motion, was highly abstract and artificial and left no room for 'real time,' or therefore for salvation history. That is why, of course, Bultmann held that *Historie* understood in this natural causalist way ruled out any thought of Incarnation or miracles or resurrection, or of God's interaction with us in history. His acceptance of the idea of an unbroken continuity of cause and effect governed by natural law made him regard the central Christian beliefs embedded in the Gospels and Epistles of the New Testament as a mythological account of reported this-worldly events in other-worldly ways lacking objective truth and reality. They were no more than subjective forms of thought devised by the Early Church in order to make existential sense of the way Jesus was reported to have appeared to his followers. Hence Bultmann devised a "programme of demythologising" and reinterpreting the New Testament existentially in which modern people can make sense of the New Testament in terms of their own self-understanding in the scientific world of classical Newtonian mechanics.

The Newtonian conception of absolute mathematical time and space clamped down upon the universe, along with its rational dualism between empirical events and theoretical constructions, gave rise to a rigidly mechanistic account of nature that Clerk Maxwell found could not explain the behaviour of light. A new scientific approach to the created universe, and a very different understanding of nature in terms of continuous dynamic fields had to be developed. This reconstruction of the foundations of science, which Albert Einstein held to be the most important in history, led him to develop his theories of special and general relativity. They shattered the determinist conceptions of classical mechanics and led to quantum theory, and a much more refined and dynamic and open-ended understanding of reality. We cannot go into that here, but it will be sufficient for our purpose to note that Einstein overthrew the dualist disjunction between empirical events and scientific theory or between physical facts and mathematics. He showed that if scientists are to be true to the nature of the space-time universe, they must not try to interpret it by crushing their understanding of it into a preconceived static frame of ideas formulated altogether apart from the physical structures of nature, as the Newtonians had done with the timeless necessary system of Euclidean geometry. Everything finally goes wrong when that is done. Rather must geometry be put into the heart of physics where it is transformed through being embedded in the dynamic world of space-time, and becomes four-dimensional. This means that geometrical patterns and physical structures in our space-time universe are bound inseparably together; conceptual and empirical factors inhere in one another both in nature and in our understanding of it, and must not be torn apart. That is why, our twentieth-century science has made such enormous advance, for it no longer imposes abstract necessary patterns of thought upon nature, but seeks to understand nature out of its own inherent rational order, and is therefore concerned with continuous dynamic fields and with real time.

There we have the immense revolution in the foundations of knowledge brought about through general relativity theory, followed up by quantum theory, which has now been built into rigorous modern science. This involves a way of thinking in which experiment and theory, empirical and theoretical factors interact with one another and must not be divorced from one another, and therefore a way of thinking in which the historical and the conceptual ingredients must be taken together in the understanding of any historical culture or religion. The extraordinary thing is that our biblical scholars seem to show very little knowledge of this revolution and correction in the foundations of rational and scientific knowledge. They still work with a dichotomy between empirical and theoretical factors in knowledge, and with the old discarded notions of split time expressed in their two kinds of history. I don't know any scientist who accepts what biblical scholars say about *Historie* and *Geschichte*. Actually even the German secular historians don't operate with this artificial concept of a two-fold history. Quite clearly biblical scholars need to turn their attention to conceptions of real time, and real history if they are to do justice to salvation history and to the intrinsic truth of Christ clothed with his gospel.

'Scientific' Method

The kind of scientific method that became dominant after the Enlightenment in the eighteenth century concentrated first upon the isolation and observation of phenomena, and then set about establishing natural laws through logical deduction from the empirical data reached in that way, but that meant, as even Kant admitted, reading laws into nature not reading them out of nature. This is known as the phenomenalist and constructivist conception of science. Scientific theories were reached through observation and analysis of phenomena and then imposing upon them the necessitarian framework of absolute mathematical time and space, in order to give the phenomenalist particulars some kind of rational coherence. This is the kind of scientific method that produced the hard determinist conception of the universe that has done so much damage to all areas of human thought.

Think what happens when that kind of scientific method governs research into the culture of the Navaho Indians. First of all you isolate and determine the empirical data, and try to describe them in strictly empirical or observationalist terms. When you have done that, you interpret them, not through a conceptuality inherent in them, but through a conceptual frame of thought derived elsewhere, e.g., from a mechanist theory of evolution. As we have noted that is the kind of scientific method which Clyde Kluckholn found to be disastrously wrong. And that is precisely the false scientific method that has now been comprehensively destroyed in physics the most rigorous of all sciences, in the rejection of a dualism between empirical and conceptual factors, or between phenomena and theory. Proper scientific method seeks to penetrate into the intrinsic rationality of any field of reality, grasping it in depth, as Einstein argued, in order to understand it in accordance with its distinctive nature, and to find appropriate ways of formulating knowledge of what is learned in this way. That is actually how scientific method normally operates today.

The Loss of Biblical Wholeness

But what have biblical scholars being doing with their so-called historical scientific method? In examining the biblical records they try to determine the truth about the historical Jesus, through giving critical attention to empirical data in isolation from any theological factors. Thus when they come to passages such as we find in Matt 11 or Luke 10 where Jesus is reported to have said, "No one knows the Son but the Father and no one knows the Father but the Son and he to whom the Son reveals him," they argue that the historical Jesus could not have said that, for in accordance with their preconceptions that must be put down to theological interpretation that came later, from the Early Church's attempt to understand Jesus. They say the same thing about the command of the risen Jesus to institute baptism in the name of the Father, of the Son, and of the Holy Spirit. Although there is no textual evidence against either passage they insist that they could not have come originally from Jesus himself! Why? Because, they argue, those reported sayings of Jesus have a theological ingredient that cannot 'scientifically' be accepted as part of the empirical data relating to the historical Jesus. Hence, for extraneous dogmatic reasons, they cut out theological elements from the Gospels and attribute them to the activity of the Christian community. Thus these biblical scholars through their historical scientific method tear the empirical and the theoretical, the historical and theological ingredients, from one another, thereby doing exactly the same thing that we find happening with inverting spectacles which disrupt vision by tearing apart the perceptual image from the conceptual image. Hence it is not surprising that New Testament scholarship today is in a rather chaotic state. It is largely due to this analytical approach dismembering the biblical witness that some scholars claim to find several 'Christologies' in the New Testament—they cannot see the wood for the trees!

How different was the early account given by St. John in his first Epistle in which the empirical events of seeing, hearing, and touching Jesus are found interwoven with the gospel message of Christ as the incarnate Son of God who gave himself in sacrifice to be the propitiation for our sins. The real Jesus of history is the Christ who cannot be separated from his saving acts, for his person and his work are one, Christ clothed with his gospel of saving grace. The so-called Jesus of history shorn of theological truth is an abstraction invented by a pseudo-scientific method.

The questionable state of affairs in New Testament scholarship today brought about through the divorce of historical and theological ingredients is such that a few years ago Professor Michael Dummet, the Oxford mathematical philosopher, wrote a couple of articles in the magazine *New Blackfriars* charging New Testament scholars with a "fraudulent" handling of the resurrection narratives in the Gospels. The foundations of New Testament scholarship are now under attack and changes are being made, not least in a reintegration of historical events and divine revelation. This is increasingly evident in the way in which the New Testament documents are being interpreted in relation to a Hebraic, and not a Hellenistic, frame of mind, so that Jesus is being understood again in the light of God's redemptive self-revelation to Israel and indeed not just in the light of the documents of Rabbinic Judaism on which some scholars have been concentrating. This is having the effect of stripping away from Jesus the clothes of Gentile culture with which he has been robed and obscured. Another of the significant changes taking place, I am told, is the questioning of the Q Hypothesis, which arose under the analytical activities of the historical scientific method and the kind of reconstruction that had to be attempted after the natural connection of empirical and theological factors was disrupted. When you tear the visual and mental images apart, or sever the connection between the perceptual and conceptual ingredients in knowledge, then some sort of extraneous matter has to be brought in order to make the dismembered results of this kind of historical critical research stick together. But all the time the real historical Jesus slips through the fingers of those critical New Testament scholars like sand. The historical Jesus and the theological Christ cannot be separated from one another without grave misunderstanding of the gospel and serious detriment to the faith of the Church.

The Divorce of Kerygma and Didache

What I am trying to say, then, is that this divorce of the empirical from the theoretical, which involves the divorce of *kerygma* from *didache*, disrupts and damages the biblical presentation of Jesus Christ in such a way that people find it difficult to preach, for all it offers is a Christ stripped bare of his divine truth. If you cannot preach the gospel didactically as well as kerygmatically, you have to invent your own theology to make these things stick together. But once humpty dumpty has fallen like that, all the king's horses and all the king's men cannot put him together again—that's the problem, and it is a far bigger problem than many people realize.

I have challenged New Testament scholars deliberately about this problem in the introduction and last chapter of my book *Space, Time, and Resurrection,* and I have raised these issues in public lectures in different universities, but not a single New Testament Scholar has offered me any answers! I can understand that, because in order to do so they have to rethink their understanding of what took place in the relation between the Early Church and Hellenistic philosophy and science, and to face up to the similar revolution in the foundations of knowledge in our own times, delivering it from the damaging dualisms of the past, which, thank God, has been brought about in our day through modern science, and that may involve some very hard thinking for them.

Let me refer again to James Clerk Maxwell, our great Scottish scientist who began this remarkable clarification in knowledge when he rejected the mechanical model of thought in his dynamical theory of the electromagnetic field. He showed that we cannot think of connections in nature in terms of action at a distance, through the bearing of atoms or particles externally upon one another. Rather must we think in terms of continuous dynamic field structures in which particles are interlocked with one another in a much profounder integrated form of rationality. That is the only way we can think in theology as well, in the light of the intrinsic intelligibility of God's interaction with us in his revealing and saving acts in space and time in history, as indeed Clerk Maxwell himself pointed out from his own deeply Christian convictions.

Well that is the first thing I want to say. I believe this to be terribly important, for to interpret Jesus Christ under the guidance of the kind of rationalist historical scientific method long discarded by science, actually destroys a proper understanding of the humanity of Jesus, and of the kerygmatic and didactic way in which he confronts us in the Gospels.

II. The Unbroken Relation between the Sheer Humanity of Jesus and God

This brings me to the second thing I want to stress in preaching Christ, *the unbroken relation between the sheer humanity of Jesus and God.*

The New Testament opens with the announcement by the angel of the Lord that the child to be born of Mary was to be called both *Jeshua* (*Jahweh* saves), and *Immanuel* (*God* with us). The Jesus of whom we read in the Gospels and whom we proclaim as Christ is both man of Israel and the Lord God, for in him God himself has come to be with us, really to be with us as one of us and as God for us, who has taken our human nature upon himself, our sin and guilt, our misery and death, in order to save and heal us, and as such really to be our God. How do we put these two facts together, that Jesus Christ is both *man* of Israel and our *God*? Everything in the gospel depends on that twofold truth.

How do you interpret the New Testament if you tear Jesus out of the revelationary context in which he is presented to us, and tear apart the empirical and the theological aspects of the gospel with which he is essentially bound up? When you do that, you inevitably interpret Jesus in terms of your own self-understanding and culture in the West or the East and so put an alien Gentile image upon the face of Jesus. When that is done our Jewish brethren cannot recognize their own promised Messiah in our Jesus. But that is not the real Jesus, for Jesus was a Jew. Properly to understand Jesus we must not detach him from the people of Israel but think of him as a Hebrew of the Hebrews who may be understood only out of the midst of God's long interaction with Israel chosen to be the medium of his self-revelation to mankind. Thank God, as I have noted, a change in the approach of scholars to Jesus is now taking place along these lines.

I once asked Matthew Black, one of the very best of our New Testament scholars, well-known from his book on *The Aramaic Origin of the Gospels*, what he thought of a passage in the Jerusalem *Talmud* where two rabbis are discussing the interpretation of a Hebrew word in Isaiah but did not know how to pronounce it, for they themselves did not speak Hebrew. And so they called in the maid from the kitchen and asked her how she pronounced the word, for she spoke Hebrew. Aramaic was a literary language, but Hebrew, as recent discoveries in archaeology and many newly discovered documents have verified, was the language of the common people. There are certainly Aramaic terms in the Gospels, but when we read that the common people heard Jesus gladly, we must think of him as having spoken to them in the ordinary day to day Hebrew with which they were familiar.

The Humanity of Jesus

It has been my custom since I was a child to read through the Bible once or twice a year, and when I come to the Gospels, I am always overwhelmed with the thought that here in Jesus it is God himself who has come among us, not just as a man indwelt by the Spirit of God like an Old Testament prophet, but actually as *Man*. I can never get over this astonishing fact. What bowls me over every time I read about Jesus in the Gospels, is not the wonderful things he did, not the so-called nature miracles in which the wind and the sea obeyed him, or even his making the dead alive again, for if Jesus really is God, as John Polkinghorne the Cambridge mathematical physicist has said, one would expect that, for he was the Creator personally present in the midst of his creation. If you really believe that Jesus is God become incarnate you will have no trouble with the miracles. No! What overwhelms me is the sheer humanness of Jesus, Jesus as the baby at Bethlehem, Jesus sitting tired and weary at the well outside Samaria, Jesus exhausted by the crowds, Jesus recuperating his strength through sleep at the back of a ship on the sea of Galilee, Jesus hungry for figs on the way up to Jerusalem, Jesus weeping at the grave of Lazarus, Jesus thirsting for water on the Cross—for that precisely is *God* with us and one of us, *God* as "the wailing infant" in Bethlehem, as Hilary wrote, *God* sharing our weakness and exhaustion, *God* sharing our hunger, thirst, our tears, pain and death. Far from overwhelming us God with us and one of us does the very opposite, for in sharing with us all that we are in our littleness and weakness he does not override our humanity but completes, perfects, and establishes it.

What I find always most breath-taking, however, is that in Jesus the Lord God Almighty, the Maker of heaven and earth and of all things visible and invisible, stoops down to be so fully one with us that he speaks to us in our *human* language, and indeed, as Calvin used to say, babbles to us in ways that even children can understand. We don't know what language God speaks in the communion of the Holy Trinity or speaks to the angels and the blessed departed, but we do learn in Jesus that God actually speaks to us in our creaturely language on earth. In Jesus the Word by whom all things in heaven and earth were created became human and communicates with us and addresses us in this frail creaturely form.

I will never forget the day after the Russian Sputnik was launched in 1957 when my young sons wanted us to visit Jodrell Bank near Manchester where we the first large radar telescope had been set up by Sir Bernard Lovell. We spent several days there on our way to visit my wife's family in Somerset. We found the radio astronomers in a state of great excitement, not because they were able to track the orbit of the Sputnik round the earth, but because through their radar telescopes they were receiving signals from what they regarded at that time to be the outermost edges of the Universe. They were so excited that they would not go home to eat or sleep, and their wives had to bring them camp beds and food and drink so that they literally lived in the laboratory for days. With their astonishing radar telescope there was opening out before them the ultimate ranges of the universe revealing its incredible ever-expanding immensity as never before.

Shortly after that we celebrated Christmas at Combe Down in Somerset, and I kept thinking of the fact that the babe born of the Virgin Mary in Bethlehem was none other than God, the Creator and Sustainer of that incredibly vast universe, he for whom the vast galaxies and nebular masses are like dust in the palm of his hand—the Lord

God Almighty, Maker of heaven and earth and of all things visible and invisible had become man in Jesus sharing to the full our littleness and weakness.

How do we link those two facts together? That is the heart of the Christmas message, *Jesus* IS *Immanuel, Jesus* IS *God with us*? Read the first chapter of St. Paul's Epistle to the Colossians, nothing in the whole Bible is more breath-taking than what is written there—the Creator and Upholder of the whole universe of visible and invisible realities is identified with *Jesus* and in him everything consists and is held together. This truth does not overwhelm or detract from the humanity of Jesus, but has the opposite effect. The transcendent deity of Jesus Christ secures and preserves his humanity in a way that no human questioning or critical research can ever undermine.

This, then, is the second thing I wish to stress in preaching Christ as *Yeshua* and *Immanuel: there is an unbroken relation in being and act between Jesus and God.* That was the supreme truth for which Christians had to struggle in the Early Church, within a culture dominated by the dualist philosophy and science of classical Greece and Rome, which prevented people from thinking of God as interacting with the world, or of incarnating himself within it. However, it is the same supreme truth for which the Western world has had to fight again and again in face of the dichotomous ways of thinking embedded in our Western philosophy and science, which were given powerful scientific formalization through Newtonian mechanics, for the determinist conception of the universe to which it gave rise led to the deistic notion of a God who does not interact with us in the world of space and time in any realist way.

The Nicene Creed

The ancient world worked with a radical dualism between the sensible world and the intelligible world, or between appearance and reality. When you work with a radical dualism in that kind of way, how can you think of there being an unbroken relationship between Jesus Christ and God? That was not possible within the framework of Greek thought, for it had the effect of driving a sharp line of demarcation between the deity and the humanity of Christ. The whole trend of Greek thinking gave rise to ways of thinking about Jesus which tore him apart, and gave rise to the various heresies all of which in one way or another sinned against the unity of Christ in his person and work, some stressing his deity at the expense of his humanity, and some stressing his humanity at the expense of his deity. That was a way of thinking with which the Church had to struggle hard in order to preserve the gospel. And so at the Council of Nicaea the fathers and theologians came up with a theological concept with which they tried to give concise expression to the supreme evangelical truth embedded in the Scriptures of the New Testament, the deity of Jesus Christ who was born of the Virgin Mary and crucified under Pontius Pilate. They knew that if Jesus Christ was not God incarnate, if the relation between Christ and God was severed, the Christian gospel would be emptied of any divine content and would quickly degenerate into some kind of moralistic philosophy with no saving value. And so the Church Fathers set about finding a way to give decisive expression to the oneness in being and act between Jesus Christ and God the Father. This they did by speaking of Christ as of one and the same being with the God Father. The word for that in Greek was *homoousios* with the Father, which is translated into Latin as "of the same substance" or as "consubstantial" with the Father. By giving conceptual expression to oneness between the Son of God become man in our world of space and time and God the Creator of heaven and earth and of all visible and invisible reality, the Early Church destroyed at a stroke the epistemological dualism of Greek thought, and did something that penetrated into and changed the very foundations of knowledge in the ancient world. They thereby laid the theological basis for their understanding of the unbroken relation between the sheer humanity of Jesus and God. The history of thought has shown us that it is only when Jesus is known and worshipped as God become man, that his humanity has been preserved—when Jesus is detached from oneness with God, what is called 'Jesus' is no more than an empty symbol into which people project their own religious fantasies and ideas. That is why the so-called historical Jesus, considered and studied apart from his divine truth, apart from the theological Christ, slips away, as I have said, like sand through people's fingers.

Preaching Christ Today

This modernist way of thinking of Jesus is the very opposite of what took place in the ancient times when the Church refused to allow Jesus of Nazareth and his intrinsic truth as the incarnate Son of God to be split apart, but took care to hold the historical and the theological factors in the Gospel account of Jesus inseparably together. What the ancient Church did, then, was in its own way just what Einstein and others have now done in the twentieth century. In their development of general relativity theory and relativistic quantum theory, they have knitted firmly into each other again the empirical and theoretical factors in knowledge that had been split apart in Newtonian physics and mechanics. It was precisely in that way that they laid the foundation for the dynamic understanding of the created universe on which present day science rests and has made such incredible progress in uniting the sub-atomic world with the world of the vast immensities of the universe, in uniting microphysics with astrophysics. Behind and below all that lies the great revolution in the foundations of human knowledge in which experience and geometry, physical events and mathematics, or empirical and theoretical factors, have been knit together again. That is precisely what the Judaeo-Christian theology in the early centuries, in its own sphere and on its own ground had done long ago, when through bringing together the doctrines of Incarnation and creation it overthrew the dualist patterns of thought in Greek philosophy and science and unified understanding in the foundations of knowledge. It was only in that way that they could give faithful theological expression to the key truth upon which the whole gospel of salvation rests, the unbroken relation in being and act between Jesus Christ and God the Father. How interesting and exciting it is that now at last modern science should carry out in its own realm of natural knowledge basically the same revolution in thought that was brought about in theological knowledge in the early centuries of the Christian era under the impact of God's self-revelation in Jesus Christ!

Let us consider the significance of that for a moment. Suppose for instance that we think of Jesus as only a man, then what are we to make of his statement to the paralyzed man reported in the second chapter of Mark's Gospel, "Your sins are forgiven you," at which the Scribes grumbled, for only God can forgive sins? Are the words of Jesus, here and elsewhere, only the words of a man or are they also the words of God? We believe that when Christ says "your sins are forgiven," they *really are* forgiven. The Jews were right, only God can forgive sins. The whole of the gospel depends on the deity of Christ, for unless he is God, all that Jesus said and did is only of passing ephemeral significance, without any ultimate divine validity. Apart from the deity of Christ forgiveness or atonement would be null and void.

The One Mediator between God and Man

The Church had to fight hard against the whole thrust of Greek thought to secure this truth that Jesus Christ is God and man, and as such the one Mediator between God and man. He really is *Jeshua/Immanuel*, God with us—when Jesus speaks and acts, God himself is present speaking and acting. As we have noted, that is the supreme truth that was secured for the Church at the Council of Nicaea in the doctrine of the *homoousion,* or *consubstantiality,* namely, that *Jesus Christ is of one being with God the Father.*

However, throughout the centuries the Church has had to fight hard for that very truth again and again. The insidious dualism of pagan thought crept back into the Western Church through the dualist thinking of people like St. Augustine in his radical distinction between the sensible and intelligible realms that came to govern the Latin concentration on the salvation of the soul and its deliverance from the world. St. Thomas Aquinas tried to tame that dualism, through Aristotelian metaphysics, but all he managed to do was to narrow the gap between the two realms. Instead of being abolished, however, the dualist way of thinking of the relation of God to the world became hardened, so that it was widely held that the Holy Scriptures have to be interpreted in various figurative ways, for the words of Holy Scripture are not as such the Word of God. In fact, it was argued, there is no 'Word' as such in God, for when God and the angels or God and the blessed departed communicate with one another, they do so through the medium of light by way of vision not of word. This had the effect of undermining the significance of the Holy Scriptures and of throwing the centre of authority upon the institutional Church in its interpretation of the Scriptures and upon the word of the Church in giving absolution for sins.

Toward the end of the Middle Ages, however, this view of the Word was challenged by John Reuchlin, who through his study of Hebrew gained a very different understanding of what the Word of God which we hear in the Holy Scriptures really is. He published a little book called *De Verbo Mirifico*, *On the Wonderful Word*, in which he expounded the Hebraic concept of the Word and its identification with Christ in the New Testament. Then with reference to the teaching of the Council of Nicaea he argued that since Jesus Christ is the Word of God as well as the Son of God, we must think of the Word of Jesus which we hear in the gospel as the incarnate Word of God that is consubstantial with God or of the same substance as God. To deny that there is Word in God is equivalent to rejecting the consubstantiality of Christ the incarnate Son of God. And so John Reuchlin charged mediaeval theology with sinning against the teaching of the Council of Nicaea. This application of the Nicene *homoousion* to the understanding of the Word of God incarnate in Jesus had a profound effect upon people's understanding of the Holy Scriptures as the inspired medium through which we hear the very Word of God, and played a very significant role in the Reformation understanding of the objectivity of the Word of God and of the authority of the Holy Scriptures.

John Major or Mair, a Scot who was then one of leading theologians in Paris, was asked by the Church authorities to examine John Reuchlin's book to see whether it was heretical or not. Major believed Reuchlin to be basically right, and reported that what he taught was in accordance with Nicene Catholic belief. It was current Thomist teaching about the Word that tended to be heretical. If according to the Nicene Creed Jesus Christ is the Son of God, that must also apply to the Word of God made flesh in Jesus Christ. Here then, at the end of the Middle Ages there was an understanding of the Word of God which radically affected the doctrine of Holy Scripture, and even before the Reformation began to revolutionize the understanding of the Bible on the ground that it is the real living Word of God that we hear in the Scriptures, for in them God speaks to us directly and personally.

That encounter with the thought of John Reuchlin left an impact on John Mair and influenced his epistemology, but it also influenced the preaching and teaching particularly of the Calvinist Reformation, because, if in the Bible people have to do with a Word that is consubstantial with God, then they read and interpret the Holy Scriptures in quite a different kind of way as the Word of God addressing them directly in and through them.

The Divine Gift and the Divine Giver

A similar change took place during the Reformation in the understanding of the doctrine of grace in the light of the Nicene Creed. In the third article of the Creed belief is confessed in the Holy Spirit, "the Lord and Giver of life who proceeds from the Father and who together with the Father and the Son together is glorified and worshipped." In line with what is said there about Jesus Christ as the incarnate Son of God, the Holy Spirit is said to be the Lord and the Giver of life. In both cases the divine Giver and the divine Gift are one and the same. At the Reformation that Nicene principle was applied not only to the Word of God and to the Spirit of God but to the grace of God. The Grace of God given to us in Christ is not some kind of gift that can be detached from Christ, for in his grace it is Christ himself who is given to us. Properly understood grace is Christ, so that to be saved by grace alone is to be saved by Christ alone. It was in a cognate way that the Reformation (I think here especially of John Calvin) regarded the gift of the Holy Spirit who is not some gift that can be detached from God and dispensed to us by the Church, for the Holy Spirit himself is the Lord and Giver of life. It is through the power of the Holy Spirit that the gift of God in Jesus Christ is mediated to us and we are savingly united to Christ.

Unfortunately due partly to a confusion between *charis*, the Greek word for grace, and *caritas*, the Latin word for love, there grew up in the Middle Ages the masterful idea that grace is a gift imparted to the Church and that the Church is endowed with power to dispense that gift. This is a notion of grace as something detached from God, but if the Nicene principle that the gift and the Giver are one applies to grace, as well as Christ and the Spirit, then it is impossible to think of grace or of the Spirit as endowments bequeathed by Christ to the Church to be administered under the authority of the Church. Hence, as in the Greek Orthodox Church much earlier, the question was raised by the Reformers whether the Church is subjected to God's grace or whether divine grace is subjected to the activity of the Church through its clergy. It was the application of the Nicene doctrine of consubstantiality, or the identity between the gift and the Giver, to the doctrine of grace that led the Reformation to depart from that damaging mediaeval conception of grace, and thereby also from the mediaeval notion of the sacraments as "causing grace physically," as Hugo of St. Victor declared.

Three times in its long history the Church has had to struggle particularly hard for the supreme truth of the deity of Christ and of the Holy Spirit. *First*, in the fourth century at the Council of Nicaea, when it was realized that if this supreme truth were given up Christianity would lapse back into paganism, or mere secularism and moralism. *Second*, in the sixteenth century in the struggle for the identity between the gift and the Giver, the consubstantiality of grace and of the Word, for it was realized that in that identity the very substance of the gospel was at stake. *Third*, in our own day in the massive upsurge of relativism, secularism, and syncretism, with its lapse back into a deistic disjunction between God and the world and questioning of the uniqueness of Christ, when once again it is the very essence of the Christian Faith that is under threat.

The Church's Continuing Struggle Today

We are still in the midst of this struggle to maintain the supreme truth of the unbroken relation in being and act between Jesus Christ and God the Father against insidious dualist or dichotomous ways of thinking, in spite of the fact that in the great scientific revolution of our times those dualist ways of thinking have been comprehensively overcome, at least among the pure sciences. The difficulties facing the preaching of Christ today come, for the most part, from the social sciences, for they still operate with dualist structures of thought and a scientific method that is a hang-over from pre-relativity science. This is very evident, for example, in the way they use statistics which in the final analysis yield determinist patterns of thought and behaviour which has the effect of excluding any thought of God's interaction with the world.

Several years ago when Lord Porter was President of the British Association for the Advancement of Science, he delivered a blistering attack on the social sciences because they really were not scientific, but operated with what he called pseudo-scientific methods. When James Clerk Maxwell began the revolution in scientific explanation and altered the rational structure of science, setting aside the use of mechanical models in research and explanation, he was accused by Lord Kelvin of lapsing into "mysticism." Clerk Maxwell had been brought up to believe in Jesus Christ as the incarnate Son of God through whom the universe had been created and endowed with its contingent rational order and beauty. Already as a teenager being taught Newtonian physics at Edinburgh Academy he began to have difficulties with mechanistic explanations of the way nature behaved. The world of nature that came from the God he knew in Jesus Christ would not have been constructed and or made to function in the mechanical way. And so even at school he began to work out new ways of scientific thinking, and produced two papers that were deemed to be so good that they were read to the Royal Society of Edinburgh. Later on when out of deference to Newtonian science he tried again and again to understand and explain the behaviour of light and electromagnetism with the help of mechanical models he found it impossible, and developed instead the concept of the continuous dynamic field described in terms of partial differential equations for which he became so famous. He succeeded so well that he laid the foundation for Einstein's theories of special and general relativity. The great Lord Kelvin had taken Clerk Maxwell under his wing, but when Clerk Maxwell found he had to reject mechanical models, Lord Kelvin accused him of tumbling into "mysticism"! Even in 1905 after Einstein published his epoch-making papers dealing with the behaviour of light, Lord Kelvin still insisted, incredibly, that Clerk Maxwell's dynamical theory of the electromagnetic field was untenable.

I have taken time to speak about this, because it shows how terribly difficult it is even for a great scientific mind like that of Kelvin to break out of its dogmatism. The mechanistic way of thinking had gained a powerful hold upon the modern mind, and even though that way of thinking has been radically undermined there are still scientists who find it difficult to break out of it—look at the school textbooks on physics! Where it continues to have its biggest hold, however, is in the new social sciences of the twentieth century, which sought to establish themselves as sciences through applying to themselves the old scientific method, and the mechanistic ways of thinking, that are now so discredited by the pure sciences. No wonder scientists like Lord Porter or Sir Alan Cook have questioned the scientific character, methods, and validity of the social sciences (excluding geography and economics).

Where does the Church today stand in all this change? The astonishing thing is that it has almost everywhere allied itself with the social sciences, and with them has laid itself open to the relativism, secularism, and syncretism, to which I have already alluded in the struggle of the Church to preach Christ and the supreme truth of the gospel. This is all too evident in some of our Theological Faculties and Colleges in the Departments of Religious Studies, where Christian dogmatics is pushed to the wall if it is taught at all. That represents a serious lapse back from rigorous theological science into the kind of rationalistic thinking that arose with the European Enlightenment and prevailed in the nineteenth century, according to which Christianity may be studied and taught in universities only as one religion in a universal class of religions. This implied that the uniqueness of the Christian faith that centres on the person and work of Jesus Christ as the incarnate Son of God could have no place in an academic discipline. Such a rejection of the concrete particularity of the Incarnation, of course, was in accord with scientific concern to discover and formulate universal timeless laws of nature through a generalization from particulars. That kind of science had no room for concrete particularities, and it abhorred the very word 'singularity.' Hence if Christianity was to have an academic place in our universities, the uniqueness of Christ or the concrete particularity of the Cross, had to be soft-pedalled to say the least.

The Singularity of the Incarnation

Into the midst of that kind of science a powerful bomb has now been exploded, the discovery of the so-called black hole, the original incredibly dense state of matter from which the universe is held to have expanded with the big bang. With the black hole, however, the concept of *singularity* has bounced back in a very big way, and has been radically transforming scientific thinking. My only concern with that here is that *singularity* is now no longer an idea abhorrent to science, but on the contrary a proper scientific concept of absolutely central importance. And as such it has become the great rock of offence upon which the old Enlightenment idea of science concerned with the generating of universal timeless laws has shattered itself, for the universal and the concretely particular have come together with comprehensive significance. The upshot of this is that today scientists are open to the absolute singularity of the Incarnation which they had hitherto rejected out of hand simply because it was a singularity. Many a scientist is now ready for the first time to entertain the Christian concept of the Incarnation, and to think seriously about the absolute significance of Jesus Christ. And increasingly not a few are ready to believe in him as the way the truth and the life apart from whom there is no way to God the Father.

When I published my little book *Space Time and Incarnation* in 1969 a very distinguished scientist wrote me a letter to thank me for presenting the Incarnation and its relation to space and time in a way that he could appreciate and in which he could believe. More than one distinguished scientist has recently become a Christian, for the advance of scientific knowledge has undermined their atheism or their agnosticism—I am constantly hearing of them and sometimes from them. They clamour for a proper understanding of creation and its openness to God. The whole intellectual climate has changed, and scientists are asking theologians to help them think out the interrelation of the Incarnation to the creation. They have in mind not least the discovery known as "the anthropic principle," that the expansion of the universe has taken place governed by a very fine tuning of both its strong and its weak forces which against all the laws of probability has adapted it as the home of mankind. But they also have in mind the fact that, as far as they are able to see, the whole of the universe in its quite incredible immensity is needed for human existence on planet earth. Let me refer only to a quite wonderful publication of only thirty-five pages by Professor David Block, the Johannesburg Astronomer, called *Our Universe: Accident or Design?*

Unfortunately, however, our theologians and biblical scholars, for the most part at least, are blissfully ignorant of what has taken place and do not seem to believe in the singularity of Christ and the Incarnation, and are therefore unable to help scientists just when they are calling out for it. It seems to be the same case with many of our missionaries who have evidently lost belief in the uniqueness of Christ and speak of Christianity only in the terms of what they call a multi-faith approach, in which Christianity is presented along with other religions, as one religion in a universal class of religions, just like the obsolete rationalists of the eighteenth century. One missionary of note who has been trumpeting the singularity of Christ is Lesslie Newbigin. He points not only to the transcendence of Christ, but argues that the twin dogmas of the Incarnation and the Trinity form the starting point for a way of understanding reality as a whole. It will be sufficient for me here to direct attention to two little books that have come from his pen which all who are concerned with preaching Christ today ought to read: *The Other Side of 1984: Questions for the Churches*, and *Foolishness to the Greeks: The Gospel and Western Culture*. What Lesslie Newbigin and his friends are now concerned with is what they call "The Gospel as Public Truth," that is, with the evangelization of our modern culture.

Evidence of Change

It may be noted here in passing that events of considerable Christian significance have been taking place in which we see evidence of the winds of God blowing across the Churches today. I think particularly of the fact that the doctrine of the Holy Trinity is now becoming the focus of attention again all over the world. I may mention that in 1989 the British Council of Churches published a report of their study commission on Trinitarian Doctrine Today, entitled *The Forgotten Trinity*. And in 1991 after years of discussion beginning with 1976 Orthodox and Reformed Churches have produced together an *Agreed Statement on the Holy Trinity*. Nothing like this has ever taken place between the Churches of the East and West, at least since the early centuries. There is now a rapidly growing literature on the doctrine of the Trinity, with which it is difficult to keep up. I think not least of books discussing ways of bringing Christian understanding of the personal relations within the Holy Trinity to bear upon social relations and structures with a view to bringing about their radical transformation and liberation from fascist and Marxist suppression.

I would like to draw attention to this movement of thought, for there are ways of thinking being pursued today which are not tied up with the Enlightenment rationalism, the pseudo-sciences, or with relativism and secularism. In connection with the doctrine of the Trinity there become disclosed ways of relational thinking in which even some scientists are becoming very interested, for they find in the Christian doctrine of the Trinity that theologians, as they express it, have been able to map the three to the one and the one to the three, which they need to do but have not been able to do in quantum theory. Moreover, it is when we consider what these scientists call "the intersection of symmetries" between the transcendent order of the divine Trinity and the contingent order of the created universe, that refined patterns of order become disclosed which may very well help scientists when they push their inquiries to the very edge of being, where being bounds on non-being, only to find chaotic states of affairs, which are probably due to the inadequacy of their conceptual instruments (e.g., a mathematics that does not have time relations built into it) as much as to the subtle dynamic nature of reality. If this kind of interrelation between basic theological concepts and basic scientific concepts could be worked out, there might well come about the most profound and startling transformation in human knowledge to the benefit of theological science and natural science alike. This kind of engagement of Christian theology with natural science is, I believe, an essential part of the missionary task of the Church in preaching Christ, for evangelization involves not only the evangelization of people but the evangelization of the structures in which they live and think.

Now let me turn back again to *the unbroken relation in being and act between Jesus Christ and God the Father* upon which the very substance of the gospel rests. Cut the bond of being and act between Jesus Christ and God and the bottom falls out of the gospel, for then all that

Jesus was, said and did is only of transient moral significance. But if Jesus Christ really is God incarnate, and divine and human nature are inseparably united in his one person in an utterly unique way, then Jesus Christ himself in the undiminished fullness of his humanity and deity becomes the very centre of the Church's mission. To preach Christ to men, women and children today we must proclaim him in his uncompromising singularity and transcendence as the one Lord and Saviour of the world.

So far I have been concerned mainly with the unbroken relation in *being* between Jesus Christ and God, now let me turn to the oneness in *act* as well as being between him and God.

III. The Cross of Christ

The third thing I would like to speak about in preaching Christ is *the Cross of Christ*. This is the most astonishing part of the Christian message, "God crucified," as Gregory Nazianzen expressed it. The identification of the man on the Cross with God himself is, as St. Paul once wrote, offence to the Jews and foolishness to the Greeks. Be that as it may, it is the preaching of Christ crucified that lies at the very centre of the Christian gospel, if only because the Cross, as H. R. Mackintosh once wrote in a gospel tract, is "a window into the heart of God." He was drawing attention there to the words of St. Paul in Rom 8:32: "He who spared not his own Son, but delivered him up for us all, how shall he not with him also freely give us all things?" St. Paul was thinking in the back of his mind of the readiness of Abraham to sacrifice his "only son Isaac, whom he loved" (Gen 22:2, 16), thereby demonstrating that he loved God more than he loved himself. In giving his own dear Son to die for us in atoning sacrifice for the sins of the world, God has revealed that he loves us *more than he loves himself*. Far from remaining detached from us in our fearful alienation and unappeasable agony, God has penetrated through the Cross into the deepest depths of our wickedness and violence and taken it all upon himself in order to judge them and redeem us from their tyranny over us.

Let me preface discussion of the Cross by referring to my visit to Israel in 1977 where I was warmly welcomed by the President, a distinguished scientist, Professor Katsir, and three ministers from the department of religion who took me to see the *Yad Vashem*, the museum of the Holocaust. I will never forget what I saw and read there. I had been in Palestine, as it was then called, in 1936 when the Grand Mufti came back to Jerusalem from visiting Hitler and spread the terrible poison of his anti-semitism all over the Middle East. *Yad Vashem* houses the most detailed account of the abominable murder of millions of Jews through the presentation of written documents, photographs, drawings, including the terrible cartoons of Julius Streicher. I was altogether overwhelmed by the massive evidence vividly placarded before my eyes of the slaughter of six million Jews, which we now know to be an underestimate. When I came out I felt numb with horror and shame that human beings in Christian Europe should have perpetrated such wickedness, and stood still for a few minutes with my three Israeli companions to get my composure. They asked me what I thought about it, and I pointed to a rough hewn rock outside the entrance, on which there had been fastened some Hebrew words taken from Ezek 16 which are cited at every circumcision, "In your blood live." By putting that there, I suggested, you are connecting the blood of Jews slaughtered in the holocaust with the covenant cut into the flesh of Israel throughout the generations. I added, somehow you have to link God with the Holocaust—if you do not do that, you cannot go on believing in God. All they did was to nod their heads in agreement. Then I said, now I must speak to you as a Christian. That is what we believe to be the significance of the Cross of Christ—in him we believe that God himself has come into the midst of our human agony and our abominable wickedness and violence in order to take all our guilt and its just judgment on himself. That is for us the meaning of the Cross. If I did not believe in the Cross, I could not believe in God. The Cross means that, while there is no explanation of evil, God himself has come into the midst of it in order to take it upon himself, to triumph over it and deliver us from it. My three friends were silent, and once more nodded their heads.

Two days later the Mayor of Jerusalem asked one of the leading archaeologists to take my wife and myself round Jerusalem and show what had been carried out. He had been engaged for some years in uncovering historic Jerusalem and opening it up for people to see as never before. The tour on which he took us ended up at the Holy Sepulchre, the place where Jesus was crucified—he had planned it that way. My wife and I knelt down with the pilgrims and prayed, while he stood back. When we got up he took hold of me by the sleeve to pull me aside and said, "I cannot understand why Christians are divided at this place." He understood the reconciling import of the Cross of Christ—he, the Jew! Whereas at the Holy Sepulchre the representatives of different Christian Communities quarrel with one another so much that the key to the Church of the Holy Sepulchre has to be kept by a Muslim. I learned much from that experience, and believe more than ever that it is still by the Cross of Christ that we Christians can have inter-relations with the Jews. But how far is the Cross really the controlling centre of our own life and thought?

The Power of the Cross

Let me now focus attention on some verses from St. Paul's First Epistle to the Corinthians.

> For Christ did not send me to baptize, but to preach the gospel, and not with eloquent wisdom, lest the Cross of Christ be emptied of its power. For the word of the Cross is folly to those who are perishing, but to us who are being saved it is the power of God. (1 Cor 1:17–18)

> I decided to know nothing among you except Jesus Christ and him crucified, and I was with you in weakness and trembling, and my speech and my message were not in plausible words of human wisdom but in demonstration of the Spirit and power, that your faith should not rest in the wisdom of men. (1 Cor 2:2–5)

It is the Cross of Christ that surely lies at the heart of our faith and of the mission of the gospel. I believe that if the Church is to be faithful to its calling it must concentrate, as I have said, on the uniqueness of Christ, but on Christ clothed with his gospel as the crucified and risen Lord. It is through the gospel of the saving love of God exhibited and enacted in the atoning sacrifice of Christ that the life and faith of the Church are found to be rooted and grounded in the incarnate act of the Son of God in becoming one with us as we really are. He made our lost and damned condition, our death under divine judgment his very own. I believe we have to stress again the fact that in the Incarnation and the Cross Christ has penetrated into the darkest depths of our abject human misery and perdition where he takes our place, intercedes for us, substitutes himself for us, and makes the atoning restitution which we could not make, thereby reconciling us to God in the Holy Spirit as his dear children.

Now in preaching this, I believe that it is concentration upon the *vicarious humanity* of Christ in the Incarnation and atonement, in death and resurrection, that is particularly important for us today. It is curious that evangelicals often link the substitutionary act of Christ only with his death, and not with his incarnate person and life—that is dynamite for them! They thereby undermine the radical nature of substitution, what the New Testament calls *katallage*, Christ in our place and Christ for us in every respect. Substitution understood in this radical way means that Christ takes our place in all our human life and activity before God, even in our believing, praying and worshipping of God, for he has yoked himself to us in such a profound way, that he stands in for us, and upholds us at every point in our human relations before God.

Galatians 2:20 has long been for me a passage of primary importance as it was for John McLeod Campbell and Hugh Ross Mackintosh: "I am crucified with Christ, nevertheless I live, yet not I. But Christ lives in me, and the life which I now live in the flesh, I live by the faith of the Son of God, who loved me and gave himself for me." "The *faith of the Son of God*" is to be understood here not just as *my* faith *in* him, but as the faith *of* Christ himself, for it refers primarily to Christ's unswerving faithfulness, his vicarious and substitutionary faith that embraces and undergirds us, such that when we believe we must say with St. Paul "not I but Christ," even in our act of faith. This is not in any way to denigrate the human act of faith on our part, for it is only in and through the vicarious faith of Christ that we can truly and properly believe. Faith in Christ involves a polar relation between the faith of Christ and our faith, in which our faith is laid hold of, enveloped, and upheld by his unswerving faithfulness. No human being can do that for another, far less give himself as a ransom from his sin, but this is precisely what the

Lord Jesus does when in giving himself for us he completely takes our place, makes our cause his very own in every respect, and yields to the heavenly Father the response of faith and love which we are altogether incapable of yielding.

It is the same conception of faith, I believe, that is found in St. Paul's teaching that we are *justified by faith* and that *the just shall live by faith*. Does this mean that the just person lives from his own faith or from God's faith? In saying that "the just shall live by faith" (Rom 1:17) the Apostle was actually citing from the book of Habakkuk (2:4), but in the Habakkuk Commentary found among the Dead Sea Scrolls this is interpreted to mean that the just live "from the faith of God," which is also, incidentally, the way that people like Athanasius, Calvin, and Barth have interpreted it. However, if we understand faith in the polar way to which I have pointed, justice can be done to both conceptions of faith! In the polar relation the primary pole is certainly God's faith or Christ's faith, for he is the faithful one who lays hold of us and brings us into a living relation with himself, but within the embrace of that relation the secondary pole is that of the believer, his responding faith. But that is an act of faith that is evoked by and sustained by the faithfulness of God—far from being of ourselves, it is a gift of God. This is how, I am sure, we are to understand the relation of our response in faith to the vicarious faith of Christ. The Pauline principle "not I but Christ" applies to faith: "I believe, yet not I but Christ."

The Reconciling Exchange

When preaching about faith in Christ and his vicarious humanity I sometimes use and develop an illustration taken from John Welsh, the son in law of John Knox, who used to point out that our grasping of Christ by faith is itself enclosed within the mighty grasp of Christ, and it is in Christ's grasp of us rather than in our grasp of him that our salvation and certainty lie. In this connection I sometimes recall what happened when my daughter was learning to walk. I took her by the hand to help her, and I can still feel her little fingers tightly clutching my hand. She was not relying on her feeble grasp of my hand, but on my strong grasp of her hand, and even my grasping of her grasping of my hand.

Is that not how we are to understand the faith by which we lay hold of Christ as our Saviour? It is thus that our grasp of faith, feeble though it is, is grasped and enfolded in the mighty grasp of Christ who identifies himself with us, and substitutes himself in our place, making what is ours wholly his own, so that we may have wholly made over to us what is Christ's. Think of that in terms of St. Paul's wonderful statement to the Corinthians: "You know the grace of our Lord Jesus Christ, that though he was rich, yet for your sakes became poor, that you through his poverty might be rich" (2 Cor 8:9). That is what the Early Church and John Calvin called the "the blessed exchange" or "the wondrous exchange," and even the Roman Missal calls *mirabile commercium*. This is in fact the New Testament doctrine of *katallage*, for it is an *atoning and reconciling exchange*, in which what is ours is displaced by Christ who substituted himself in our place and yet is restored in a new way to us.

A very important point must be noted here, relating to the fact that in his becoming one of us and one with us as we actually are, *Christ takes our sins upon himself in such a way as to make them serve our healing and salvation*. Think of the incident in the Gospel when James and John quite selfishly asked for the privilege of being at the right hand and left hand of Jesus at the inauguration of his Kingdom, which made the other disciples angry. Jesus did not rebuke them, except to ask if they could drink of the cup that he drank of and be baptized with the baptism with which he was baptized. When they said they could, he promised that they would indeed drink of the cup that he drank of and be baptized with the baptism with which he was baptized (Mark 10:35-40).

A little later, Jesus sat down with his disciples at the Passover Meal at which he specifically *linked his body and blood with the covenant*. Then when Jesus was betrayed and crucified the disciples found themselves in utter disarray standing before the Cross in a crowd of people who mocked and jeered at Jesus and laughed at the helplessness of Jesus nailed to the Cross. Jesus was now utterly alone, abandoned by them, and they the disciples were now separated from him by an unbridgeable chasm of shame and betrayal and horror, for they had all forsaken him and fled. They had betrayed the very love with which he had bound them to himself. Then they remembered what had happened at the Upper Room and the covenant Jesus had forged with them in his body and blood. *Jesus had meant them to remember, for in that act he took their very sins, even their denial of him, and used it as the very means by which to bind them to himself.*

Then the disciples understood the significance of the vicarious Passion of Christ as something undertaken not for the righteous, but precisely for the sinner. It was their very sin, their betrayal, their shame, their unworthiness, which became in the inexplicable love of God the very material he laid hold of, and turned into the bond that bound them to the crucified Messiah, to the salvation and love of God forever. *That is the way in which the* katallage, *the wondrous exchange of the atoning and reconciling Cross of Christ operates, by making the shameful things that divide us from him, into the very things that bind us to him in life and death for ever. Such is the unlimited power of the Cross of Christ.*

The Gospel at the Lord's Supper

It is not easy to preach the truth that we are saved by the grace of Christ alone, and it is through the vicarious humanity of Jesus and in its substitutionary bearing upon faith that we can properly believe, but this is what may be proclaimed at Holy Communion as nowhere else. In our Scottish tradition the great revivals have often taken place in connection with the celebration of the Lord's Supper, for example the great revival in the middle of the eighteenth century at Shotts Kirk (where incidentally, my grandparents are buried).

I have found in my own ministry that it is easiest to preach the unconditional nature of grace, and the vicarious humanity and substitutionary role of Christ in faith, at the celebration of the Eucharist, where the call for repentance and faith is followed by Communion in the body and blood of Christ in which we stretch out *empty hands* to receive the bread and wine: "Nothing in my hands I bring, simply to thy Cross I cling." There at the Holy Table or the altar I know that I cannot rely on my own faith but only on the vicarious faith of the Lord Jesus in the total substitution of his atoning sacrifice on the Cross. Salvation and justification are by the grace of God alone. Faith, as John Calvin taught, is an empty vessel, so that when you approach the table of the Lord, it is not upon your faith that you rely, but upon Christ and his Cross alone.

That is what the covenant in his body and blood, which the Saviour has forged for us, actually, practically, and really means. It is of the very essence of the gospel that salvation and justification are by the grace of Christ alone, in which he takes your place, that you may have his place.

I believe this emphasis in the mission of the Church may well be more important than anything else in Scotland today. There is a kind of subtle Pelagianism in preaching and teaching which has the effect of throwing people back in the last resort on their own act of faith, so that in the last analysis responsibility for their salvation rests upon themselves, rather than Christ. In far too much preaching of Christ the ultimate responsibility is taken off the shoulders of the Lamb of God and put upon the shoulders of the poor sinner, and he knows well in his heart that he cannot cope with it. Is that not one of the things that keeps pushing people away from the Kirk? I think here of the reluctance of many people in the Highlands to approach the holy table, but this is something that sadly happens all over the land when people fail to understand the absolutely free and unconditional nature of the Grace of the Lord Jesus Christ who came not to call the righteous but sinners to repentance, and who through the miracle of his Cross turns our sins and failings into the very means he uses in order to save us and bind us to himself—that is precisely what he pledges to us in the communion of his body and blood.

Unconditional Grace

Let us pause for a minute to reflect on the nature and implications of unconditional grace as it is freely extended to us in forgiveness. One does not forgive an innocent person but only a guilty one—by its very nature forgiveness involves a judgment on the wrongdoer. Total forgiveness involves total judgment, and it is total forgiveness that Christ gives us that involves a total judgment upon us. Think of that in terms of the Cross, on which Christ died for us, all of us, and the whole of each one of us, not just a part of us. Hence we must think that the whole of our being comes under the judgment of the Cross. That is why, as H. R. Mackintosh used to say, at the Lord's Supper as we partake of the body and blood of Christ, we feel ashamed of our whole being, for our goodness as well as our badness. In the atoning exchange of grace in which Christ gave himself for us, *all* that we are and claim to be, is called in question. There is no such thing as a partial substitution, or therefore a partial forgiveness and a partial judgment. Each one of us comes unreservedly under the judgment of the Cross, for in his act of total self-substitution Christ took the place of each one of us in making our sin his own and in bearing it along with the judgment of God upon it. Christ Jesus died for us when we were yet sinners; hence we must think him as having died for all people while they are yet sinners irrespective of their response. Just as the Cross is proclaimed to all, so the total forgiveness and the total judgment it involves are proclaimed to all, whether they believe or not. But unconditional forgiveness involves unconditional judgment. Just as divine forgiveness is not given on the ground of some condition being met by us, so the judgment it involves—the judgment enacted and exhibited on the Cross, once for all—is likewise unconditioned.

This unconditional grace of the Lord Jesus Christ, which is proclaimed to us in the gospel, summons us to repent and believe. But in our very act of believing and repenting, *we* with our faith, with our believing and repenting *self*, come under the unconditional judgment of Christ's forgiveness. Face to face with the Lord Jesus whose eyes search out the deepest secrets of our being and whose Spirit discerns the thoughts and intents of the heart, all our acts of faith and repentance, our prayer and worship, are found to be unclean in God's sight, so that if divine forgiveness were conditional on our responses, we would never be saved. Even the exercise of our free-will in believing and repenting in response to the summons of the gospel is not separable from our self-will, for it is the *self* in our free-will and self-will, the subtle Pelagianism of the human heart, that comes under the judgment of Christ's unconditional forgiveness. We sinful human beings are trapped by our sin within the circle of our hearts which are turned in upon themselves, so that we cannot even repent of our faith or repent of our repentance, but are cast wholly and unreservedly upon the unconditional forgiveness of Christ Jesus. Indeed it is because the judgment inherent in his forgiveness falls upon the innermost self in all our acts of faith and repentance, that we are thrown upon Christ alone and are saved by grace alone.

Without any doubt the gospel of unconditional grace is very difficult for us, for it is so *costly*. It takes away from under our feet the very ground on which we want to stand, and the free-will which we as human beings cherish so dearly becomes exposed as a subtle form of self-will—no one is free to escape from his self-will. It is the costliness of unconditional grace that people resent. Martin Luther once said that when he preached justification by faith alone, people responded to it like a cow staring at a new gate, but he also said that when he preached justification by grace alone it provoked tumults. I find this kind of disturbance again and again in the reaction not only of people outside the Church, but even of would-be evangelical people within the membership of Church, for their refusal to accept unconditional grace seems to be due to the fact that it cuts so deeply into the quick of their souls. This is part of what I meant a short time ago when I pointed out that there is a subtle form of Pelagianism in the way people often preach the gospel and claim that people will be saved only if they believe, or on condition that they believe. Hidden deep down beneath all that there is a failure to take the New Testament teaching about the power of the Cross of Christ and his substitutionary role seriously, a reluctance to allow it to apply to the whole of their being and to all their human activity before God, even to their believing and praying and worshipping. We need to learn and learn again and again that salvation by grace alone is so radical that we have to rely upon Christ Jesus entirely in everything, and that it is only when we rely on him alone that we are really free to believe: "Not I but Christ" yet "Christ in me." Because he came as man to take our place, in and through his humanity our humanity is radically transformed, and we become truly human and really free to believe, love and serve him. That is the wonderful message of the Cross and resurrection.

I have been laying the emphasis upon the unconditional nature of salvation by grace grounded in the fact that Christ gave himself freely in atoning sacrifice for all people without exception, for that is what we are sent by our Lord to preach. But what of those who turn away from the gospel and its summons to repent and believe? They do not thereby nullify the unconditional nature of the grace of Christ, or therefore the unconditional nature of the divine judgment that it involves. The judgment of God upon sinners remains when they spurn his grace. While the preaching of the gospel, in the vivid expression of St. Paul, is to some people a vital fragrance that brings life, to others it is a deadly fume that kills (2 Cor 2:16). That is to say, if people are damned, they are damned by the gospel. Why anyone who is freely offered the unconditional grace and love of God in the Lord Jesus should turn away from him, is something quite inexplicable and baffling to those who are "on the way to salvation," but it is a fearful fact that the New Testament will not allow preachers of the gospel to ignore or forget its teaching about damnation. It is at the final judgment that the dark side of the Cross, the unconditional judgement of God upon all sin and evil, will be unveiled, for people will be judged by what took place once for all in the finished work of Christ on the Cross, when he was crucified as the Lamb of God to bear and bear away the sins of the world. Is that not what the New Testament speaks of as "the wrath of the Lamb"?

It was one of the lovely and refreshing things about the preaching of Billy Graham in Scotland recently that in preaching Christ, he directed people to Christ and to Christ alone as Lord and Saviour, in such a direct and blunt way, not through brilliant preaching, that through the Holy Spirit thousands and thousands of people who were not members of the Church, and thousands who were under thirty years of age, were challenged by the gospel, and turned in their utter helplessness too Christ Jesus, to find in him one who has wholly taken their place so that they might freely be given his place. It is in this message of the unconditional grace and vicarious humanity of the Lord Jesus Christ that people have often told me that they have found the healing and liberation that they never thought possible.

The Wisdom and Power of God

Let me now end by directing attention back to those two passages in Paul's First Epistle to the Corinthians (1:17–18 and 2:2–5) and through them to the Cross of Christ as the power of God, and to the kind of faith that does not stand in the wisdom of men, but in the power of God.

I believe that emphatic focus upon this truth is precisely what is very much needed in the Church today in its calling to preach Christ. This is the central truth that we must surely stress in the ministry of ministers, and elders, and deacons, and church workers alike, and in the Christian witness of every member of the Church. It is the one message that really reaches the multitudes that are outside the Church, the young as well as the old. Unfortunately the kind of evangelism that is so often most vociferous actually seems to blur the radical nature of Christ's vicarious humanity and the New Testament gospel that proclaims it. That kind of 'evangelism' itself needs to be evangelized! The gospel must be proclaimed in an evangelical way! It is the proclamation of the Cross as the power of God, and teaching about faith standing in the power of God not in the wisdom of men, foolish as it may look before the wisdom of the world, that will open wide the gates and point the way ahead for a radical renewal of the Church and its mission. That is the kind of wisdom, the wisdom of God, as St. Paul called it, that we in the Kirk desperately need today.

In the celebration of the Eucharist in the Orthodox Church, it is when the Holy Gospel is lifted up and carried forth that there rings out through the Church a loud shout from the priest standing in front of the congregation, "Here is wisdom." Yes, it is in the celebration of the Eucharist or the Lord's Supper that proclamation of the Lord's death and the wisdom of God come so effectively together in the life and ministry of the Church, for it is at the Eucharist where we rely wholly upon Christ, and his Cross, not at all upon ourselves, that true wisdom is to be found, the wisdom of God!

Increase, O God, the faith and the zeal of all thy people, that they may earnestly desire and more diligently seek, the salvation of their fellow-men through the message of thy love in Jesus Christ our Lord. Send forth a mighty call unto thy servants to preach thy Word, and multiply the number of those who labour in the gospel; granting unto them a heart of love, sincerity of speech, and the power of the Holy Spirit, that they may be able to persuade people to forsake sin and turn unto thee. And so bless and favour the work of thine evangelists, that multitudes may be brought from the kingdom of evil into the Kingdom of thy dear Son, our Saviour Jesus Christ.

(Prayers for Divine Service)

CHAPTER 12

Legal and Evangelical Priests: The Holy Ministry as Reflected in Calvin's Prayers[1]

TOWARD THE END OF his life John Calvin published two sets of commentaries in which we find his biblically grounded mature thinking on the ministry of Word and Sacrament. These were his *Commentaries on the Harmony of the Pentateuch*, and his *Homilies*[2] *on the Minor Prophets*. Both these works reached John Knox in Scotland at the beginning of the Reformation and had a role in shaping the slant of the ministry in the development of distinctive trends in Scottish theology. In them Calvin was concerned to expound the teaching of the Old Testament on the worship of God and the character of the kind of priesthood appropriate to it, and to draw out its theological and practical implications for the ministry of the gospel and the pastoral care of the Church as the body of Christ. This essay will concentrate on Calvin's expositions of the prophecy of Malachi, "the messenger of the Lord" who pointed ahead to the advent of Christ, and his trenchant criticism of the behaviour of the Levites and priests after their return from exile and the restoration of the temple in Jerusalem. Here are some words from the second chapter of Malachi (vv. 7–9), which are an epitome of Calvin's teaching: "The

---

1. Published in *Calvin's Books: Festschrift for Peter de Klerk*, edited by W. H. Neuser, H. J. Selderhuis, and W. Van't Spilker (Heerenveen: Uitgeverij J. J. Groen en Zoon, 1997), 63–74.

2. *Praelectiones* in the original.

lips of the priest should guard knowledge, and men should seek instruction from his mouth, for he is the messenger of the Lord of hosts."

Particularly illuminating, however, are several of the prayers with which Calvin concluded his homilies, for they not only refer face to face with God to principal aspects of truth in the chapters he had been expounding, but reflect in an unusual personal way what he thought of his own ministry as a priesthood within the royal priesthood exercised by the Church as the body of Christ, in the service of our great high priest who is the one mediator between God and man. Here Calvin showed that priesthood, properly understood, is a primary form of the ministry of the gospel.

John Calvin's Prayers (selected)[3]

(1) On Malachi 1:2-6

Grant, Almighty God, that as thou hast been pleased to adopt us as thy people for this end, that we may be ingrafted as it were into the body of thy Son, and be made conformable to our head, O grant that through our whole life we may strive to seal in our hearts the faith of our election, that we may be the more disposed to render thee true obedience, and that thy glory may also be made known through us; and those also whom thou hast chosen together with us may we labour to bring with us unanimously to celebrate thee as the author of our salvation, and so ascribe to thee the glory of thy goodness, that having cast away and renounced all confidence in our own virtue, we may be led to Christ only as the fountain of our election, in whom also is set before thee the certainty of our salvation, through thy gospel, until we shall at length be gathered into that eternal glory which he has procured for us by his own blood. Amen.

(2) On Malachi 1:6-10

Grant, Almighty God, that as thou hast been pleased in thine infinite mercy not only to choose from among us some to be priests to thee, but

---

3. Because of Calvin's repetition in the original prayers, I have selected only the ones that best illustrate the points he is making.

also to consecrate us all to thyself in thine only-begotten Son, O grant that we at this day may purely and sincerely serve thee, and so strive to devote ourselves wholly to thee, that we may be pure and chaste in mind, soul, and body, and that thy glory may so shine forth in all our performances, that thy worship among us may be holy, and pure, and approved by thee, until we shall at length enjoy that glory to which thou invitest us by thy gospel, and which has been obtained for us by the blood of thine only-begotten Son. Amen.

(3) On Malachi 1:11–14

Grant, Almighty God, that since thou does not keep us at this day under the shadows of the law, by which thou didst train up the race of Abraham, but dost invite us to a service far more excellent, even to consecrate ourselves, body and soul, as victims to thee, and to offer not only ourselves, but also sacrifices of praise and prayers, as thou hast consecrated all the duties of piety which thou dost require from us through Christ thy Son, O grant that we may seek true purity, and study to render, by a real sincerity of heart, our services approved by thee, and so reverently profess and call upon thy name, that really fulfilled in us may that be which thou hast declared by thy prophet, that thy name may be magnified and celebrated in the whole world, as it was truly made known to us in the person of thine only-begotten Son. Amen.

(5) On Malachi 2:6–9

Grant, Almighty God, that since thou hast deigned to receive us into priesthood, and hast chosen us when we were not only of the lowest condition, but even profane and alien to all holiness, and hast consecrated us to thyself by thy Holy Spirit, that we may offer ourselves as holy victims to thee, O grant, that we may bear in mind our office and our calling, and sincerely devote ourselves to thy service, and so present to thee our efforts and labours, that thy name may be truly glorified in us, and that it may really appear that we may been ingrafted into the body of thine only-begotten Son; and as he is the chief and only true and perpetual priest, may we become partakers of that priesthood with which thou hast been *pleased to honour him, so that he may take us as associates to himself; and may thus by name be perpetually glorified by thy whole body as well as by the head. Amen.*

(7) On Malachi 2:13–16

Grant, Almighty God, that though we daily in various ways violate the covenant which thou has been pleased to make with us in thine only-begotten Son, so may we nevertheless not yet be dealt with according to what our defection, yea, the many defections by which we daily provoke thy wrath against us, do fully deserve; but suffer and bear with us kindly, and at the same time strengthen us that we may persevere in the truth and uphold to the end the pledge of faith we have given to thee, and which thou didst require from us in our baptism, and that we may each of us so conduct ourselves toward our brethren, and husbands toward their wives, that we may cherish that unity of spirit which thou hast consecrated between us by the blood of thine own Son. Amen.

(10) On Malachi 3:4–8

Grant, Almighty God, that since thou hast been pleased to choose us as priests to thyself, not that we may offer beasts to thee, but consecrate to thee ourselves, and all that we have, O grant that we may with all readiness strive to depart from every kind of uncleanness, and to purify ourselves from all defilements, so that we may duly discharge this holy priesthood, and thus conduct ourselves toward thee with chasteness and purity; may we also abstain from every evil work, from all fraud and all cruelty towards our brethren, and so to deal with one another as to prove through our whole life that thou art really our Father, ruling us by thy Spirit, and that true and holy brotherhood exists between us; and may we live justly towards one another, so as to remember to each his own right, and thus show that we are members of thy only-begotten Son, so as to be owned by him when he shall appear for the redemption of his people, and shall gather us into his celestial kingdom. Amen.

Legal and Evangelical Priests

(12) On Malachi 3:15–17

Grant, Almighty God, that as Satan strives to draw us away from every attention to true religion, when things in the world are in a state of disorder and confusion, O grant that we may know that thou carest for us; and if we perceive not this by what we find in the world, may we rely on thy Word, and doubt not but that thou ever watchest over our safety; and being supported by this confidence, may we ever go on in the course of our calling: and as thou has deigned to make us partakers of that evidence of thy grace, by which we know that we are reconciled to thee in thine only-begotten Son; and being thus made his members, may we never hesitate cheerfully to offer to thee our services, however defective they may be, since thou hast once promised to be a propitious Father to us, so as not rigidly to try what we offer to thee, but so graciously to accept it, that we may know that not only our sins, which justly deserve condemnation, are forgiven and remitted to us, but that thou also so bearest with our infirmities and our defects in our imperfect works, that we shall at length receive the reward which thou hast promised, and which we cannot attain through our own merits, but through the sanctification of thy Spirit, and through the sprinkling of the blood of our Lord Jesus Christ. Amen.

(14) On Malachi 4:3–6

Grant, Almighty God, that as nothing is omitted by thee to help us onward in the course of our faith, and as our sloth is such that we hardly advance one step though stimulated by thee, O grant that we may strive to profit more by the various helps which thou hast provided for us, so that the Law, the Prophets, and the voice of John the Baptist, and especially the doctrine of thine only-begotten Son, may more fully awaken us, that we may not only hasten to him, but also proceed constantly in our course, and persevere in it until we shall at length obtain the victory and the prize of our calling, as thou hast promised an eternal inheritance in heaven to all who faint not but wait for the coming of the great Redeemer. Amen.

In his account of the ministry in *The Institute of the Christian Religion* Calvin showed that in the order which God has appointed for the

Church to be governed, while it is he himself who rules and reigns in the Church through his Word, he nevertheless uses the service of men to fulfil as it were a vicarious work (*quasi vicariam operam*) in his name, not by transferring to them his own right and honour, but nevertheless to function as his ambassadors to interpret his will and represent his own person (*personam suam repraesentent*).[4] In his commentaries on four books of the Pentateuch Calvin gave considerable attention to the role of the Levitical priests as reconcilers, advocates, intercessors, and mediators whose task it was, in representing the Mediator, to offer sacrifices and entreat divine pardon in the name of the whole people.[5] But as such they were set apart and consecrated to God in such a way that it was given to them by God to bear the iniquity of the holy things and of the congregation and even to bear their judgment before God. That applied particularly to the High Priest on the Day of Atonement in the supreme liturgical act of sacrifice once a year on which the renewal of the covenant and the validity of the sacrifices and offerings of the congregation throughout the year depended.[6] There was an intimate and a fearsome tie between the offerings and the offerers. This was reflected in the immensely solemn consecration of priests for liturgical acts of worship in the name of the people before God, recounted in the Pentateuch, which was a terrifying experience.

It was in this light that Calvin read and commented on the prophecy of Malachi in which the corruption of pure worship was traced to the behaviour of the priests who were responsible for the integrity and purity of the worship prescribed by God. Thus the blame for deceptions and transgressions of people in bringing to the temple polluted sacrifices and offerings was laid on the priests—they bore the guilt of the people so that the strictures of the prophet fell most heavily upon them, for their office was to see that nothing polluted or profane should be received into the temple or offered to God. Even though the priests did not sin themselves, says Calvin, they were nevertheless regarded as the chief in wickedness, for it was their office to correct what the

---

4. Calvin, *Inst.* 4.3.1.

5. See Commentaries on Exodus 28 and 29; Numbers 8 and Leviticus 6; and cf. Mal 2:13 and 3:1.

6. Exod 28:38; Lev 16:17; Num 18:1, 23, etc.

people did amiss. In fact the dissimulation of the priests in condoning the transgressions of the common people had the effect of encouraging them to sin, so that the prophet accused them especially as the authors of impiety.[7] Thus in commenting on the fact that the prophet blames the whole people, Calvin reiterates that in the first place the severest criticism is directed to the priests, for "the greater portion of the guilt belongs to them."[8]

In the Church of the New Testament it is not animal sacrifices that are offered, but sacrifices of prayer, praise and thanksgiving for the one unique self-sacrifice of Christ the Lamb of God who bears away the sins of the world. The Lord has called and set apart some people to represent him in "spiritual worship," and thus to engage, along with their own self-offering to God, in a sacred office in which, after the analogy of the Levitical priests, they share the guilt of the congregation and bear the responsibility for the spiritual manner of worshipping God on the ground of the only true and perpetual sacrifice of Christ on the Cross. However, the analogy between the priesthood and the worship of God prescribed by the Word of God in the Old Testament Scriptures, and what has been prescribed in the Old Testament in the Church's celebration of the author of salvation, meant that Calvin took the prophecy of Malachi the Old Testament messenger of God deeply to heart. In one passage of his Commentary about acts of the Levitical priesthood in offering sacrifice, Calvin points out that the prophet seems to be alluding to the person of the Mediator. Christ had not yet appeared, but when the priest presented himself before the altar, it was the same thing as though God looked on the face of a mediator, and became thus propitious to all.[9]

While in the New Testament we learn that the whole Church has been called to be a royal priesthood in Christ,[10] nevertheless Calvin

---

7. In Mal 2:1f.
8. In Mal 2:1–2.
9. In Mal 2:1–5.

10. In 1 Pet 2:9. See the concluding prayer to the Homily 139 on Zech 3:34: "Grant, Almighty God, that as thou hast made us a royal priesthood in thy Son, so that we may daily offer to thee spiritual sacrifices, and be devoted to thee, both in body and soul ..." etc.

held that God has chosen some people to stand before him in a priestly capacity: "Grant, Almighty God, that as thou hast been pleased in thine infinite mercy not only to choose from among us some to be priests to thee, but also to consecrate us all to thyself in thine only-begotten Son . . ."[11] Again: "Grant, Almighty God, that as thou hast been pleased to choose us at this day as thy priests, and hast consecrated us to thyself by the blood of thine only begotten Son and through the grace of thy Spirit, O grant that we may rightly and sincerely perform our duties to thee, and be so devoted to thee that thy name may be really glorified in us . . ."[12]

Two points must be noted here. In the first place, Calvin allows a distinction between the general priesthood of the whole membership of the Church, and the priesthood of certain people within it; and in the second place, Calvin clearly regards himself as chosen to be a priest. He regarded himself as consecrated to act in a special way as a messenger, intercessor, advocate, or mediator (terms he uses of evangelical priests) between God and his people. He felt himself called to consecrate himself, body and soul, as a "victim" to God, to offer not only himself, but sacrifices of praise and prayers.[13]

Of course, in thinking of himself (along with other ministers of the gospel) as a priest, Calvin drew a clear distinction between true and legitimate priests and false priests, and between the kind of legal priesthood that obtained in the old covenant and the kind of evangelical priesthood that obtains in the new covenant. It is to the office of priesthood that his Homily 174 on Malachi is devoted.[14] The difference between the two priesthoods is that one is appropriate to the preparatory form that divine revelation took in the Old Testament and the other is appropriate to the nature of the final self-revelation of God in Jesus Christ his incarnate Son. But there are basic features common to both, and helpful analogies may be drawn between them. Commenting on the institution of Levi, in connection with the statement, "the law of truth was in his mouth." Calvin insists that the offices of priesthood and

---

11. Homily 171 on Mal 1:6–10.
12. In Mal 1:11–14.
13. See the concluding prayers at Mal 1:13 and 3:7–8.
14. In Mal 2:6–9.

teaching are inseparable: "He is not worthy of the honour of priesthood who is mute; nothing is more preposterous, or even more ridiculous, than that those should be counted priests, who are no teachers. These two things are, as they say, inseparable—the office of priesthood and teaching."[15]

"The priest's lips should keep knowledge, and they should seek the law at God's mouth; for he is the messenger of the Lord of Hosts." The faithful priest does not apply to himself the honour due to God, but stands in his own place as the minister of God, and the teacher of his chosen people: "The priest is the messenger of Yahweh. Malachi briefly defines here what the priesthood is, even an embassy which God commits to men, that they may be interpreters in teaching and ruling the Church. What then is a priest? A messenger of God and his interpreter. It hence follows that the office of teaching cannot be separated from the priesthood."[16] That is to say, while the office of the priest is to teach, the office of the prophet, teacher, or pastor on its part is an essentially priestly office. While both the priest and the teacher fulfil their office in ministering the things of God from God to man, they also fulfil their office by ministering the responses of man to God. As such they are messengers of God to man as well as messengers of man to God—which is why Calvin spoke of the priest also as advocate and mediator.

"The prophet includes two things of great importance—that there is no priesthood without doctrine or teaching and no priest except he who faithfully performs his office as a teacher, and secondly, that God does not resign his own right and power when priests are set over the Church; for God commits to them the ministration only, on this condition that the authority remains in himself alone; for otherwise the priest would not be the messenger of the God of hosts."[17] That is to say, neither as priest nor as teacher does a person act or prophesy in his own name, but only "out of the mouth of God." It cannot be emphasized enough, therefore, that teaching the Word of God is itself an intrinsically priestly act. Here, then, Calvin adds, there is set before our eyes a pattern by which we may know what God requires from us who would be pastors

15. In Mal 2:6.
16. In Mal 2:7.
17. In Mal 2:9.

over his Church. And so Calvin concludes this homily with the following prayer:

> Grant, Almighty God, since thou hast deigned to receive us into priesthood, and hast chosen us when we were not only of the lowest condition, but even profane and alien to all holiness, and has consecrated us to thyself by thy Holy Spirit, that we may offer ourselves as holy victims to thee, O grant that we may bear in mind our office and our calling, and sincerely devote ourselves to thy service, and may so present to thee our efforts and our labours, that thy name may be truly glorified in us, and that it may really appear that we have been ingrafted into the body of thine only-begotten Son; and as he is the Chief and only true and perpetual priest, we may become partakers of that priesthood with which thou hast been pleased to honour him, so that he may take us as associates to himself; and may thus thy name be perpetually glorified by the whole body as well as by the head.[18]

It should be pointed out here that what differentiates the evangelical priesthood sharply from the Roman Catholic conception of it has to do with delegation and succession in the exercise of power. And so Calvin recalls that all papal priests are inaugurated into their office, that they may sacrifice, with the words: "We give to you the power to offer appeasing sacrifices."[19] This was the sacerdotal notion of priesthood in which priests were bequeathed the authority to teach (*munus doctrinale*), to govern (*munus regale*), and to sacrifice (*munus sacerdotale*). For Calvin this called in question the uniqueness, completeness, and finality of the priesthood and sacrifice of Christ, whose person and word, person and act are indivisibly one. God may not be separated from his Word nor Christ separated from his mediatorial work—hence Calvin's unremitting attention to the kind of representation involved in the consecration of ministers of the gospel or evangelical priests and the difference between them and Jesus Christ the one mediator between

---

18. In Mal 2:6–9.
19. In Mal 2:9. (See Homily 175).

Legal and Evangelical Priests

God and man. Nevertheless within that relation of representation Calvin was ready to regard ministers, including himself, as priests, for all the activity to which they are ordained and consecrated is of an essentially priestly nature, both in the proclamation the gospel from the mouth of God, and in the oblation of prayer as a memorial before God and of the blessing the people in the name of the Lord Jesus the only-begotten Son of God. In both cases he could speak of the fulfilment of a minister's priestly office in the Church as that of *interpres* and even of *mediator*.

The question must now be asked: how did Calvin think of this priestly activity in offering and oblation before God? For an answer we may turn to his *Commentary on Four Books of the Pentateuch in the Form of a Harmony*, in which his discussion of the various sacrifices, offerings and oblations prescribed for the Mosaic Liturgy, was concerned to draw out their Christological and evangelical significance for the benefit of the Christian Church.

Here is a theologically interesting and illuminating passage from his Comments on Num 19:2f., which had to do with the sacrifice of the "red heifer."

> The command to offer was given to the whole people, because in order that they may partake of ablution, it was necessary that each of them should offer Christ to the Father. For, although he only, and that but once, has offered himself, still a daily offering of him, which is effected by faith and prayers, is enjoined to us, not such as the Papists have invented, by whose impiety and perverseness the Lord's Supper has been mistakenly turned into a sacrifice, because they imagined that Christ must be daily slain, in order that his death might profit us. The offering, however, of faith and prayers, of which I speak, is very different, and by it and by it alone we apply to ourselves the virtue and fruit of Christ's death.
>
> A clear distinction is here made between two offerings; for the people are not permitted to kill the heifer, for this is the peculiar office of the priest; and in this way also at present, although we set Christ before God's face in order to propitiate him, still it is necessary that Christ

himself should interpose, and exercise the office of a priest. Again the heifer was to be taken outside the camp, as a sign that it was accursed, since it was an atonement. On which account, too, the atoning victims, whose blood was carried into the Holy of Holies, were burnt without the camp; the truth of which was completed in Christ, who therefore suffered outside the gates of the city, as the Apostle testifies.[20]

The same thing is most clearly seen in Christ; for although he was made a curse for us, he was our atoning victim, yet nothing was thereby taken from his purity, so as to prevent his holiness from being the sanctification of the whole world. He offered himself through the Spirit, and by his own blood entered into the holy place, and his death is elsewhere called by Paul a sacrifice for a sweet-smelling savour.[21]

Beside this passage may be set another in which Calvin has in mind the words: "And Aaron shall make an atonement upon the horns of it once a year with the blood of the sin-offering of atonements; once in the year shall he make atonement upon it, throughout your generations: it is most holy unto the Lord." Calvin comments: "Although this was only done once a year, yet it was daily to be called to mind, in order that they might offer the death of Christ by faith and prayer, and yet might know that their prayers had no sweet savour, unless in so far as they were sprinkled with the blood of atonement."

While operating with "the analogy between the sign and the thing signified," with its recognition of an utter difference as well as likeness between the atoning sacrifice of the Levitical liturgy and the atoning sacrifice of Christ, Calvin nevertheless holds that in the Christian Church it is necessary that each of us should "offer Christ to the Father," in a "daily offering," which we effect through by faith and prayer, and indeed "offer the death of Christ by faith and prayer." That is to say, Calvin is saying that although Christ has once for all died in his atoning

---

20. Heb 13:11–12.
21. Heb 9:11–12; Eph 5:2; Phil 4:18.

self-offering for us on the Cross, nevertheless in our daily worship and prayer for cleansing and forgiveness, we are to offer him and his death to the Father. That is how Calvin understood the Eucharistic sacrifice of praise and thanksgiving at the celebration of the Lord's Supper, but how also he regarded the daily devotions of members of the Church which is the body of Christ, the crucified, risen and ascended Lord. And when we recall Calvin's insistence on the unity of the priestly and teaching offices, together with his distinction between legal and evangelical priesthood, stressed so strongly in his Commentary on Malachi and the concluding prayers to his Homilies, we can understand again in this light how he could regard the sermon not only as a proclamation of the gospel from the mouth of God but as an offering made to God, assimilated to Christ's one self-offering as the Word become flesh now ascended to the Father.

Here in the biblical expositions which Calvin penned and published toward the end of his life, we find him using terms and expressions in speaking of the ministry and worship, such as he had not been in the habit of using before, but with no less an evangelical meaning. We are reminded of the views of John Knox, who studied these writings during the Scottish Reformation, and who constantly referred to the highpriestly prayer of the Lord Jesus, recorded in the seventeenth chapter of St. John's Gospel, in which he spoke of sanctifying or consecrating himself before the Father that we might be sanctified and consecrated in him, thereby constituting us with him in his priestly self-presentation to God. That was the passage to which Knox turned again and again in his teaching about the Lord's Supper or Eucharist, the passage to which he turned on his deathbed, for it was there, he said, that "I first cast my anchor."[22]

---

22. Reported by Knox's secretary and man-servant Richard Bannatyne in *The Last Days of John Knox*. Edited by D. Hay Flemming (Edinburgh: Knox Club, 1913).

General Index

A

Aaron, 112–14, 116, 120–21
Aberdeen, 3
Abihu, 114
advent. *See* Jesus Christ; *parousia*
Alexandria, 202–19
Alyth, 3, 27–73
anamnesis. See Lord's Supper
Anderson, Charles, 31
angels, 34
Angus Theological Club, 41
anthropic principle, 242
anthropology, 22, 222, 226
apostles, 119–21, 130
Apostolic Constitutions, the, 128
apostolic succession, 108, 119, 121, 125–26, 130–32
Aquila, 201, 204
Aquinas, Thomas, 236
Arabs, 19, 173
army chaplaincy, 25. *See also* Torrance, army chaplain
Articles, Thirty-nine, 89
ascension. *See* Jesus Christ
Athanasius, 11, 22, 86, 210, 221
Athanasius, *De Incarnatione*, 210
atonement, 91, 149, 218–19, 250, 267–68. *See also* Jesus Christ; soteriology
and substitution, 248

Atonement, Day of, 113, 120–21, 262
Augustine, 138–39, 183, 215
Auschwitz, 177
Augustine, *De Trinitate*, 206
Ayton, Thomas, 31

B

Baillie Commission, 6, 74
Baillie, John, 7, 9
baptism, 87, 119, 166, 260
Barnabas, 124–25
Barth and Brunner, 70
Barth, Christoph, 66, 68
Barth, *Church Dogmatics*, Vol. 1, Part 2, 207
Barth, Karl, 6, 10, 18, 26, 41, 44, 64, 108, 207, 221
Barth, Peter, 184
Basil, *De Con. Hom.*, 206
Beechgrove, 3, 71
Bell, David, 27, 51
Beza, Theodore, 185
Bible, 210. *See also* word of God
Bible reading, 169
biblical criticism, 222–24, 227
bishops, 12, 20, 134–35, 184, 199
bishop, single, 202–19
Black, John, 31
Black, Matthew, 231
Blanshard, Brand, 9

General Index

Block, David, 243
British Weekly, the, 42
Bruce, Alastair, 61
Bruce, Robert, 9, 89
Brunner, Emil, 41, 56
Bucer, Martin, 183-84
Bullinger, Johann, 89
Bultmann, Rudolf, 13, 64, 85, 221
Buri, Fritz, 221

C

Cairns, David, 63, 73, 89
Calvin, *Commentary on Malachi*, 269
    Institute of the Christian Religion, 12, 261
calvinism, 90
Calvin, John, 8, 11, 23, 24, 34, 38, 86, 87, 89, 92, 127, 168, 183, 221
    and ordination, 127, 136-39
    Commentaries, 257-69
    Homilies. *See* Commentaries
    not a presbyterian, 189
    prayers of, 257-69
    view of church, 23
Campbell, George, 29, 57
Campbell, McLeod, 9, 90, 248
Campbell, Peter Cohn, 184
Campbell, Peter John, 188-89
Carey, George, 209
change, 162, 166
China, 8
Christ. *See* Jesus Christ
    clothed with his gospel, 158, 221, 247
    clothed with human need, 158
Christian faith, unique, 241, 243
Christie, Lucy, 49, 67
christology, 15, 227, 230. *See also* Jesus Christ
church, 84, 97-110. *See also* theology, church order, church worship
    and hospitals, 180
    and human need, 155-61
    and Israel, 14
    and mission, 102, 161
    and ordination, 129
    and pastoral ministry, 170
    and politics, 81
    and power, 154
    and reconciliation, 160-61
    and reform, 166
    and service of response to the word, 156-61
    and service of the word, 156-61
    and state, 7, 43, 75, 76, 78, 82
    and time and space, 136. *See also* church order
    authority of, 132, 139
    doctors of, 134
    formalism and legalism, 171
    intercession of, 158-61
    message of, 167
    mission to Jews and Arabs, 179
    royal priesthood, 119
    temptations of, 154-61
    unity of, 12, 16, 161, 179
    weakness of, 84
    witness of, 159-61
Church and Nation Committee, 7, 17
church discipline, 184
church finance, 76, 81
Church of Scotland General Assembly, 162-72, 186
church order, 10-11, 11, 12, 14, 93-110, 183, 186-99
    and space and time, 99, 101-10
    provisional, 97, 98
Church Service Society, 9
church unity. *See* church, unity of
church worship, 9, 13, 24, 60, 92
circumcision, 113
Clark, Jacob, 30
Clark, Sibbald, 52
communication, 80
communion, 79, 85-92. *See also* Lord's Supper, the
    preaching at, 47

General Index

Communism, 162–72. *See also* Marxism
congregation, limit to 600, 171
consecration, 116, 121. *See* ordination
  filling the hands, 12, 115, 117
consubstantiation, 89
conversion, 220
Cook, Sir Alan, 241
Copts, 174–81
covenant, 93, 96, 250
  new, 94, 108, 120
  of salt, 113–14, 117
Craig, John, 89
creation, 94
  order lost, 10
  restored, 95, 97
cross, 246–56. *See also* Jesus Christ, death
  and judgment, 255
Crossraguell, Abbot of, 88
Cullmann, Oscar, 66
Cunningham, William, 89
Curtis, W.A., 29
Cyprian, 183–84
Cyril of Jerusalem, 86, 92

D

Daube, David, *The New Testament and Rabbinic Judaism*, 122
David, 117
deaconess, 204
deacons, 184
  ministry of, 157–61
Dead Sea Scrolls, 249
de Klerk, Peter, 23
demythologising, 221–24
Denney, James, 220
destiny, 173–81
determinism, 225, 226, 233
diaconate, 14, 15, 16, 144, 189
diakonia, 16, 20, 140–61, 152
dialogue
  Orthodox and Reformed, 243
  with Jews, 175–81

Dickie, Edgar, 57
didache, 220–56
Didymus, *De Trinitate*, 206
Dodd, C. H., 85
Donaldson, Gordon, 186, 192
doulos, 141–44
dualism, 225, 226, 233–36, 239
Dummet, Michael, 228
Du Moulin, Pierre, 90
Duncan, J. M. B., 29

E

Early Church, 166, 167
Edinburgh Medical Missionary Society, 18, 173–81
education, 76, 78, 225, 229
Edwards, Bella, 48, 52
Egypt, 173–81
Ehrhardt, *The Apostolic Ministry*, 121
Einstein, Albert, 225, 235
elders, 20, 29–34, 40, 47–48, 182–99
  and pastoral care, 170
  ordination of, 132–33
  role of, 190–91
  service of response to the Word, 194
  service of the Word, 194
  women as, 48
Eleazar, 127
election, in Christ, 258
epiclesis, 138
eschatology, 85
evangelism, 16, 43, 79, 160–61, 256
exorcism, 5, 35

F

faith, 6, 7, 47, 168, 250, 251. *See also* Jesus Christ
faith-healing, 11
fascism, 77, 80
Ferguson, James, 31, 40
Fison, Joe, 26
Fleming, Jim, 33

273

General Index

Forbes, John, 184
forgiveness, 236
Foster, W R, 186–99
Fraser, Ian, 6
freedom, 10
freemasonry, 51

G

Gellatly, Mrs., 33, 36
General Assembly (of Church of Scotland), 16, 18, 162–72
genomenos and *gennomenos*, 209
Gillespie, George, 187, 190, 191
Glen Isla, 53, 55, 69
God, 19. *See also* Jesus Christ
    and gender, 212
    and prayer, 168
    language about, 211
    mercy of, 152
    nature of, 175–81
gospel, 24, 78, 84, 145–47, 157, 158, 166, 168, 220–56
Gossip, A. J., 71
grace, 114, 238, 254–56
    unconditional, 252–56
Graham, Billy, 8, 18, 255
Grant, Douglas, 65
Greek Orthodox Church, 174–81
Grieve, David, 27
Grieve, MacKenzie, 49

H

Handsel Press, 182
Hastie, Robert, 27, 38
Hayek, Friedrich, 10
Helvetic Confession, second, 89
Henderson, Alexander, 186
Henderson, Ian, 6, 44, 63
Hendry, George, 64
Heron, John, 45
Hetherington, Sir Hector, 64
Hewitt, Gordon, 69
Hippolytus, 11

history, 85, 221–22
Hodge, Charles, 188–89
Hodges, H. A., 42
holiness. *See* ordination; Jesus Christ, obedience
Holy Land, the, 175
Holy Spirit, 98, 100, 105, 117, 238
    and Christ, 129
    and ordination, 126, 127
    anointing of, 118
Hugo of St. Victor, 239
human nature, 95
    and anxiety, 146–49
    and spirituality, 165
    sinful in mind and will, 146–49
Hunter, Archie, 73

I

idolatry, 211
incarnation, 148, 167. *See also* Jesus Christ; christology
infant baptism. *See* baptism
intercession, 15, 139, 265, 268
inter-Church conversations, 134–39
Inter-Varsity Fellowship, 26, 42
Irenaeus, 86, 87
Isidore of Seville, 183
Islam, 19, 173–81
Islamism, 19, 173–81
Israel, 19, 101, 113, 246–56
    and Six-Day War, 176–81
    God's first-born, 112–14, 117
    new, 13, 120–21
    Presbytery of, 124

J

James, brother of Jesus, 202
Jaspers, Karl, 26
Jehoiada, 117
Jesus Christ, 118
    advent of, 11, 12
    and Adam, 149, 208

ascension of, 12, 99, 101, 102, 218–19
atonement, 12
baptism of, 118
death of, 120, 179, 245
divinity of, 9, 87
faith of, 6, 47, 251–52
head of creation, 172
healer, 146–149
historical and risen, 130–32
humanity of, 8, 85–92, 95, 98–110, 248, 255
incarnation, 10, 12, 147–49, 148
intercession, 15
king, 118, 144
language of, 22, 231, 232
life of, 103, 141–61
mediation, 87, 236, 263. *See also* Jesus Christ, intercession
mission of, 144
obedience of, 93, 95, 97, 143–44
one with the Father, 234, 236, 244–56
priesthood of, 23, 87, 92, 116, 117, 144, 218–19, 259
prophet, 118, 144
prophet, priest, and king, 144
resurrection of, 12, 106, 130–32, 149, 180
servant, 14, 95, 96, 118
son of God, 117, 230
son of Man, 208, 213, 230, 231
Jewish synagogue, 196
Jews, 19, 173
and the Land, 175–81
mission to, 19
John, first Letter, 41
Josephus, 196
Joshua, ordination of, 123, 127
Judaean Scrolls, the, 118
Judaism, 122–23
and laying on of hands, 126
judgement, 146–49, 255
Junia, 204, 205

Justin Martyr, *Dialogue with Trypho*, 219

K

Kelly, J. N. D., 193
Kelvin, Lord, 240
Kemp Smith, Norman, 42
kerygma, 220–56
and *didache*, 126
Kidd, Willie, 51
Kierkegaard, Søren, 40, 44
king, consecration of, 117, 126
kingdom of God, 75, 79, 92, 101
Kluckholn, Clyde, 226
Knox, John, 24, 88, 92, 138, 249, 257
and ordination, 137–39
deathbed testimony, 269

L

Laidlaw, John, 89
Lamont, Daniel, 6, 44
language about God, 211
Last Supper, 120, 127
law, 93–110
Levison, Fred, 37
Levites, 112–14
Life and Work, 42
Lightfoot, John, 196
Lindsay, Jim, 31, 36, 62
Lindsay, T. M., 196
Lithgow, Sir James, 65
liturgy, 92. *See also* church worship
Lords of the Congregation, 185
Lord's Supper, the, 11, 12, 24, 47, 88, 106, 128, 214–19, 251–56
anamnesis, 217–19
and Orthodox Church, 256
and real presence, 100, 107, 212
and Roman Catholic Church, 267
and vestments, 217–19
in homes, 47
institution of, 213
practice at, 186–97

275

General Index

love. *See* service; mission; God, nature of
love as service, 141–44
Lovell, Bernard, 164
Lunan, Janet, 49
Lunan, John, 42, 44
Luther, Martin, 40, 51
Lutterworth Press, 69, 70

M

Macaulay, A. B., 45
Mackenzie, Kenneth and Margaret, 46, 58
MacKinnon, Donald, 26
Mackintosh, H. R., 2, 6, 41, 44, 45, 71, 245, 248, 252–56
MacLaren, Alexander, 39
MacLeod, George, 45
Major, John, 237, 238
Makey, William, 186–99
manichaeism, 207
Manson, William, 64
Martyr, Justin, 11
Martyr, Peter, 183
Marxism, 4, 16, 92, 162–72
Maxwell, Clerk, 224, 229, 240
McConnachie, John, 41, 42
McCord and Parker (ed.), *Service in Christ: Essays Presented to Karl Barth on his 80th birthday*, 191
McCormick, Neil, 17
McEwen, James, 44, 56
McGrath, Alister, 9
McGrath, *T. F. Torrance: An Intellectual Biography*, 2, 12, 22
Meigle, Presbytery of, 3, 29, 42, 74
Meikle, James, 31
Melville, Andrew, 185
Messiah, 118
 in O.T., 117
Middle East, 19, 173–80
 and church property, 177–81
Miller, Samuel, 188

Milton, John, 23
ministry. *See also* ordination
 and preaching, 169
 order of, 133, 134
Mishnah, 197, 201
mission, 2, 83, 84, 144, 161, 245. *See also* seaside mission
 as religious technology, 4, 18
mission, foreign, 8, 43, 83
Mohammed, 174
Moltmann, Jürgen, 68
Moody, D. L., 40, 50
Moses, 114, 123
 appointment of, 120
 servant of the Lord, 114
Muir, William, 50, 58
Mumford, Louis, 32
Murchison, Tom, 65
Muslims, 19. *See also* Islam

N

Nadab, 114
nationalism, 17
Nestorianism, 215–19
Newbigin, Lesslie, 243
New Testament scholarship, 227–29
Newton, Isaac, 224, 235
Nicaea, Council of, 234–39
Nicene Creed, 9, 233
Niebuhr, Reinhold, 85
Niesel, Wilhelm, 184
Nympha, 204, 205

O

Ogilvy, John, 28
Ogilvy, Lloyd, 35
oikonomia, 10, 94–95
Oldham, J. H., 42
Oliver & Boyd, 64
Optatus, 183, 184, 197, 198, 202–19
ordination, 11, 13, 21, 111–39
 age for, 125
 and communion, 128, 136–39

General Index

and different churches, 132
and fasting, 128
and Judaism, 122
by presbytery, 125, 135
in the N.T., 126–28
laying on hands, 113, 121, 122, 137
of elders, 190–91
through prayer, 121, 137–39
Origen, 183
Oxford Inter-Collegiate Christian Union, 7

P

parish ministry, 4, 18, 33, 171
Parker, Joseph, 39
parousia, 109, 110, 149
Passover, 111
pastoral care, 33
  lay, 51
Patterson, Barbara, 49
Paul, 124–25, 133
  ordination of, 124–25
Pelagianism, 252, 253
Pentecost, 14, 118
pentecostalism, 17, 165
person, 215–219
Peters, *From Time Immemorial*, 19
Polanyi, Michael, 164
politics, 43, 59. *See also* Torrance, and politics
Polkinghorne, John, 231
Porteous, Norman, 25
Porter, Lord, 240
prayer, 34, 87, 91, 92
prayer meeting, 31, 92
preaching, 5, 12, 21, 43, 46, 83, 169, 220–56. *See also* ministry
presbyters, 20, 24, 134–35, 184, 187–89, 199
presbytery. *See* ordination
priest. *See* priesthood
  consecration of, 112–16

priesthood, 23, 24, 112–14, 257–69
  Roman view of, 266
Priscilla, 201–4
  Catacomb of, 21, 197, 201
prophet. *See* Jesus Christ
  consecration of, 118, 126
propitiation, 267
Pseudo-Ambrose, 183, 188
psychology and spiritual counsel, 170

Q

Q Hypothesis, 228
quantum theory, 225
Quest of the historical Jesus, 221–23

R

recapitulation, 208
reconciliation, 16, 22, 99
reform, 16, 17, 78, 80, 84. *See also* Torrance, reformer
Reformation, 166, 168, 183–84, 238
Reid, Denis, 60
Reid, Henry, 30, 33
Reid, J. K. S., 6, 29, 44, 184, 193
Reid, Thomas, 42
relativity, general, 225
Rennie, Alastair, 45
resurrection, 167. *See also* Jesus Christ
Reuchlin, John, 237, 238
Revelation, book of, 39
Ritschl, Albrecht, 91
Robertson, John, 31
Ross, Donald, 29, 36
Ross, John, 29, 67
Ross, Sir David, 26, 63
Russell, Sir Patrick, 65
Rutherford, Samuel, 191

S

sacraments. *See* baptism, Lord's Supper
  seals of the word, 133, 140–61

General Index

salvation, 147
sanctification, 116, 116–18. *See also* ordination; *See also* ordination; Jesus Christ, obedience
Sanhedrin, 196, 201–19
Saul, 117
Schleiermacher, Friedrich, 91
Schmidt, Karl Ludwig, 44, 66
science, 21, 164
    and open structures, 163
    and singularity, 242
    and theology, 242, 244–56
scientific method, 223, 224, 226–56
Scots Confession, 44, 88, 89
Scottish Church Theology Society, 6, 44, 65, 220
Scottish Journal of Theology, 44, 64, 111–39
Scottish Order of Christian Unity, 3
seaside mission, 49
Second Book of Discipline, 185
Septuagint, 114, 115
service, 14, 20, 140–61
    of response to the Word, 156–58
    of the Word, 156–58
Sillars, Jim, 17
sin, 10
    and expiation, 148
    and the law, 147–49
    as contempt of mercy, 145–49
singularity, 241–43
Smith, Ritchie, 27, 42
Smith, Ronald Gregor, 64
social justice, 50
social sciences, 240
society, 7, 15, 17, 18, 43, 75, 76
Solomon, 117
soteriology, 15, 86–88, 245–51
space, 99
    and time, 107–10
Spear, Margaret Edith, 14, 65, 66, 72
Spirit. *See* Holy Spirit
spiritual awakening, 165, 172
state, 77. *See also* church and state

Steuart of Pardovan, 185
Stewart, James, 22, 26, 71, 220
Stewart, Tommy, 68
Storrar, *Scottish Identity*, 17
Strasbourg, 183
Streicher, Julius, 246
Student Christian Movement, 7, 26
suffering, 173–81
Synod of Dort, 90

T

Talmud, Jerusalem, 22
Theodora, 205
theology., *See also* christology, etc
    and church, 3, 4
    and experience, 2, 4
    and mission, 2
    and science, 8, 9, 229
    conservative, 7, 22
    forensic, 91–92
    liberal, 7, 9, 44, 60, 91, 92
    natural, 60, 82
    practical, 14, 24
Theology in Scotland, 10, 12
Thin, Ainslie, 65
Thomas, Charles, 68
Thompson, Sol and Nan, 27, 50, 55, 62
Thomson, Annie, 72
Thomson, D. P., 18, 37
Thomson, Ian, 26
Tillich, Paul, 85
time, 85, 101–10, 224. *See also* space
Timothy, 124–25
Todd, Marcus, 25, 63
Torrance, *Atonement*, 11, 13, 16
Torrance, *Calvin's Doctrine of Man*, 41, 70
Torrance, *Conflict and Agreement*, vol. 2, 93
Torrance, David, 18, 54
Torrance, *God and Rationality*, 4, 9
Torrance, Herbert, 180
Torrance, *Incarnation*, 13, 16

Torrance, *Royal Priesthood*, 12
Torrance, *Space, Time and Incarnation*, 11, 242
Torrance, *Space, Time and Resurrection*, 11, 13, 229
Torrance, T. F.
   and nationalism, 17
   and pastoral care, 33, 35, 50, 67
   and politics, 6, 7, 17, 43, 50, 76
   and prayer, 31, 34-35, 67
   and youth work, 53, 54
   Basel dissertation, 44, 64
   evangelist, 2, 5
   ministry to Germans and Poles, 56, 68
   parish minister, 4
   preacher, 5. *See also* preaching
   reformer, 8, 15, 60, 65, 78, 79
   stipend, 52, 71
   war service, 49, 57, 58, 60
Torrance, *The Apocalypse Today*, 39
Torrance, *The Doctrine of Grace in the Apostolic Fathers*, 64
Torrance, *Theological Science*, 9
Torrance, Thomas and Annie, 46, 70
Torrance, Thomas S., 70, 71
Torrance, *When Christ Comes and Comes Again*, 11, 12
Trinity, doctrine of, 164, 232, 243, 244-56
   and science, 164
Turkey, 173-81

U

universities
   and dogmatics, 5, 14, 241
   and practical theology, 14

V

vicarious humanity. *See* Christ, humanity; atonement etc
virgin birth, 207, 218-19

Vitringa, 184

W

Walker, Jamie, 39
Walker, Robert, 2, 23
Walker, Robert and Grace, 46, 52, 70
Wallace, Ronald, 44, 53
Walls, Roland, 14
war, 79
War (1939-45), 36, 53, 77
Warr, Charles, 57
Watt, Hugh, 30
Weber, Max, 32
Welch, John, 31, 39, 50
Welsh, John, 249
Westminster Assembly, the, 187-89
Westminster Confession, 9, 89, 90
Westminster, Documents, 137-39
White, Bill, 51
Williamson, Colin, 12
Williams, William, 31
woman bishop, 205
Woman's Guild, 48, 83
women, ministry of, 15, 20, 201-19
   and God's image, 206
   and Roman Catholic view, 21
word of God, 105, 236-37
   sceptre of Christ, 137-39
World Alliance of Reformed Churches, 192
worship. *See* church worship
Wotherspoon and Kirkpatrick, *Manual of Church Doctrine*, 189
Wright, Selby, 29, 45

Y

Yad Vashem, 177, 246
youth, 78, 171

Z

Zurich, 183
Zwingli, 183

Scripture Index

1 Chronicles
29:22f. — 117

1 Corinthians
1:17 — 13
1:17–18 — 247, 255
1:24 — 256
2:2–5 — 247, 255
3:9 — 204
11:7–8 — 206, 209
11:31 — 203
12:28 — 186, 187
14:33–35 — 203
15:47 — 208
16:19 — 203

1 John
1:1–2 — 228
2:2 — 83
2:20,27 — 119

1 Kings
1:33ff. — 117
13:33 — 115
19:16 — 118

1 Peter
2:9 — 263

1 Samuel
10:1 — 117

16:13 — 117
26:11 — 117

1 Timothy
2:11–12 — 203
3:2 — 204
3:11 — 204
4:14 — 121, 124
5:3–16 — 204
5:17 — 186
5:22 — 121

2 Chronicles
6:42 — 117
13:9 — 113, 115
19:8–10 — 195
19:8f. — 187
29:31 — 115

2 Corinthians
1:21 — 119
2:16 — 255
8:9 — 250
8:19 — 121

2 Kings
11:12,17 — 117

2 Samuel
2:4 — 117
5:3 — 117

2 Timothy
1:6   121, 124

Acts
1:15   196, 202
1:17   195, 198
4:26   117, 118
6:1–7   123, 195
6:6   121
10:38   118
13:1–3   124
13:3   121
14:23   121
15:13   197
15:23   187
21:18   197

Colossians
1:15   212
3:10   212

Deuteronomy
7:6   112–14
14:21   112
17:18–20   117
18:2   195
26:19   112
28:9   112
34:9   123

Ephesians
1:23ff.   116
3:14–15   212
3:19   116
4   186
4:11   204
4:12   7
5:2   268

Exodus
19:6   112
28   111
28:41   115
29   111
29:29   115
31:13   114
35:35   115

Ezekiel
16:1–6   177
16:6   246

Galatians
2:20   6, 47, 248, 254
3:28   206

Genesis
1:2   93
1:27   206
3:16   207
22:2,16   245

Habakkuk
2:4   249
3:13   113, 117

Hebrews
1:9   118
2:11   116
7:28   116
9:11–12   268
13:8   139
13:11–12   268
13:15   128

Isaiah
43:26   115
61:1   118
62:12   112

Jeremiah
6:14   160

John
1:13   207
3:6   231
3:7   29
3:30   217
3:35   115
4:24   211, 212
4:34   116

Scripture Index

John (*continued*)
5:26	86
5:36	116
6:53–56	213
10:36	118, 119
11:35	231
11:38	152
13–17	111
15:16	30
17	88, 120
17:2–4	115, 116
17:11	127
17:17–19	116
17:23	116

Judges
17:5,12	115

Leviticus
6	111
7	111
8	111
8:33	115
9	111
10:1–2	114
16:32	115
20:8	114
20:26	112
21:10	115

Luke
4:18	118
9:28–36	214
10:1	202
10:17	202
11:20	152
12:42–46	102
19:11–27	102
22:29f.	198

Malachi
1:2–6	258
1:6–10	258, 264
1:11–14	259, 264
2:1f	263
2.6	265
2:6–9	259, 264, 266
2:7	265
2:7–9	257–269
2:9	265
2:13–16	260
3:4–8	260
3:15–17	261
4:3–6	261

Mark
2:1–12	235
4:38	231
8:35	84
10:6f.	207
10:35–40	250
10:45	83, 198
11:12	231
14:62	208
16.19–20	11

Matthew
1:21–23	230, 233
5 – 7	143
5:48	143
11:27	227
19:4f.	207
19:28	198
25:1–3	11
25:14–30	102, 112
27:46	147, 178
28:19–20	227
35.31–46	150

Numbers
3:3	115
3:5	134
3:12f.	112
8:5–26	113
11:16	123
18:7	114
19:2f.	267
27:18,23	123

Philippians
1:1	193
4:3	204
4:18	268

Scripture Index

Philemon
24 — 204

Psalms
2:2 — 117
45:7 — 117
51 — 34
84:9 — 113
89:38, 51 — 113
105:15 — 118

Revelation
3:20 — 11
6:16 — 255

Romans
1:17 — 249
8:32 — 245
12:7f. — 187
12:8 — 186
16:1 — 204
16:3, 21 — 204

Zechariah
3:34 — 263

www.ingramcontent.com/pod-product-compliance
Lightning Source LLC
Chambersburg PA
CBHW070237230426
43664CB00014B/2337